Green Finance and Investment

OECD Review on Aligning Finance with Climate Goals

ASSESSING PROGRESS TO NET ZERO AND PREVENTING GREENWASHING

OECD
BETTER POLICIES FOR BETTER LIVES

Please cite this publication as:
OECD (2024), *OECD Review on Aligning Finance with Climate Goals: Assessing Progress to Net Zero and Preventing Greenwashing*, Green Finance and Investment, OECD Publishing, Paris, https://doi.org/10.1787/b9b7ce49-en.

ISBN 978-92-64-75672-4 (print)
ISBN 978-92-64-37289-4 (PDF)
ISBN 978-92-64-40824-1 (HTML)

Green Finance and Investment
ISSN 2409-0336 (print)
ISSN 2409-0344 (online)

Revised version, December 2024
Details of revisions available at: https://www.oecd.org/en/publications/support/corrigenda.html

Photo credits: Cover © HelloRF Zcool/shutterstock.com.

Corrigenda to OECD publications may be found at: https://www.oecd.org/en/publications/support/corrigenda.html.

Foreword

Aligning finance with climate policy goals is crucial for-achieving net-zero greenhouse gas emissions and resilience to-climate change, as called for by Article 2.1c of the-Paris Agreement. Evidence-based policymaking and-investment decisions towards such alignment need to-be informed by robust assessments. To support such efforts, this inaugural OECD Review on Aligning Finance with Climate Goals brings together best-available evidence on three core questions: (i) How is climate alignment of finance assessed? (ii) What do we know about current finance flows and-stocks? (iii) What evidence exists on the role of financial sector policies and actions? The report identifies actions policymakers and financial sector stakeholders can take to improve the evidence base and better align finance with climate goals. It further sets out good practices to prevent greenwashing and inaccurate claims of climate alignment.

This work was conducted under the OECD Working Party on Finance and Investment for Environmental Goals (WPFIEG) as part of the Sustainable Finance output of the Programme of Work and Budget of the OECD Environment Policy Committee (EPOC). The analysis results from and contributes to a multi-year body of work designed to advance and share knowledge for improving the assessment of the consistency and alignment of finance with climate policy goals, including to inform finance-related information needs and discussions under the United Nations Framework Convention on Climate Change (UNFCCC).

The report was prepared by the Finance, Investment, and Global Relations Division within the OECD Environment Directorate. This publication was co-ordinated and co-authored by Jolien Noels, Economist/Policy Analyst, together with and under the supervision of Raphaël Jachnik, Finance for Climate Action Team Lead, with contributions from Bentje Böer (independent consultant), Angela Zha (OECD), Paola D'Orazio (Chemnitz University of Technology) and Coline Pouille (OECD). Ria Sandilands provided editorial support.

The OECD Secretariat is thankful to delegates to the WPFIEG for comments on earlier versions of this report, and to delegates who participated in the Informal Reflection Group on Aligning Finance with Climate Goals and provided further feedback and suggestions in this context.

This report also benefitted from comments and inputs from OECD colleagues at various stages of advancement: Geraldine Ang, Valentina Bellesi, Riccardo Boffo, Miguel Cardenas Rodriguez, Bopha Chhun, Joseph Cordonnier, Caio De Oliveira, Chiara Falduto, David Gaukrodger, Sirini Jeudy-Hugo, Yuval Laster, Elisa Lanzi, Etienne Lepers, Virginie Marchal, Catrìona Marshall, Ariola Mbistrova, Mathilde Mesnard, Hugh Miller, Benjamin Michel, Daniel Nachtigall, Isabella Neuweg, Kilian Raiser, Dirk Röttgers, Mohammed Saffar, Toon Vandyck, Stephanie Venuti, Isabelle Ynesta, and Robert Youngman.

The authors are also grateful to the following organisations for sharing data and insights to inform specific sections of the report: BloombergNEF, Climate Policy Initiative (CPI), MSCI, Net-Zero Data Public Utility (NZDPU) and S&P Global.

Finally, the OECD Secretariat would like to thank OECD member countries providing funding to support this body and area of work (Austria, Canada, the European Union, Germany, Italy, Norway, Switzerland, the United States of America) and in particular the German Federal Ministry for Economic Affairs and Climate Action (BMWK), which provided the bulk of the funding for the preparation of the present report.

Table of contents

FIGURES

INFOGRAPHICS

TABLES

Abbreviations and acronyms

2DII	2 Degrees Investing Initiative
AEs	Advanced economies
AEC	Absolute emissions contraction
ASCOR	Assessing Sovereign Climate-related Opportunities and Risks
AUM	Assets under management
BIS	Bank of International Settlements
BoE	Bank of England
CAT	Climate Action Tracker
CCS	Carbon capture and storage
CDM	Clean Development Mechanism
CDR	Carbon dioxide removals
CO_2	Carbon dioxide
CPI	Climate Policy Institute
CCUS	Carbon Capture, Utilisation and Storage
DEFRA	United Kingdom Department for Environment Food and Rural Affairs
DGI	Data Gaps Initiative
EBA	European Banking Authority
ECB	European Central Bank
EIC	Economic intensity contraction
EMDEs	Emerging market and developing economies
ESG	Environmental, social, and governance
EU	European Union
GDP	Gross domestic product
GECO	Global Energy and Climate Outlook
GHGs	Greenhouse gas emissions
GFANZ	Glasgow Financial Alliance for Net Zero
GFCF	Gross fixed capital formation
ICMA	International Capital Markets Agency
IEA	International Energy Agency
IEEFA	Institute for Energy Economics and Financial Analysis
IFCMA	Inclusive Forum on Carbon Mitigation Approaches
IFRS ISSB	International Finance Reporting Standards Foundation's International Sustainability Standards Board
IIGCC	Institutional Investors Group on Climate Change
IMF	International Monetary Fund
IPCC	Intergovernmental Panel on Climate Change
IRENA	International Renewable Energy Agency
ISF-UTS	Institute for Sustainable Futures of the University of Technology Sydney
ITR	Implied temperature rise
JRC	European Commission Joint Research Centre
LSEG	London Stock Exchange Group
MEPS	Minimum energy performance standards

NDCs	Nationally Determined Contributions
NGFS	Network for Greening the Financial System
NZAM	Net Zero Asset Managers Initiative
NZAOA	Net-Zero Asset Owner Alliance
NZBA	Net Zero Banking Alliance
NZDPU	Net-Zero Data Public Utility
OECD	Organisation for Economic Co-operation and Development
PAAO	Paris Aligned Asset Owners
PACTA	Paris Agreement Capital Transition Assessment
RBA	Reserve Bank of Australia
SBTi	Science Based Targets Initiative
SDA	Sectoral decarbonisation approach
SIFMA	Securities Industry and Financial Markets Association
SMEs	Small to medium enterprises
SNA	System of National Accounts
TCFD	Task Force on Climate-related Financial Disclosures
TPI	Transition Pathway Initiative
UK	United Kingdom
UN	United Nations
UNEP FI	United Stations Environment Programme Finance Initiative
US	United States of America
UNFCCC SCF	United Nations Framework Convention on Climate Change Standing Committee on Finance
WFE	World Federation of Exchanges
WWF	World Wide Fund for Nature

Executive Summary

Achieving net-zero emissions and resilience to climate change requires aligning finance with such goals, going beyond climate-related financial risk management. Financial flows and stocks could be considered aligned with the Paris Agreement if they support socio-economic systems that are consistent with low-greenhouse gas emissions and climate-resilient development pathways. This involves scaling up finance for activities contributing to climate goals (including climate solutions and transition activities), and redirecting finance away from activities undermining climate mitigation and resilience goals.

Public and private actions to better align finance with climate goals need to be informed by robust assessments of progress. In the absence of a common framework to track progress, available evidence on best practices, finance volumes, and actions is currently scattered and incomplete. This inaugural edition of the OECD Review on Aligning Finance with Climate Goals contributes to an improved and more coherent knowledge base by bringing together best-available evidence in relation to three core questions: (i) How is climate alignment of finance assessed? (ii) What do we know about the current climate alignment of finance? (iii) What financial sector policies and actions influence the climate alignment of finance?

Climate-alignment assessments require methodological transparency and a set of complementary metrics to address greenwashing risks. Different methodological assumptions, such as the choice of reference scenario, can lead to diverging results. Where assumptions are not communicated, this can lead to greenwashing, as preferred results can be cherry picked. Relying on a robust set of complementary metrics provides a more complete and accurate view on progress towards transition plans and alignment.

While data and methodologies have improved, comprehensive alignment assessments for climate mitigation are not yet possible for all layers of finance and remain exploratory for climate resilience. Such assessments would need to cover all layers: real-economy investments, financial assets across asset classes, financial institutions, and financial jurisdictions. Methodologies and data availability across layers and metrics are still maturing. As climate-alignment assessments are currently not possible for all finance flows and stocks, blind spots can hide misaligned activities, thus contributing to greenwashing. However, remaining gaps should not prevent progress assessments based on best-available estimates of finance contributing to or undermining climate goals placed in the context of total finance volumes.

Available evidence on finance flows and stocks remains very partial but points to a continued overall low degree of alignment of finance with climate change mitigation goals. For real-economy investments, new investments in clean energy reached USD 1.7 trillion in 2022, surpassing USD 1.5 trillion for fossil fuels but representing a small share of total investments. Across financial asset classes, while many significant blind spots persist, especially for private equity and loans, estimates for listed equity and corporate bonds highlight a low degree of alignment. For example, low-carbon energy supply accounted for only 4% of global listed equity, compared to 10% for fossil fuel supply. At the level of financial institutions, available estimates of climate alignment also remain limited, despite the involvement of commercial banks and institutional investors in various climate coalitions. Banks continue to finance fossil fuel supply heavily, with an estimated USD 1 trillion allocated in 2022, compared to USD 0.7 trillion for low-carbon energy. Tracking efforts at the level of financial jurisdictions and national financial accounts are ramping up and can more coherently bring together all layers of finance.

Real-economy policies remain fundamental levers to increase the climate alignment of finance, but the role of financial sector policies cannot be ignored. Governments use a range of real-economy policies that influence the attractiveness of climate-relevant investments. As climate change poses risks to financial and price stability, as well as market integrity and efficiency, climate considerations are being integrated in financial sector policies. However, climate-related financial sector policies may also influence the climate-alignment of finance, either as an unintended consequence or, depending on the mandate, an intention to contribute to aligning finance with climate goals.

Financial sector policies integrating climate change-related considerations have more than quadrupled since the Paris Agreement, mainly in the form of transparency and information policies. By 2023, 77 countries had adopted climate-related transparency and information policies, 41 had climate-related prudential policies, and 16 had climate-related credit allocation policies. Climate-related transparency and information policies were mainly adopted by supervisory and regulatory authorities or governments. Within this policy area, 55 countries had put in place disclosure policies and 70 countries established climate-related finance guidelines, which can include taxonomies. Climate-related prudential policies have mostly taken the form of climate-related risk management and supervision policies adopted by central banks. There is no consistent data collected on climate-related monetary policies yet.

Common understanding of the effects of climate-related financial sector policies remains primarily based on conceptual analysis and assumptions. Limited theoretical and empirical analysis is available on the effects of climate-related financial sector policies on financial and climate policy objectives. For example, current analysis expects strong trade-offs for climate-related capital prudential policies and monetary credit operations. It also assumes that some leverage, risk management and supervision, and large exposure policies could positively contribute to both policy objectives. Where available, expected effects based on conceptual analysis are not always confirmed by theoretical and empirical research.

Policymakers can take individual and coordinated actions to better align finance with climate policy goals and improve evidence that informs practices with impacts in the real economy. Based on the evidence compiled in this review, they can consider the following key actions.

- Governments can: (a) develop mandatory disclosure requirements that are interoperable across jurisdictions, covering key complementary metrics that relate to impacts on emissions and resilience; (b) support assessments through improved availability of granular input data and reference points, including for climate resilience; and (c) identify and revise policies incentivising and enabling domestic and international financial flows going to climate-misaligned activities.
- Financial system policymakers can: (a) collect and make public, to the extent possible, detailed data on finance exposed to activities contributing to or undermining climate goals, (b) develop disclosure requirements of core complementary metrics for financial institutions, and (c) where consistent with their mandates, consider the impacts of existing policies on climate goals.

Financial sector stakeholders need to mainstream climate-related considerations and better understand impacts on real-economy emissions and resilience. Investors and financial institutions can assess and disclose impacts of climate-related actions and unintended consequences of existing practices. Data and rating providers need to develop assessments across all asset classes and layers of finance to address current blind spots, especially for climate-misaligned finance. Researchers can develop further theoretical and empirical analysis on impacts of climate-related policies to inform their design.

Evidence informing policies and actions to better align finance with climate goals should be based on robust assessments, following good practices on methodologies and metrics. This review identifies five good practices to ensure the integrity and policy relevance of alignment assessments: (i) place best-available estimates of finance to activities contributing to or undermining climate goals in the context of total finance flows and stocks; (ii) rely on a set of core complementary metrics across layers of finance; (iii) disclose methodological assumptions; (iv) assess the reliability and comparability of input data; and (v) rely on credible and ambitious reference points against which to assess climate alignment.

Infographic 1. Approaches and estimates of climate alignment of finance

Achieving net-zero greenhouse gas emissions and resilience to climate change requires aligning all financial flows and stocks with such outcomes, as called for in the Paris Agreement.

How is the alignment of finance with climate goals assessed?

For mitigation, assessments compare the climate performance of financial flows and stocks with a scenario, reflecting asset characteristics and the level of ambition needed to reach policy goals.

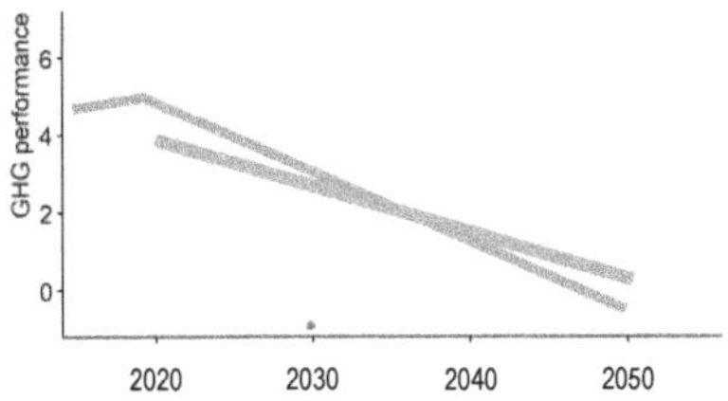

For adaptation, methodologies are underdeveloped.

Such assessments are not yet available for most layers of finance. For listed equity, **assessment providers find diverging results**. Complementary metrics and transparent methodologies can help address greenwashing concerns.

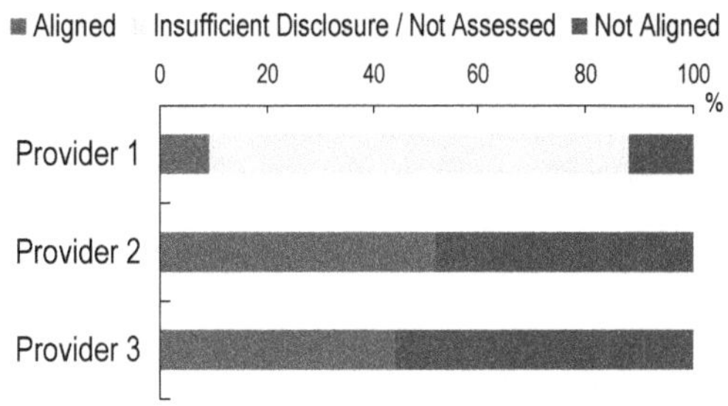

What do we know about finance contributing to or undermining climate mitigation?

Available evidence across layers of finance remains very partial but points to a **continued low degree of alignment** of financial flows and stocks with climate mitigation goals. Awaiting full alignment assessments, estimates of finance to low-GHG emissions activities and emissions-intensive sectors need to be compared to total finance volumes, including to understand **blind spots**.

2022 data, except for debt assets (2023)

Real-economy investments

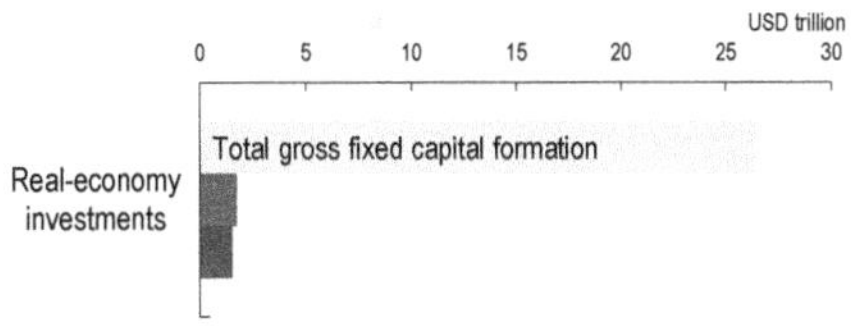

Real-economy investment flows for clean energy have grown to outpace fossil fuel investments but remain a small share of total investment flows.

Financial asset classes

Stocks of listed equity and corporate bonds for renewable energy and fossil fuel sectors highlight a continued low degree of alignment with many blind spots for other economic sectors. There are almost no estimates of volumes undermining or contributing to climate goals for corporate loans, private equity, and sovereign bonds.

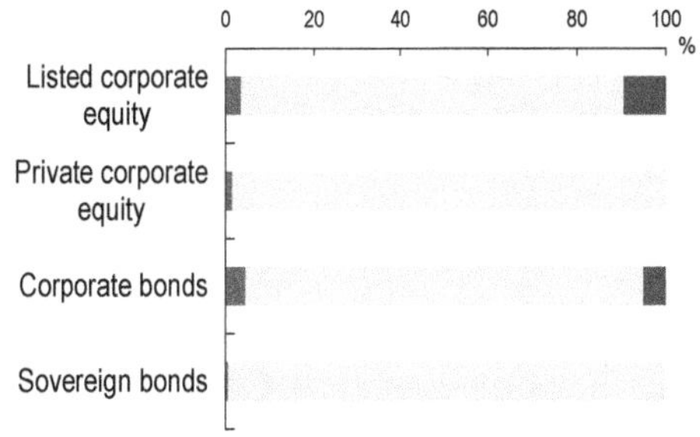

Financial institutions

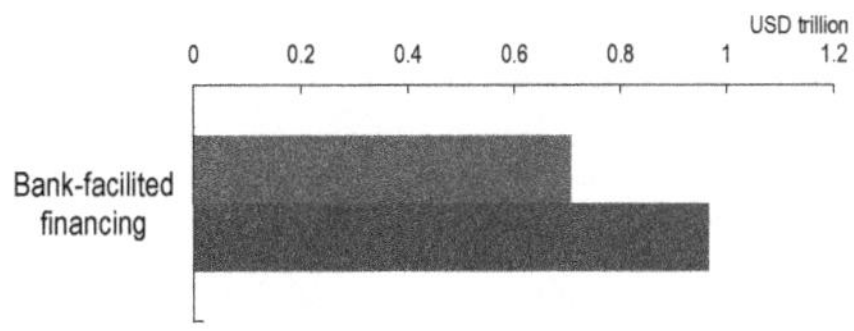

Bank-facilitated financing flows for fossil fuel activities still outweigh those for low-carbon energy activities, but evidence remains too scarce to comprehensively assess portfolios of investors and financial institutions.

Financial jurisdictions

Upcoming updates to the System of National Accounts intend to include "green" breakdowns for debt securities, loans, equity, and investment fund shares but not in relation to potentially misaligned finance.

Infographic 2. Policies and actions influencing climate alignment of finance

What policies and actions influence the climate alignment of finance?

Aligning finance with climate policy goals requires an ecosystem of public policies and private sector actions that incentivise financing and investments towards activities aligned with climate goals, and revisiting the most misaligned policies.

Real-economy policies

Real-economy policies remain crucial drivers of investments in activities contributing to or undermining climate goals.

Economic policies – Regulatory policies – Government investment and consumption – Voluntary approaches – Information policies

Financial sector policies

By 2023, **81** countries had adopted 466 financial sector policies identified as integrating climate change considerations.

Financial sector policies integrating climate change considerations more than **quadrupled** between the adoption of the Paris Agreement and 2023, primarily in the form of transparency and information policies (including disclosure requirements).

Understanding of the effects and potential trade offs of such policies on financial and climate policy goals remains largely based on conceptual research and assumptions rather than on empirical evidence.

Country with at least one climate-related financial sector policy? Yes No

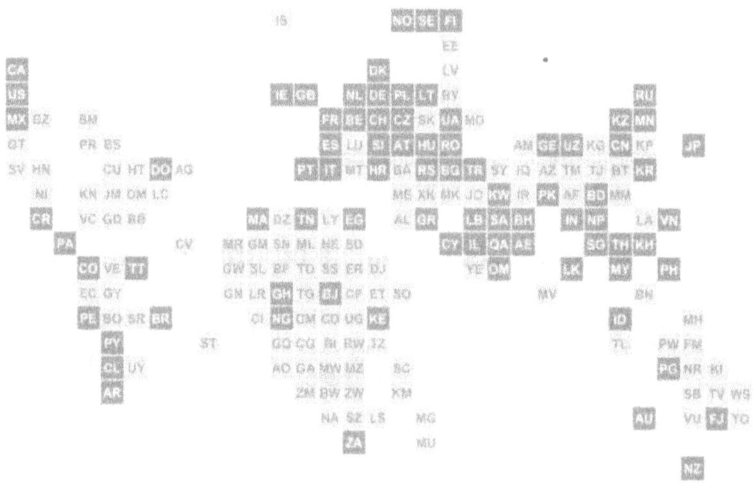

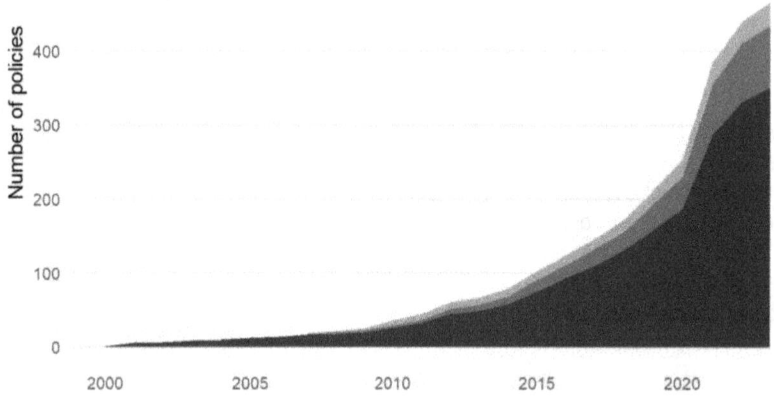

Climate-related credit allocation policies
► adopted in **16** countries as of 2023

Climate-related prudential policies
► adopted in **41** countries as of 2023

Climate-related transparency and information policies
► adopted in **77** countries as of 2023

No consistent data collection yet for climate-related monetary policies.

Private financial sector actions

Investors increasingly adopt climate-related strategies. Evidence indicates that engagement actions have not necessarily resulted in real emissions reductions yet, while divestment and exclusion policies are faced with trade-offs and unintended consequences.

Engagement – Divestment and exclusion – Tilting – Other portfolio construction practices

1 Introduction: the need to align finance with climate goals and enhance the evidence base

Climate change brings enormous challenges to societies and economies. Climate change mitigation scenarios leading to temperature outcomes aligned with the Paris Agreement goals highlight the need for significant shifts in sectoral characteristics (IPCC, 2022[1]; Pouille et al., 2023[2]; IEA, 2023[3]). At the same time, increasing the ability to adapt to the adverse impacts of climate change and fostering climate resilience requires adaptation and resilience considerations to be embedded in all economic and human activities. While climate change and policies to mitigate climate change and its effects can pose significant risks to the financial system, finance also plays a crucial role in addressing climate change challenges. Required transformations and opportunities across economic sectors need large investments.

The scale of investment and financing needs for climate action require significant shifts in the financial system. Estimates of global climate mitigation and adaptation finance needs are between USD 5.9 and 12 trillion annually by 2030 (CPI, 2023[4]). Such a wide range can be explained by the fact that such estimates may be based on different scopes, methodologies, and data (UNFCCC SCF, 2021[5]; Kreibiehl et al., 2022[6]; CPI, 2024[7]). In any case, these figures do not only highlight the need to scale up and mobilise climate-aligned investments, but also to actively finance the climate transition of indispensable economic sectors, as well as to progressively phase out finance for certain activities incompatible with low-greenhouse gas (GHG) and climate-resilient development.

Article 2.1c of the Paris Agreement set a specific goal on "making finance flows consistent with a pathway towards low greenhouse gas emissions and climate-resilient development" (UNFCCC, 2015[8]), through which policymakers highlighted the critical role of finance in reaching the temperature goal (Article 2.1a) and climate resilience goal (Article 2.b). The formulation of Article 2.1c of the Paris Agreement, which sets a goal of making finance consistent with climate policy goals, contributed to the development of the concept of "climate alignment" of investments and financing – a term that has been picked up by policymakers, financial sector players, and civil society. More recently, the G7 stressed the need to accelerate efforts to make finance consistent with the goals of the Paris Agreement (G7, 2024[9]). The G20, through its Sustainable Finance Working Group, also developed approaches to align finance with the Paris Agreement and ways to operationalise them across jurisdictions (World Bank Group, IMF and OECD, 2023[10]).

As aligning finance with climate policy goals is crucial for a successful net-zero transition and enhanced climate resilience, there is a clear need to assess progress on such alignment. Indeed, evidence-based policymaking and investment decisions towards aligning finance with climate goals need to be informed by robust assessments. In this context, credible, transparent, and comparable metrics and data are required to prevent greenwashing and inaccurate claims of climate alignment or positive impacts (UN, 2022[11]; OECD, 2023[12]). As climate-related progress metrics are often based on complex methodologies with a range of assumptions (Noels and Jachnik, 2022[13]; Noels et al., 2023[14]), their transparency and credibility provide the foundation for accurate progress assessments of aligning finance with climate goals.

Efforts to increase the climate alignment of finance are currently fragmented, in part due to the absence of a common framework to track progress. Different stakeholders that can inform and influence assessments of and developments in the alignment of finance with climate goals include environmental and financial policymakers, financial sector participants, and private sector decision makers. These different stakeholders are increasingly implementing climate-related actions and policies. However, such actions and policies are often taken to address risks from climate change, which may not always contribute to aligning finance with climate goals. In the private and financial sector, the focus tends to be more on climate-related risk management, which does not always result in financial decisions aligned with climate policy goals, notably in the absence of mechanisms to properly price climate externalities in investment decisions. Moreover, a range of existing policies still incentivise and result in investments and financing in high-GHG and non-climate resilient activities.

While further methodological and data developments are needed, progress towards aligning finance with climate goals should already be assessed based on best-available estimates and data examples. Such assessments of the current climate alignment or misalignment of finance can help identify priorities to close the financing and investment gaps, finance the transition, and fulfil the goals of Article 2 of the Paris Agreement.

To contribute to addressing these challenges, this report takes stock of progress in aligning finance with climate goals by answering three questions related to assessing, tracking, and incentivising the climate alignment of finance, each addressed in a dedicated chapter:

- How is the climate alignment of finance assessed, and what gaps and greenwashing risks remain? (Chapter 2)
- What does existing partial available evidence about financial flows and stocks tell us about the current climate alignment or misalignment of finance? (Chapter 3)
- What is the state of adoption of climate-related financial sector policies and actions, and what evidence exists on their effects? (Chapter 4)

Chapter 5 concludes by providing suggestions for how answers to these questions and further actions by policymakers and the financial sector can, over time, inform a common and improved framework to better assess and inform progress on the climate alignment of finance.

References

CPI (2024), *Top-down Climate Finance Needs*, https://www.climatepolicyinitiative.org/publication/top-down-climate-finance-needs/. [7]

CPI (2023), *Global Landscape of Climate Finance 2023*, https://www.climatepolicyinitiative.org/publication/global-landscape-of-climate-finance-2023. [4]

G7 (2024), *Climate, Energy and Environment Ministers' Meeting Communiqué*, https://www.g7italy.it/wp-content/uploads/G7-Climate-Energy-Environment-Ministerial-Communique_Final.pdf. [9]

IEA (2023), *Net Zero Roadmap: A Global Pathway to Keep the 1.5 °C Goal in Reach*, IEA, https://www.iea.org/reports/net-zero-roadmap-a-global-pathway-to-keep-the-15-0c-goal-in-reach. [3]

IPCC (2022), *Climate Change 2022: Mitigation of Climate Change*, https://www.ipcc.ch/report/ar6/wg3/. [1]

Kreibiehl, S. et al. (2022), "Investment and Finance", in *Climate Change 2022: Mitigation of Climate Change*, Cambridge University Press, https://doi.org/10.1017/9781009157926.017. [6]

Noels, J. and R. Jachnik (2022), "Assessing the climate consistency of finance: Taking stock of methodologies and their links to climate mitigation policy objectives", *OECD Environment Working Papers*, No. 200, OECD Publishing, Paris, https://doi.org/10.1787/d12005e7-en. [13]

Noels, J. et al. (2023), "Climate change mitigation scenarios for financial sector target setting and alignment assessment: A stocktake and analysis of their Paris-consistency, practicality and assumptions", *OECD Environment Working Papers*, No. 223, OECD Publishing, Paris, https://doi.org/10.1787/bcd25b82-en. [14]

OECD (2023), "Assessing net-zero metrics for financial institutions: Supporting the monitoring of financial institutions' commitments", *OECD Business and Finance Policy Papers*, No. 37, OECD Publishing, Paris, https://doi.org/10.1787/dedcfe56-en. [12]

Pouille, C. et al. (2023), "Paris-consistent climate change mitigation scenarios: A framework for emissions pathway classification in line with global mitigation objectives", *OECD Environment Working Papers*, No. 222, OECD Publishing, Paris, https://doi.org/10.1787/0de87ef8-en. [2]

UN (2022), *Integrity Matters: Net zero commitments by businesses, financial institutions, cities and regions*, https://www.un.org/sites/un2.un.org/files/high-level_expert_group_n7b.pdf. [11]

UNFCCC (2015), *The Paris Agreement*, https://unfccc.int/process-and-meetings/the-paris-agreement. [8]

UNFCCC SCF (2021), *First report on the determination of the needs of developing country Parties related to implementing the Convention and the Paris Agreement*, UNFCCC Standing Committee on Finance, https://unfccc.int/topics/climate-finance/workstreams/determination-of-the-needs-of-developing-country-parties/first-report-on-the-determination-of-the-needs-of-developing-country-parties-related-to-implementing. [5]

World Bank Group, IMF and OECD (2023), *Activating Alignment: Applying the G20 Principles for Sustainable Finance Alignment with a Focus on Climate Change Mitigation*, World Bank, https://www.imf.org/external/np/g20/091323.htm. [10]

2 Current approaches and metrics to assess the alignment of finance with climate goals

This chapter provides an overview of how the degree of alignment of finance with climate policy goals – primarily those of the Paris Agreement – is currently assessed. It explains the scope, dimensions and assumptions that underpin such assessments at the level of financial assets, portfolios, and institutions. The chapter further reflects on different complementary metrics that are being proposed, the methodological approaches behind such metrics, as well as different data and information needs and remaining gaps. It highlights where further efforts are needed on methods, metrics, and data, including to address remaining greenwashing risks and strengthen environmental integrity.

Key insights

- **To assess progress in aligning finance with climate goals (Chapter 3) and inform the development of more effective policies and actions (Chapter 4), credible and interoperable metrics need to be further developed.** Since the adoption of the Paris Agreement, significant progress has been made in this area, notably in relation to climate mitigation alignment assessments, but greenwashing risks remain due to a lack of comparability and transparency of underlying methodologies as well as coverage gaps.
- **Financial flows and stocks could be considered aligned with the Paris Agreement if they support socio-economic systems that are consistent with low-greenhouse gas emissions and climate-resilient development pathways.** This involves scaling up finance for activities contributing to climate goals (including climate solutions and transition activities) and redirecting finance away from activities undermining climate mitigation and resilience goals. There is not yet a common agreed-upon framework to track progress towards climate alignment of finance.
- **A range of complex methodological choices and assumptions influence the results of climate-alignment assessments of finance.** Assessments can be based on different metrics, temporal perspectives, activity scopes, scenarios, and aggregation approaches among other dimensions. For example, the inclusion of offsets in corporate-related alignment assessments can be a strong driver of alignment results but should be treated with caution due to opacity and additionality concerns. Where methodologies and assumptions are not transparent enough, this can lead to greenwashing, as preferred results can be cherry-picked.
- **Climate-alignment assessments of finance notably require the selection of a benchmark, such as climate scenarios.** For such assessments, granular data on investment and financing needs to be matched with climate-related characteristics of underlying assets, and compared against climate policy goals. Climate change mitigation scenarios enable such comparisons. However, care should be taken to select scenarios that can be considered aligned with the Paris Agreement, and transparency should be ensured when downscaling global scenarios to sectors and jurisdictions, which requires further assumptions, notably about burden sharing. Relevant benchmarks for climate change resilience remain very scarce.
- **While data and methodologies have improved, comprehensive climate-alignment assessments for mitigation are not yet possible for all layers of finance and remain exploratory for climate resilience.** Methodologies and data are not yet mature for several large asset classes, such as private equity and loans. Blind spots could hide large amounts of financing continuing to go to climate-misaligned activities, raising greenwashing concerns. Such concerns increase further when attempting to aggregate asset-level alignment assessments at the level of financial portfolios, institutions, and financial jurisdictions.
- **Different metrics and methodologies, based on complementary perspectives, provide a more holistic and nuanced assessment of the climate alignment of finance.** Taking the example of alignment assessments at the level of financial institutions, emissions-related metrics need to be complemented with metrics reflecting portfolio composition practices, including investments in climate solutions and GHG-intensive assets, as well as more qualitative information about engagement, strategy, and governance.
- **Compared with climate change mitigation, conceptual and data gaps to assess the alignment of finance with climate-resilient development remain much more acute.** Initial analyses identify several gaps, particularly in asset-level data on climate exposure and vulnerability and in the availability of relevant policy goals as reference points.

To assess progress in aligning finance with climate goals (Chapter 3) and inform the development of more effective policies and action (Chapter 4), credible data, methodologies, and metrics are needed. Significant efforts have been made since the adoption of the Paris Agreement to develop such inputs into climate-alignment assessments, but further work is required towards a more comprehensive and common framework.

2.1. Assessment aspects and definitions of climate-aligned finance

As introduced by Jachnik, Mirabile and Dobrinevski (2019[1]) and summarised in Figure 2.1, the scope of Article 2.1c is all-encompassing. It covers any economic transaction by private and public actors, both domestically and internationally. While approaches to assess the climate alignment of finance can be considered for financing sources by both actors, the focus in this review is on approaches to assess alignment of finance issued or underwritten by private actors.

Assessing progress towards the climate alignment of finance requires analyses across all layers of finance, including real-economy investments, financial assets, financial institutions, and financial jurisdictions. Climate alignment of financial assets is inherently linked to that of real-economy assets and investments. More aggregate assessments at the level of financial institutions and jurisdictions are especially policy relevant. Within each of these layers of finance, both financial stocks and flows need to be tracked. Assessments of financial flows and stocks provide complementary and interrelated insights into trends over time, as the accumulation of flows, measured per unit of time, results in stocks, observed at a given point in time (Kreibiehl et al., 2022[2]).

Figure 2.1. Scope and aspects of finance covered in climate-alignment assessments

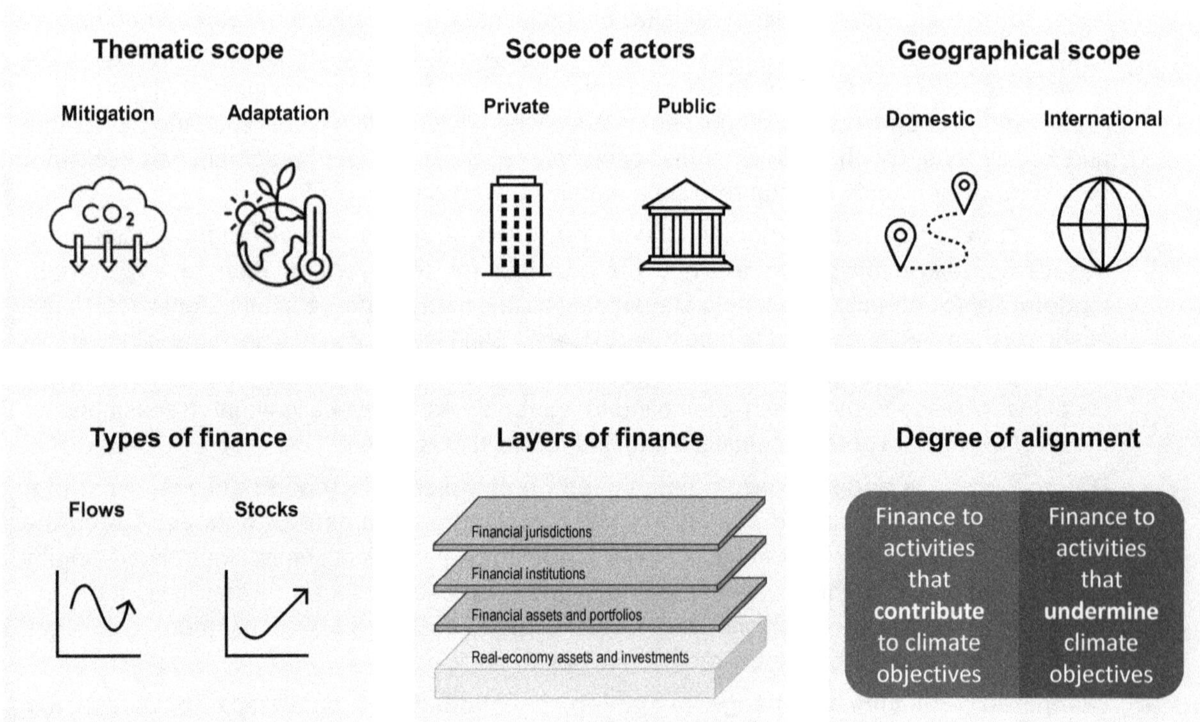

Source: Authors.

At a conceptual level, financial flows and stocks could be considered aligned (or misaligned) with the Paris Agreement mitigation and adaption climate policy goals if they contribute to socio-economic systems that are consistent (or inconsistent) with low-greenhouse gas and climate-resilient development pathways. The notion of climate alignment of finance, hence, not only relates to mobilising and scaling up finance towards activities contributing to climate policy goals, but also progressively driving finance away from activities that undermine such goals.

In practice, the climate alignment of finance to activities contributing to or undermining climate goals is assessed by comparing against one or more reference point(s) reflective of the level of ambition needed to reach climate policy goals and targets (Noels and Jachnik, 2022[3]; Jachnik and Dobrinevski, 2021[4]). For climate change mitigation, such a reference point has mainly taken the form of climate change mitigation scenarios that translate the temperature goal of the Paris Agreement into specific pathways (see more in Section 2.2.1).

Complementing outcome-based approaches based on climate mitigation scenarios, another practical approach to potentially define alignment is based on activity classifications, such as those provided by some taxonomies (Noels and Jachnik, 2022[3]). In practice, approaches based on activity classifications often explicitly or implicitly build on outcome-based approaches, e.g., by defining a specific criterion based on a threshold derived from a scenario. However, such approaches may not necessarily make it possible to make comprehensive assessments (e.g., many taxonomies only define activities contributing to climate goals but not those undermining such goals). As such, they underpin some of the partial data points presented in Chapter 3 to take stock of available evidence to assess progress.

Article 2.1c of the Paris Agreement refers to aligning all finance with both a pathway towards low greenhouse gas emissions and climate-resilient development. So far, efforts have focussed more on assessing alignment with mitigation policy goals. For climate change adaptation, there is much less availability and consensus on the types of reference points that could be used to assess alignment. This remains an area where definitions and concepts will continue to evolve as new reference points and evidence become available. While this chapter reflects such a state of development and thus primarily focuses on climate change mitigation (Section 2.2 at the level of financial assets and Section 2.3 at the level of financial portfolios, institutions, and jurisdictions), its last section (Section 2.4) addresses early developments for climate change resilience. Over time, such assessments could become integrated into one alignment assessment with climate goals. However, current practices treat both mostly separately, as different information is required to make such assessments.

2.2. Assessing climate mitigation alignment for different financial asset classes

Climate-alignment assessments are typically developed for specific financial asset classes (listed and private equity, corporate debt, sovereign bonds, real estate, infrastructure) due to differences in underlying asset characteristics and data sources (Noels and Jachnik, 2022[3]). However, existing methodologies assessing the alignment of finance with climate mitigation goals for different asset classes have common dimensions (Institut Louis Bachelier, 2024[5]; Noels and Jachnik, 2022[3]; PAT, 2020[6]). After the selection of the financial asset class coverage, these common dimensions include a selection of climate change mitigation scenario(s), choice of climate performance metric(s), and aggregate alignment analysis (Figure 2.2). Unpacking these different methodological dimensions, as done in the remainder of this chapter, helps enhance understanding of differences in the results of alignment assessments.

The composition of financial portfolios differs greatly depending on the type of investor or financial institution, its mandate, and strategy. A complete coverage of financial asset classes in climate alignment assessment methodologies is, therefore, desirable to avoid hidden pockets of climate-misaligned finance and set aligned incentives for investment strategies and decisions.

Figure 2.2. Dimensions of climate mitigation alignment assessment methodologies

Financial asset class coverage	Selection of climate mitigation scenario(s)	Choice of climate performance metric(s)	Aggregate alignment analysis
Listed equity Private equity Corporate debt Sovereign bonds Real estate Infrastructure Other	Consistency with Paris Agreement goals Scope and granularity (sectoral, geographic, temporal, emissions) Mitigation strategies and assumptions Techniques to allocate scenarios to entities	Type of climate performance metric Temporal perspective Types and scopes of emissions in metric Treatment of carbon offsets and avoided emissions	Metric at aggregate levels: financial portfolios, institutions, and jurisdictions Aggregation approach Double counting
	Section 2.2	**Section 2.2**	**Section 2.3**

Source: Updated from (Noels and Jachnik, 2022[3]).

Existing climate-alignment assessment methodologies across financial asset classes have focussed more on listed corporate equity than other asset classes (Table 2.1). In principle, these methodologies can be used for other types of corporate-related financial assets, such as private equity and corporate bonds and loans. In practice, however, different data and application considerations need to be made. While all asset classes are covered by at least one methodology provider, the lack of more systematic coverage across asset classes shows that such methodologies are still maturing. On that basis, this section reviews approaches for corporate-related financial assets (Subsection 2.2.2) and sovereign bonds approaches (Subsection 2.2.3).

Climate-alignment assessments for individual financial assets were originally designed mostly with emissions metrics in mind, as they relate more clearly to the Paris Agreement temperature goal. Some climate-alignment assessments consider non-emissions-based metrics, such as investments in climate solutions (e.g., renewable energy), which can also be compared to reference points tailored for each asset class. Moreover, complementary metrics have been developed to consider progress on concrete actions that can be taken to influence emissions. Such complementary metrics are discussed in the following subsections where relevant, as well as in the context of alignment assessments at the level of financial portfolios and institutions (Section 2.3).

As highlighted by Figure 2.2, the choice of climate change mitigation scenarios is, for any asset class, a critical methodological dimension in climate-alignment assessments and other climate-related analysis of finance. This section, therefore, starts with an overview of key considerations of relevance to inform accurate use scenarios for such assessments (Subsection 2.2.1).

Table 2.1. Financial asset classes covered by climate-alignment assessment methodologies

Asset class coverage by methodology provider: Covered | Developing | Not covered

Methodology	Listed equity	Private equity	Corporate debt	Sovereign bonds	Real estate	Infra-structure
2DII PACTA	■	■	■		■	
ESG Book Temperature Score	■					
Carbone 4 Finance Carbon Impact Analytics (CIA)	■		■	■		■
Carbon Risk Real Estate Monitor (CRREM)					■	
CDP-WWF Temperature Ratings	■					
EcoAct ClimFIT temperature	■		■			
I Care & Consult SB2A/SBAM	■					
LO Portfolio Temperature Alignment Tool (LOPTA)	■					
LSEG Beyond Ratings' method				■		
Mirova Alignment Method	■		■			
MSCI's Implied Temp Rating	■	■	■			
Ninety One Net Zero Sovereign Index				■		
Ortec Finance Climate ALIGN	■	■	■	■	■	
right. based on science XDC model	■	■	■	■	■	
S&P Sustainable1 Paris Alignment	■	■	■		■	
TPI (Carbon Performance)	■		■	■		

Note: Last updated in August 2024. LSEG was formerly included as FTSE, S&P Sustainable1 was formerly Trucost. ESG Book was formerly Arabesque.

Source: Authors, updated from (Noels and Jachnik, 2022[3]) based on publicly-available information and, for some providers, bilateral consultations.

2.2.1. Using climate change mitigation scenarios as reference points

Climate change mitigation scenarios can serve multiple purposes related to finance and investments. Many climate-related analyses and metrics in the financial sector rely on such scenarios, both in the context of climate-related risk assessments and management and for assessing the contribution to and alignment of finance with climate goals. For instance, model-based scenario assessments have been used to quantify the investment needs and the associated reallocation of the investment portfolio to align the energy system with the mitigation actions implied by the Paris Agreement (McCollum et al., 2018[7]). However, as climate-related assessments and metrics based on scenarios are highly sensitive to the characteristics of such scenarios, their choice and use needs to be made with care to avoid unintended incentives, maximise environmental integrity, and minimise greenwashing risks.

Several conditions are important to enhance the relevance, applicability, and use of scenarios in finance. This section provides a succinct update on the analysis done by Noels et al. (2023[8]), which analysed common practices and gaps of scenarios commonly used in the financial sector, which stem from the International Energy Agency (IEA), the Network for Greening the Financial System (NGFS), the Institute for Sustainable Futures of the University of Technology of Sydney (ISF-UTS), and the European Commission Joint Research Centre (JRC). The dimensions analysed and summarised below relate to: (1) the degree of consistency of climate mitigation scenarios with the Paris Agreement's long-term temperature goal and emission reduction objective; (2) their applicability for use in the financial sector, notably in terms of sectoral and geographical granularity; and (3) the characteristics of mitigation strategies and input assumptions, including in relation to feasibility and uncertainty. After selecting an ambitious, fit-for-purpose scenario(s) with certain characteristics, it needs to be downscaled to the financial asset level.

Selecting climate change mitigation scenarios consistent with the Paris Agreement

To ensure environmental integrity, climate change mitigation scenarios used in financial sector alignment assessment must be consistent with the Paris Agreement temperature goal and long-term emissions objective. The formulations of this goal and objective are, however, not specific enough to define emissions levels or benchmarks as such and, thus, leave room for a range of interpretations, pathways, and underlying scenarios (Schleussner et al., 2022[9]). Against this backdrop, Pouille et al. (2023[10]) provide a set of criteria to assess the Paris consistency of scenarios' level of ambition:

- To be in line with the Paris Agreement's Article 2.1 long-term temperature target scenarios must remain below 1.5°C by 2100 with limited overshoot (<0.1°C), with 50% chance and remain well-below 2°C throughout the century (i.e., have very high likelihoods of not exceeding 2°C).
- In addition, to be in line with Article 4 of the Paris Agreement, scenarios must see an early peak in GHG emissions and reach net-zero GHG emissions in the second half of the century. A higher level of stringency filters scenarios that peak at the latest in 2025 and achieve net-zero GHG emissions in the second half of the century, and a lower level of stringency filters those scenarios that peak at the latest in 2030 and achieve close to net-zero GHG emissions in the second half of the century.

Table 2.2 summarises the extent to which scenarios commonly used in the financial sector are consistent with these criteria. For each criterion, a scenario is assessed as consistent with either the stringent application (dark blue) or less stringent application (light blue), or as not consistent (purple). Out of the nine scenarios considered (based on their most recent available version), three are fully consistent with all temperature and emissions criteria (black rectangles). The criterion that is least complied with across all scenarios is the limitation of temperature overshoots of 1.5°C over the century. However, the updated results displayed in Table 2.2 compared to Noels et al. (2023[8]) make it possible to observe that the most recent versions of the scenarios are more consistent than their previous iterations.

Table 2.2. Assessment of scenarios based on five criteria reflecting the Paris Agreement goals

Consistent (stringent) | Consistent (less stringent) | Not consistent | Insufficient information

Criteria	Scenarios								
	IEA NZE	JRC GECO 1.5°C	NGFS4 NZE 2050			NGFS4 LD			UTS-ISF NZE
			G	M	R	G	M	R	
Criterion 1: 1.5°C in 2100									
Criterion 2: limited overshoot of 1.5°C									
Criterion 3: well-below 2°C									
Criterion 4: early peak GHG emissions									
Criterion 5: net-zero GHG emissions									

Note 1: The black boxes indicate the scenarios that are consistent with the less stringent interpretation of the Paris Agreement.
Note 2: IEA NZE is the International Energy Agency Net Zero Emissions by 2050 Scenario. JRC GECO 1.5°C is the EU's Joint Research Centre GECO 1.5°C scenario. NGFS4 NZE 2050 is Network for Greening the Financial System Net Zero 2050. NGFS4 LD is Network for Greening the Financial System Low Demand. UTS-ISF NZE is University of Sydney Institute for Sustainable Futures Net Zero. G, M, and R are three different models through which the scenarios are run, respectively GCAM, MESSAGE, REMIND.
Source: Authors', updated in August 2024 from (Noels et al., 2023[8]).

Table 2.2, however, also shows that several scenarios do not provide sufficient information to allow for a full assessment of their Paris consistency (grey boxes). This is in particular the case for features of GHG emissions pathways (early peak and net zero in the second half of the century), which are an important aspect of the Paris Agreement's emissions objectives in Article 4.1. It is also challenging to assess whether scenarios keep temperatures well below 2°C throughout the century, as this requires information on temperature outcomes at several levels of likelihoods, rather than the median outcome only.

Matching the granularity and scope of financial assets with that of scenarios

After identifying the degree of Paris consistency of scenarios at an aggregate level, understanding whether scenarios are fit-for-purpose to be used in climate-alignment assessments of finance requires looking at their applicability. This depends on the scopes and granularity of the models behind the climate scenarios with respect to sectoral, geographical, emissions, and temporal dimensions. Where the scenarios' scope and granularity are insufficient for assessments at the level of financial assets or asset classes, further methodological assumptions need to be made (Noels and Jachnik, 2022[3]). Notably, providers of target setting and alignment assessment methodologies have developed several techniques to downscale scenarios, primarily to the company-level for corporate-related assessments (Subsection 2.2.2), but increasingly so as well to country-level for assessments of sovereign bonds (Subsection 2.2.3).

The selected models have broadly similar sectoral granularity for emissions pathways and in particular more details for energy supply than for, e.g., industry (IPCC, 2022[11]). In practical terms, however, alignment assessments must address a mismatch between sectoral classifications used in the financial sector and by scenario providers. The nature of activities and actors that underpin financial assets is better characterised by granular (4-digit) sub-sectors, typically based on international sectoral classifications (e.g., ISIC, NACE, NAICS, GICS) also used for corporate and financial accounting purposes (Noels and Jachnik, 2022[3]). However, climate change mitigation scenarios rely on sector classifications defined for tracking GHG emissions, such as the IPCC classification (Battiston et al., 2022[12]; Teske, 2022[13]).

Different scenario providers model and disclose pathways for different regions and countries (Figure 2.3). These pathways are also not directly comparable due to different coverage of emissions sources and assumptions. Most scenario providers model national pathways for a handful of large countries, such as the US and China. However, few provide such pathways for a wide range of countries. National pathways for developing countries may differ more from one scenario to the other as illustrated for South Africa in Figure 2.3, possibly reflecting larger uncertainty in the underlying data on which it is build.

For the scenarios in scope, models differ in their temporal scope in terms of start and end year and intermediate data points. Some only have data until 2050 while others do so until 2100. A long-term horizon is needed to identify short-, medium-, and long-term changes consistent with a long-term climate objective (UNEP FI & CICERO, 2021[14]). However, the further into the future, the more uncertainty there is around a given datapoint. Further, most models have a modelling start year at or before 2010, meaning that recent years are already projections from an earlier point in time. Only the UTS-ISF OECM model has a more recent start date, meaning it includes more recent information on emissions-relevant variables.

Figure 2.3. Geographically granular GHG emissions pathways for China, France, South Africa, US

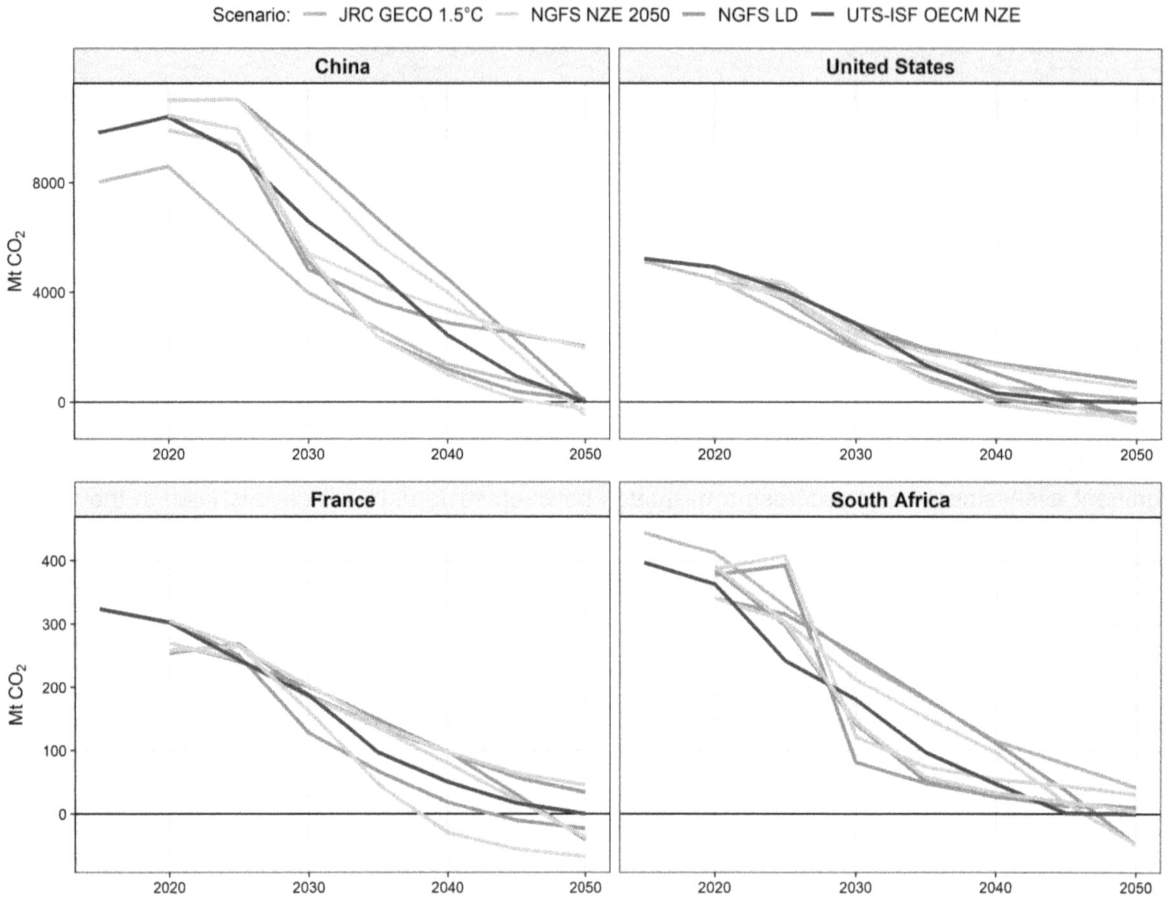

Note: Emissions pathways cover energy-related CO_2 emissions.
Source: Authors', updated in August 2024 from (Noels et al., 2023[8]).

Characteristics of mitigation strategies and assumptions of climate mitigation scenarios

Different climate change mitigation scenarios used in financial sector alignment assessments rely on various combinations of key mitigation options to achieve a given level of ambition (Figure 2.4). As points of comparison, Figure 2.4 also displays four Illustrative Mitigation Pathways used by the IPCC, each focussing on different mitigation options. By gaining insights into the mitigation options that underpin the scenarios they rely on, financial institutions can identify potential inconsistencies with their own transition plans and strategies. Understanding the plausibility of scenarios and sensitivities of scenario assumptions can help enhance engagement with investees toward achieving climate targets. Such information can also inform investment priorities.

Overall, all scenarios that achieve stringent climate goals imply rapid scale-up and large-scale deployment of new technologies and mitigation options, with trade-offs between the different options (Noels et al., 2023[8]). Decarbonising the energy supply is a first essential aspect of all mitigation scenarios that limit global warming. All scenarios considered here see a significant decrease in fossil fuel energy supply and large increases in renewable energy sources (Figure 2.4, Panel A). Some scenarios maintain a higher reliance on fossil fuels combined with a large deployment of CCS technologies (Figure 2.4, Panel B).

Figure 2.4. Mitigation strategies across scenarios

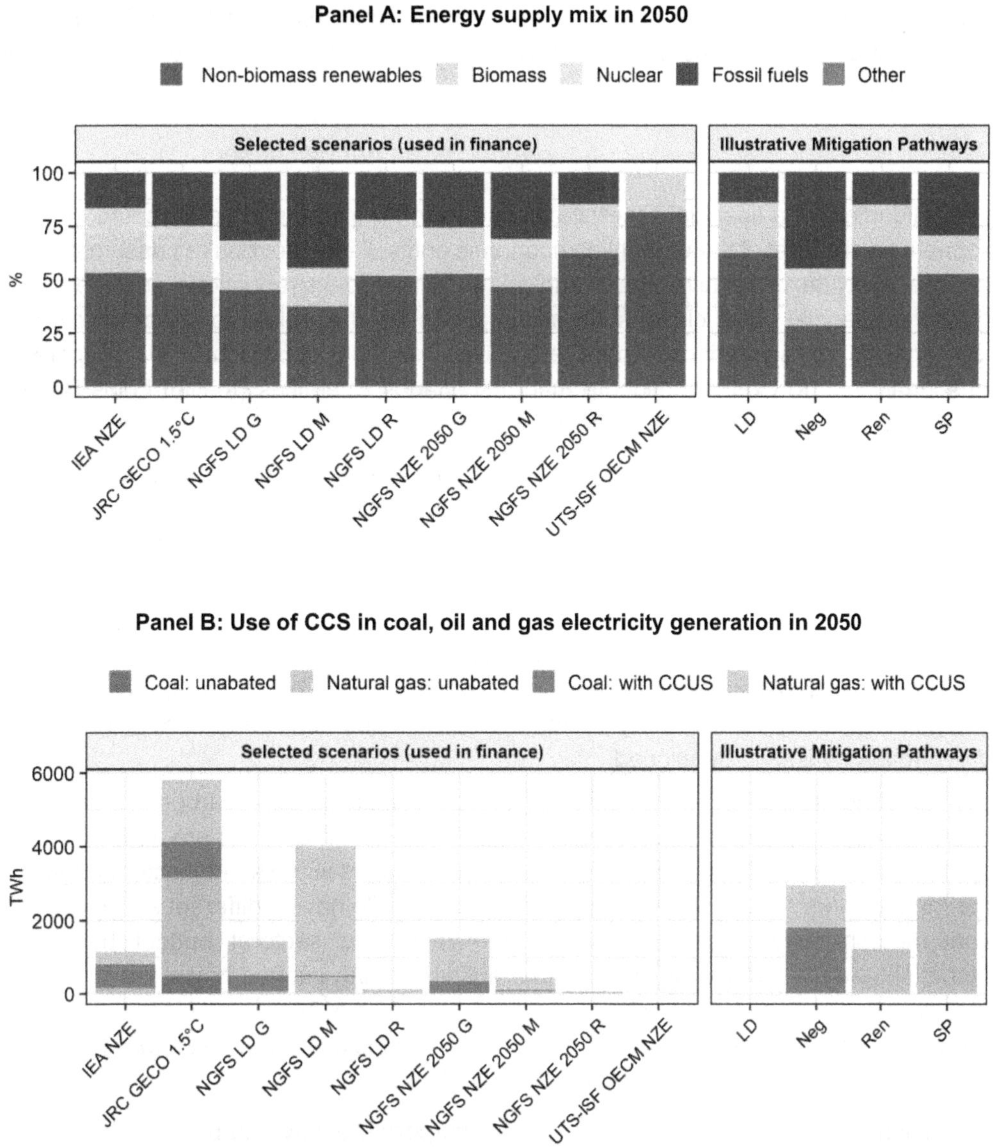

Note: The right-hand side part of the figure represents four Illustrative Mitigation Pathways used by the IPCC, with three of them allowing to keep temperatures below 1.5°C with limited overshoot (IMP Ren, IMP LD, IMP SP).
Source: Authors', updated in August 2024 from (Noels et al., 2023[8]).

Other mitigation levers include demand-side mitigation levers, carbon dioxide removals[1] (CDR), and agricultural and land use emissions reductions. The latter is, however, not considered by all selected scenarios as most models used in the considered scenarios do not cover the agricultural and land use sector. Demand-side mitigation levers are relied upon in all scenarios considered here. These include gains in energy efficiency as well as electrification of energy use across sectors (including transportation, industry, and buildings), and for some models, other demand-side interventions leading to behavioural and lifestyle changes and reduced energy demand.

CDR is a mitigation strategy most scenarios assessed in the IPCC AR6 rely on to reach stringent mitigation goals. All the scenarios commonly used in finance studies here show a limited reliance on CDR in the first part of the century (0-7Gt in 2050), but some scenarios largely rely on negative emissions thereafter, as is the case for GECO and NGFS delayed transition scenarios. Negative emissions achieved through CDR allow reaching long-term net negative emissions to ensure a long-term decline in temperatures (Riahi et al., 2022[15]), but scenarios that achieve stringent temperature limits highlight that CDR deployment can compensate for residual emissions in hard-to-abate sectors but not replace substantial emissions reductions in all sectors.

Downscaling scenarios to the level of economic and financial assets

To assess the alignment of a financial asset, the chosen scenario needs to be allocated, or scaled down, to the appropriate level of that of the underlying economic entity. Doing so requires assumptions on burden sharing, i.e., the absolute or relative share and speed of emission reductions assigned to the entity. Depending on the financial asset class, such assumptions need to relate to geographical downscaling and/or sector-specific considerations. There are a few existing approaches to compare entities to sector-level scenarios or to explicitly allocate macro scenarios to entities (Institut Louis Bachelier et al., 2020[16]; Schwegler et al., 2022[17]; SBTi, 2021[18]).

- In the contraction approach (Figure 2.5, Panel A), an entity is considered aligned if it reduces emissions at the same speed as the scenario (at the relevant sectoral and geographical granularity). In this case, a fixed reduction rate is set for absolute emissions or carbon intensities for all entities in each sector and or region.
- In the convergence approach (Figure 2.5, Panel B), an entity is considered aligned if it converges towards the (sectoral and/or geographically relevant) scenario by a given point in time. In this case, every entity in each sector/geography needs to achieve the same climate performance, typically in intensity-based terms, at that point in time. Hence, entities that are already performing well must improve relatively less to be aligned.
- In the fair share approach (Figure 2.5, Panel C), an entity-specific carbon budget or scenario is allocated to each entity based on chosen criteria. The market share criterion (by revenue, production, or capacity for example) implies that two entities in the same sector/geography with the same market share receive the same carbon budgets while having different emissions profiles. The historic responsibility criterion distributes the remaining sectoral budget based on historic contributions, which implies for instance that entities having emitted below the budget level in the past may temporarily surpass the budget in the future. The economic efficiency criterion distributes the sectoral scenario based on relative least cost or efficiency (the need for entity-level data on abatement costs makes this approach challenging).

Most climate-alignment assessment methodologies for corporate equity and bonds follow a convergence approach (Noels and Jachnik, 2022[3]). On that basis, companies that are currently more emissions-intensive will need to reduce emissions faster than companies that are already closer to the scenario. The convergence approach may be best suited for large companies with global operations where activities may be less clearly linked to specific countries. On the other hand, a contraction approach is common for absolute emissions-based metrics, where companies need to reduce emissions at the same rate, regardless of their current and past emissions. However, companies may have different abatement cost curves, investment capacities, and access to financing, especially in developing countries, which could call for a differentiated approach.

The challenges relating to using downscaled scenarios and considering fair shares are particularly pertinent for sovereigns. Geographic variations among countries imply a need to incorporate equity considerations when assessing the alignment of sovereign bond portfolios, given different countries decarbonise at different rates (Noels et al., 2023[8]). While some scenarios include fair share considerations to some degree, some providers make additional changes to reflect this. For example, TPI's ASCOR framework includes fair share considerations by relaxing certain indicator thresholds depending on the development status of a country (ASCOR, 2023[19]).

Figure 2.5. Stylised examples of different approaches to compare entities against scenarios

Panel A: Contraction approach

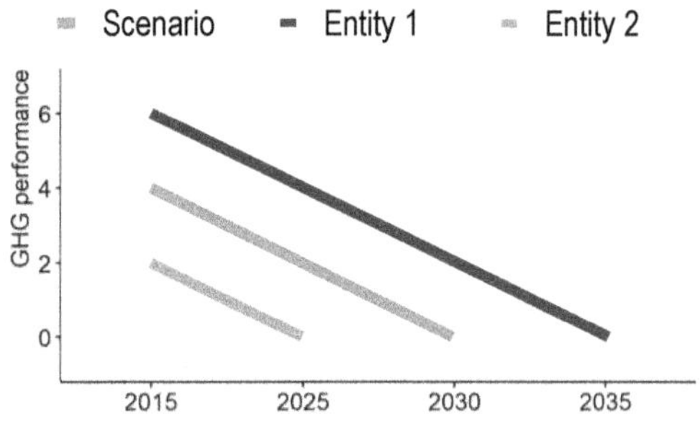

Alignment when the reduction rate is the same as in the scenario.

Panel B: Convergence approach

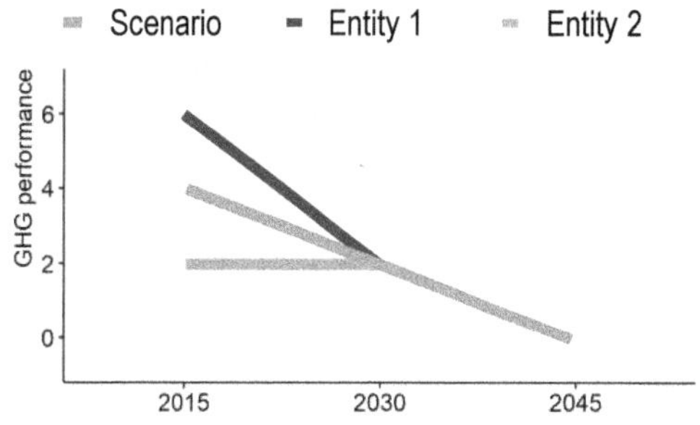

Alignment when the performance level is the same as in the scenario at time x, here 2030.

Panel C: Fair-share approach: example for two entities with the same market share

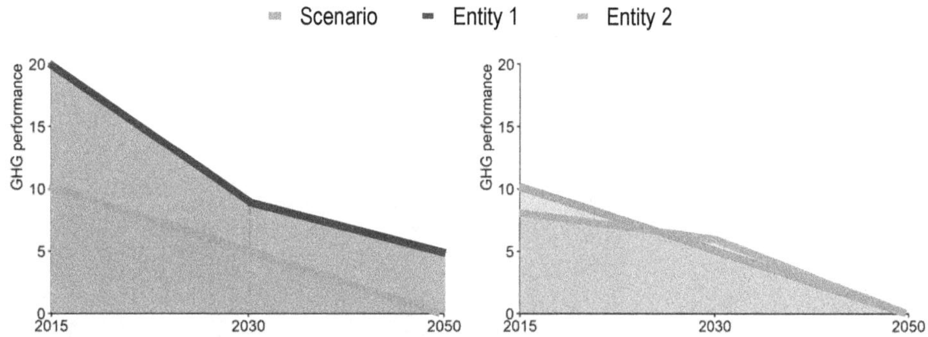

Alignment when the carbon budget of an entity is the same as or less than the carbon budget under the scenario. In this example, entity 1 and 2 must comply to the same scenario, as they have the same market share in the same sector/geography.

Note: GHG emissions performance could be in terms of absolute emissions (e.g., tCO_2e) or emissions intensity (e.g., tCO_2e per ton of steel). Contraction approach is typically used for absolute-based metrics, convergence for intensity-based metrics.
Source: Authors, adapted from (Schwegler et al., 2022[17]).

2.2.2. Alignment and complementary metrics for corporate-related financial assets

At an aggregate level, existing climate-alignment assessments of finance for corporate-related financial assets find a high degree of misalignment (as shown in Chapter 3 Subsection 3.2.2). At the financial asset level, however, Table 2.3 indicates that results frequently differ across assessment providers for the same asset. Indeed, a company assessed as aligned with a 1.5 degrees scenario by one provider can be assessed as not aligned by others. These divergences can be explained by differences in methodology and scope across the dimensions introduced in Figure 2.2, notably, as discussed in the previous section, in terms of choice and use of a climate mitigation scenario. Most providers also run into some data availability issues, but clear progress has been made compared to a previous stocktake (Noels and Jachnik, 2022[3]). Hence, even for listed corporate equity, where methodologies are more available, there is a continued need for increased transparency and comparability. Currently, the correlation and comparability among assessments for the same company are low.

Existing climate-alignment assessments of corporate listed equities are based on different **climate performance metrics**. Most rely on GHG emissions performance metrics, although some consider non-emissions-based metrics such as capital expenditure plans in certain technologies (Noels and Jachnik, 2022[3]). Different metrics reflect different perspectives, and each has advantages and disadvantages (Table 2.4). For example, absolute emissions contraction metrics can be directly related to the remaining global GHG budget, are simpler, and require less data. However, emissions reductions can be the consequence of a decline in output instead of an improvement in climate performance. To address this concern, intensity-based metrics are typically considered. Physical intensity metrics reflect emissions performance and efficiency improvements regardless of entity size and growth. On the other hand, data requirements are higher, and comparability between companies with diverse activities may be limited. While all these metrics rely on expanding the currently limited climate data disclosure (see Chapter 4 Subsection 4.2.1), data availability for absolute emissions metrics is better than for intensity metrics.

Table 2.3. Alignment assessments results across providers for selected non-financial corporates

Anonymised company	Sector	Region	Provider 1	Provider 2	Provider 3	Provider 4
Company A	Airlines	Asia	Not aligned	Not aligned	Not aligned	Not aligned
Company B	Airlines	Pacific	2 Degrees	Not aligned	1.5 Degrees	Not aligned
Company C	Airlines	North America	1.5 Degrees	2 Degrees	1.5 Degrees	2 Degrees
Company D	Autos	Asia	2 Degrees	2 Degrees	1.5 Degrees	1.5 Degrees
Company E	Autos	Europe	1.5 Degrees	Not aligned	Not aligned	1.5 Degrees
Company F	Autos	North America	1.5 Degrees	2 Degrees	Not aligned	1.5 Degrees
Company G	Shipping	Europe	1.5 Degrees	2 Degrees	2 Degrees	1.5 Degrees
Company H	Shipping	Asia	Not available	Not aligned	1.5 Degrees	1.5 Degrees
Company I	Shipping	Asia	Not aligned	Not aligned	1.5 Degrees	1.5 Degrees
Company J	Steel	Latin America	1.5 Degrees	Not aligned	Not aligned	1.5 Degrees
Company K	Steel	Asia	Not aligned	Not aligned	Not aligned	Not aligned
Company L	Steel	Europe	1.5 Degrees	Not aligned	2 Degrees	2 Degrees
Company M	Chemicals	Africa	Not available	Not aligned	Not aligned	2 Degrees
Company N	Chemicals	Asia	Not available	Not aligned	Not aligned	Not aligned
Company O	Chemicals	Europe	Not available	Not aligned	Not aligned	Not aligned
Company P	Cement	Latin America	1.5 Degrees	2 Degrees	1.5 Degrees	1.5 Degrees
Company Q	Cement	Europe	1.5 Degrees	Not aligned	2 Degrees	1.5 Degrees
Company R	Cement	Africa	Not aligned	Not aligned	Not aligned	Not aligned
Company S	Aluminium	Middle East	Not aligned	Not aligned	Not available	Not available
Company T	Aluminium	Europe	1.5 Degrees	Not aligned	Not aligned	2 Degrees
Company U	Aluminium	North America	Not aligned	Not aligned	2 Degrees	Not aligned
Company V	Electric Utilities	Asia	2 Degrees	2 Degrees	1.5 Degrees	2 Degrees
Company W	Electric Utilities	North America	1.5 Degrees	Not aligned	1.5 Degrees	1.5 Degrees
Company X	Electric Utilities	Pacific	2 Degrees	Not aligned	Not aligned	2 Degrees
Dimensions of assessments	Metric type		SDA	AEC, SDA	SDA, EIC	AEC, SDA, EIC
	Time period		2050	2050	2050	2035
	Temporal perspective		Point-in-time	Cumulative	Cumulative	Cumulative
	Emissions scopes included		1, 2, 3	1, 2, 3	1, 2, 3	1, 2
	Scenario sources		IEA	NGFS	IEA & IPCC	IPCC

Note: Results are latest available assessments for alignment in 2050, anonymised for companies and providers. ITR results are assigned to the relevant category as this illustration aims to show the level of alignment and exact temperature results come with a higher level of uncertainty. 'Not aligned' means not aligned with a 2 degrees or below scenario as assessed by the methodology provider. 'Not available' means either not enough data to apply the methodology or no methodology available for that sector by the provider.
Source: Authors', updated in August 2024 from an initial version in (Noels and Jachnik, 2022[3]) based on data provided by four selected providers (CDP-WWF, 2024[20]; MSCI, 2024[21]; S&P, 2024[22]; TPI, 2023[23]).

As each metric type comes with pros and cons and provides a complementary perspective, existing climate-alignment methodologies consider one or the other depending on their target audience and, in some cases, use a combination of metrics (Noels and Jachnik, 2022[3]). If providers are transparent about their approach, different assessments can complement each other to have a more comprehensive analysis. However, when providers are not transparent about their metric choice, greenwashing risks arise, including as corporates or financial sector players can cherry-pick assessment results.

Table 2.4. Overview of emissions performance metrics for corporates and related financial assets

Metric type	Advantages	Disadvantages	Data needs	Data availability
AEC: Absolute Emissions Contraction *(Difference in GHG emissions)*	• Is a less complex metric • Is a less data intensive metric • Can be applied to all asset classes • Relates more to the remaining carbon budget and climate impacts of cumulative carbon emissions • Could initially incentivise efficiency improvements and substitution of higher emitting products or technologies with lower-emitting alternatives	• Could reflect decreased output rather than improved performance • Could disincentivise business growth, even for activities with a better climate performance. This particularly affects start-ups and young companies, or those that have already made a significant improvement previously	Low	High
SDA: Sectoral Decarbonisation Approach *(GHG emissions divided by physical output)*	• Reflects GHG performance and efficiency improvements regardless of entity size, business growth and price changes • Applies to homogenous sectors, companies, and asset classes • Incentivises both efficiency improvements and growth into or expansion of lower-emitting products or technologies	• Is more data-intensive • Is difficult to apply to companies with diverse activities and in heterogeneous sectors • Absolute emissions could still increase while intensity-based climate performance improves • Difficult to compare across sectors	High	Low
EIC: Economic Intensity Contraction *(GHG emissions divided by economic output)*	• Reflects GHG performance and efficiency improvements regardless of entity size • Applies to non-homogenous sectors and companies • Understood more easily by investor audience due to economic/financial denominator • Relates more closely the decoupling between emissions and the economy • Incentivises both efficiency improvements and growth into or expansion of lower-emitting products or technologies	• Is sensitive to volatility in macroeconomic conditions making it difficult to track true changes in GHG performance • Absolute emissions could still increase while intensity-based climate performance improves • Assessing the PA consistency of projections for economic denominators (e.g., GDP) is difficult	Medium	Medium

Note: Data needs refers to both needs on corporate GHG emissions data and other corporate output data such as production volumes, value added or financial performance. Data availability is generally higher for listed than unlisted companies.
Source: (Noels and Jachnik, 2022[3]).

The **temporal boundary** of an alignment assessment, one of the core dimensions introduced in Figure 2.2, significantly influences assessment results (Thomä, Dupré and Hayne, 2018[24]). The three key temporal characteristics of a greenhouse gas performance metric relate to whether it is backward- or forward-looking, whether it considers a short, medium, or long period, and whether the metric is only compared with a scenario at a certain point in time or across a period. Stylised examples in Figure 2.6 illustrate how such characteristics drive alignment results.

- Backward- and forward-looking metrics serve different yet complementary purposes. Backward-looking metrics can be used for an ex-post assessment of alignment, analysing whether an entity has followed a scenario in the past (Institut Louis Bachelier et al., 2020[16]). Forward-looking metrics are more dynamic as they aim to assess if an entity is on track to comply with the remaining carbon budget for a certain goal. Metrics based on historical data are not enough on their own to assess climate-alignment due to non-linearity, non-stationarity, path-dependencies and endogeneity issues that imply that extrapolations of past trends do not provide an accurate benchmark for forward-looking assessments (Bingler, Colesanti Senni and Monnin, 2021[25]).
- In terms of period, 2025, 2030, and 2050 are all important policy milestones towards reaching the Paris Agreement temperature goal. The most recent IPCC assessment indicates 2025 as the year when global emissions should peak, as early action is essential in reducing risks of crossing climate tipping points. Further, global emissions need to reach net-zero between 2045 and 2055, in order to limit warming to 1.5°C with no or limited overshoot (IPCC, 2022[26]). Methodological recommendations for corporate-related financial assets are consistent with these considerations. SBTi requires that corporate targets and mitigation performance assessments should cover a minimum of five years and a maximum of 10 years (SBTi, 2021[18]). SBTi further recommends companies set long-term targets and near-term milestones at five-year intervals, thereby combining advanced planning (including for large capital investments) with mid- and near-term-actions.
- In relation to the point of measurement, a comparison of a GHG performance metric with a scenario can happen at a point-in-time or over a period. As such, the degree of (mis)alignment will depend on the choice of year (Institut Louis Bachelier et al., 2020[16]). Assessments over time provide a more dynamic and nuanced perspective, highlighting changes in trends and allowing for cumulative analysis of divergence between the entity's performance and the scenario over the years.

Figure 2.6. Stylised examples of temporal perspectives in alignment assessments

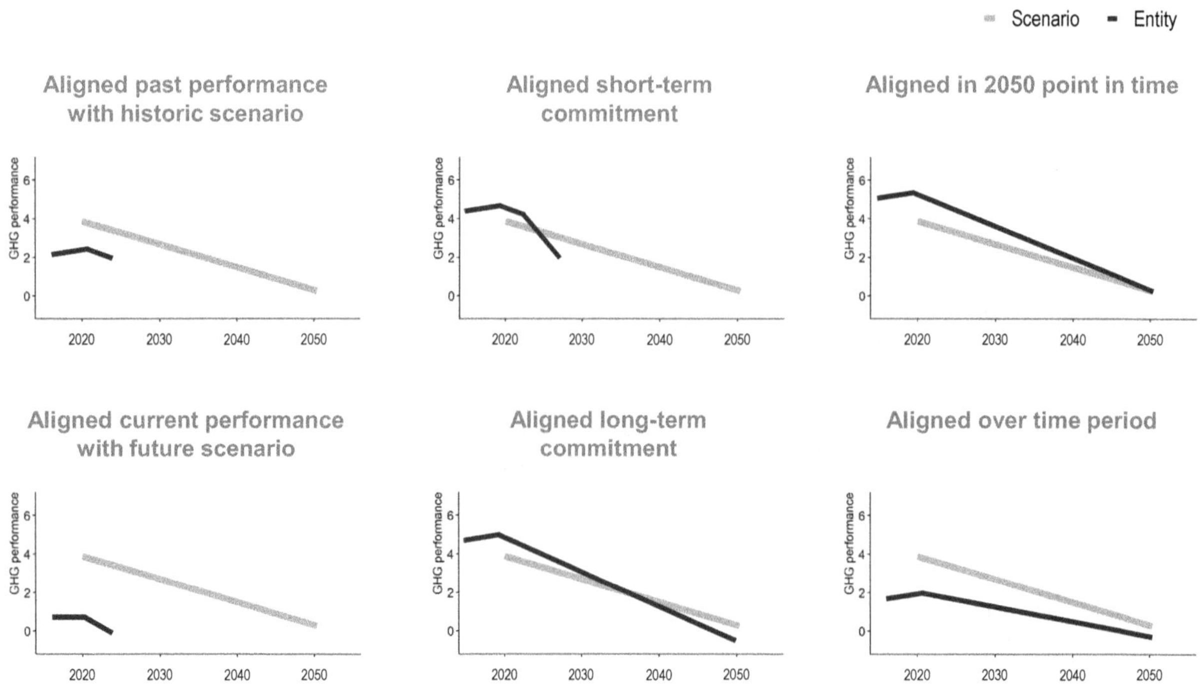

Source: Authors.

The **coverage of GHG emissions** in climate-alignment assessment methodologies relates both to the types of GHGs and the scope of emissions covered. Most climate-alignment assessment methodologies consider all types of GHGs and the widest scope possible based on available data.

- To understand the full extent of global warming, economic actors should measure and disclose emissions of all types of GHGs, i.e., both GHGs with lifetimes around 100 years or longer, notably CO2 and nitrous oxide, as well as Short-Lived Climate Forcers, notably methane and some hydrofluorocarbons (IPCC, 2022[26]). Some research further suggests that economic actors should indicate the separate contribution of each type of GHG to total (or CO2-equivalent) emissions in their targets and measurement of progress (Allen et al., 2022[27]).
- In contrast to national GHG accounting, which is based on a territorial approach, corporates account for GHG emissions according to the scope 1, 2 and 3 categorisation[2]. For corporates, building on the GHG Protocol, the SBTi requires that GHG performance metrics (both historic and targets) cover at least 95% of company-wide Scope 1 and 2 emissions and account for all relevant Scope 3 emissions (SBTi, 2021[18]) . Scope 3 emissions relate to the responsibility of companies along their value chain, both upstream and downstream. The relevance of Scope 3 emissions depends on the sector and where the company sits within the value chain. Estimates indicate they are especially important in sectors such as oil and gas and car manufacturing, for which they account for most emissions across the three scopes (Hertwich and Wood, 2018[28]).

Climate science and literature treat **offsets** with caution, in terms of risk of delaying or replacing actual GHG reductions, as well as in relation to their environmental integrity and additionally. Reach net-zero emissions requires urgent absolute emission reductions (Fankhauser et al., 2021[29]). As highlighted in Subsection 2.2.1, these reductions need to be front-loaded and to cover all emission sources. This means CDRs should be used cautiously, and the use of carbon offsets should be regulated effectively. There are many questions about the integrity and additionally of offsets. For example, over half of the carbon offsets allocated in the Clean Development Mechanism (CDM), the largest crediting mechanism under the Kyoto Protocol, went to projects that would very likely have been developed anyway, highlighting a lack of additionally (Calel et al., 2021[30]). The sale of offsets in the CDM may in fact have significantly increased global emissions. Moreover, across carbon credit market segments, independent assessments find that a large share of carbon credit supply is currently of low quality (Wetterberg, Ellis and Schneider, 2024[31]).

In this context, the current SBTi standard states that offsets cannot be counted as reductions towards meeting a near-term target set by corporates (SBTi, 2021[18]). Companies must account for reductions resulting from direct action within their operations or value chains. Moreover, the GHG protocol treats biogenic CO_2 (both sequestration, e.g., uptake by forests, and emissions, e.g., burning biomass) as separate from Scope 1, 2 and 3 emissions (World Resources Institute & World Business Council for Sustainable evelopment, 2004[32]).

Avoided emissions are currently defined and understood differently by different communities. For a country, in the context of international carbon markets, avoided emissions refer to activities that avoid potential sources of stored GHG emissions from being emitted to the atmosphere within its territory, such as the nonexploitation of fossil fuel reserves, maintaining land use and agricultural practices that retain already-stored carbon, and avoided deforestation (Jeudy-Hugo, Lo Re and Falduto, 2021[33]) (see also Subsection 2.2.2). For corporates, avoided emissions typically refer to emissions avoided during the use phase by a company's customer compared to using a more carbon-intensive product than the less-carbon intensive product from the company.

Table 2.5. Climate mitigation information points and metrics considered by selected frameworks for corporates

Included / Not included

	EU Taxonomy	China Taxonomy	South Africa Taxonomy	US SEC	UK TPT	ISSB	SBTi	CDP	CA100+
GHG emission metrics									
Historic and current GHG emissions	Not included	Not included	Included	Included	Included	Included	Included	Included	Included
GHG emission targets (short, medium, and long term)	Not included	Not included	Not included	Included	Included	Included	Included	Included	Included
Alignment assessment with a benchmark, inc. Paris Agreement	Not included	Not included	Not included	Not included	Included	Not included	Included	Included	Included
Use of offsets (current and future)	Not included	Not included	Not included	Not included	Included	Not included	Included	Included	Included
Composition of activities and related financing and investment metrics									
Composition of low-carbon and carbon-intensive products or services	Not included	Not included	Not included	Included	Included	Included	Not included	Included	Not included
Capital expenditure in low-carbon and carbon-intensive activities	Included	Not included	Included	Not included	Not included	Included	Not included	Included	Included
Operational expenditure	Included	Not included	Included	Not included	Not included	Included	Not included	Included	Included
Turnover from low-carbon and carbon-intensive activities	Included	Not included	Included	Not included	Not included	Not included	Not included	Included	Not included
Investment in R&D for low-carbon and carbon-intensive activities	Not included	Not included	Not included	Not included	Not included	Not included	Not included	Included	Not included
Financial plans, budgets, and targets supporting decarbonisation	Not included	Not included	Not included	Not included	Included	Not included	Not included	Included	Included
Disclosure on use of proceeds of green bonds	Not included	Included	Not included	Not included	Not included	Not included	Not included	Not included	Not included
Engagement metrics									
Value chain engagement	Not included	Not included	Not included	Not included	Included	Not included	Included	Included	Not included
Climate policy engagement	Not included	Not included	Not included	Not included	Included	Not included	Not included	Included	Included
Other	Not included	Not included	Not included	Not included	Included	Not included	Not included	Not included	Not included
Governance and strategy metrics									
Strategic ambition and transition planning	Not included	Not included	Not included	Included	Included	Included	Included	Included	Included
Board oversight and reporting	Not included	Not included	Not included	Included	Included	Included	Not included	Included	Included
Management incentives and remuneration	Not included	Not included	Not included	Included	Included	Included	Not included	Included	Included
Climate governance	Not included	Not included	Not included	Included	Included	Included	Not included	Included	Included
Climate scenario and sensitivity analysis	Not included	Not included	Not included	Included	Included	Included	Not included	Included	Included
Other	Not included	Not included	Not included	Included	Included	Included	Not included	Included	Included

Note: Last updated in August 2024.
Source: Authors, analysis based on publicly-available information of selected frameworks, including (European Commission, 2023[34]; IPSF, 2022[35]; National Treasury, 2022[36]; Securities and Exchange Commission, 2022[37]; Transition Plan Taskforce, 2023[38]; IFRS ISSB, 2023[39]; SBTi, 2024[40]; CDP, 2024[41]; CA100+, 2024[42]).

In all cases, there are no agreed methods or standards to count counterfactuals and calculate avoided emissions. For corporates, as avoided emissions do not occur during the product's life cycle inventory, SBTi does not allow them to be included in GHG performance metrics and requires that they are accounted for and reported separately from Scope 1, 2 and 3 emissions, including any Scope 3 metric or target (SBTi, 2021[18]). Further, assumptions regarding avoided emissions are vulnerable to the risk of non-permanence of the underlying activities. In the case of countries for instance, "fossil fuels could be kept in the ground (or deforestation avoided) for the time of the financial support from the sale of international credits, but then extracted (or deforested)" (Jeudy-Hugo, Lo Re and Falduto, 2021[33]).

To provide a more comprehensive and nuanced perspective on progress and actions by corporates towards contributing and aligning their business activities with climate goals, an increasing number of frameworks provide guidance on information points and metrics to be disclosed. For nine such frameworks, issued by either civil society organisations, industry associations, or public authorities in specific jurisdictions, Table 2.5 presents an overview of the respective information and metrics they recommend. These are grouped in four categories: GHG emission metrics (including but not limited to alignment assessments), composition of activities and related financing and investment metrics, engagement metrics, and governance and strategy metrics. Many such frameworks have been developed in the context of incentivising corporates to develop and implement credible transition plans, for which broader guidance has also been developed, e.g., (OECD, 2022[43]).

2.2.3. Alignment and complementary metrics for sovereign bonds

While sovereign bonds represent an important asset class within the portfolios of many investors and financial institutions, fewer climate-alignment assessment methodologies are available. This is, however, an area of active development. Climate-alignment assessments of sovereign bonds relate directly to underlying countries. Available assessments of countries for use in the financial sector follow different approaches (Noels and Jachnik, 2022[3]), finding different degrees of alignment (Table 2.6. As for corporate-related financial asset classes, such variations result from different assumptions and perspectives on methodological dimensions (as outlined in Figure 2.2). When such assumptions and perspectives are transparently disclosed and explained, different assessments may be complementary and, if combined, provide a more holistic assessment (Noels and Jachnik, 2022[3]).

Existing climate-alignment assessments of sovereign bonds are based on different GHG **emissions performance metrics**. Similar to corporate-related financial assets, both absolute and intensity-based emissions metrics can be considered. Absolute emission levels can be measured from the perspective of the amount produced within a country or the amount consumed by a country. Intensity-based emissions can be calculated on a per capita or per GDP basis for example. Additionally, changes in emissions trends across various years are also considered for alignment assessments, as they could be compared to changes in emissions pathways over the years.

The **temporal boundaries** for assessing the climate alignment of sovereign bonds are largely the same as for corporate-related financial assets. It is possible to take a backward- or forward-looking perspective, a short-, medium-, or long-term horizon, as well as a point estimate or time-series comparison with a climate change mitigation scenario. Choices of different perspectives can lead to different results, similar to how such perspectives may impact alignment results of corporate-related assets. For sovereign bonds, existing climate-alignment assessments consider both historical information and targets. For example, they may calculate emissions gaps between projected emissions under current policies and a stated 2030 target, or between emission pathways of Nationally Determined Contributions (NDCs) and a 1.5°C warming scenario (LSEG, 2024, p. 13[44]). They also tend to have a greater focus on medium-term timeframes, most commonly publishing results for 2030 (Table 2.6).

Table 2.6. Climate-alignment assessment results across providers for selected sovereign bonds

Income group	Region	Provider 1			Provider 2	
		Alignment of current policies to 2030	Alignment of NDC targets to 2030	Alignment of Net zero targets to 2050	Alignment with 1.5°C benchmark to 2030	Alignment with 1.5°C fair share to 2030
Lower-middle income	Africa	Not aligned	Not available	Not available	Not aligned	Not aligned
Low income	Africa	Aligned	Aligned	Not available	Not available	Not available
Upper-middle income	Africa	Not aligned	Not aligned	Aligned	Not aligned	Not aligned
High income	Asia	Not aligned	Not aligned	Aligned	Not aligned	Not aligned
Lower-middle income	Asia	Aligned	Aligned	Aligned	Not aligned	Not aligned
Low income	Asia	Not aligned	Not available	Not available	Not available	Not available
High income	Europe	Not aligned	Not aligned	Aligned	Not aligned	Not aligned
Upper-middle income	Europe	Not aligned	Not aligned	Aligned	Not available	Not available
Upper-middle income	Middle East	Aligned	Not aligned	Not available	Not available	Not available
High income	North America	Not aligned	Not aligned	Not aligned	Not aligned	Not aligned
Upper-middle income	North America	Aligned	Aligned	Aligned	Not aligned	Not aligned
High income	Oceania	Not aligned	Not aligned	Not available	Not available	Not available
Upper-middle income	Oceania	Aligned	Not available	Not available	Not available	Not available
Lower-middle income	South America	Not aligned	Not available	Not available	Not available	Not available
Upper-middle income	South America	Not aligned	Aligned	Not available	Not available	Not available

Note: 'Not aligned' means not aligned with a 2 degrees or below scenario as assessed by the methodology. 'Not available' means that the country was assessed by the methodology as having a non-quantifiable target. Countries and methodology providers are anonymised.
Source: Authors' calculations based on data from selected providers (LSEG, 2021[45]; LSEG, 2023[46]; TPI, 2024[47]) and income group classifications from the World Bank.

Like for corporate asset classes, the complementarities that exist between different perspectives imply the need to rely on a range of indicators for a more holistic and nuanced assessment. Aside from alignment assessment methodologies developed with the financial sector in mind, a range of methodologies have been developed within the climate policy research community to assess the climate performance of countries. These put forward additional metrics, e.g., relating to the adoption of climate policies (also discussed in Chapter 4) or to innovation and infrastructure investments (Table 2.7). Further qualitative information can, for instance, relate to 'willingness' measures that examine a country's commitments and progress towards net zero, such as NDCs and engagement in environmental conventions (Barrahhou, Ferreira and Maalei, 2023[48]).

Table 2.7. Metrics considered by providers assessing the climate performance and alignment of countries

■ Included　　□ Not included

	LSEG	RIGHT	ASCOR	CAT	CCPI	ETI	EPI	GFI
GHG emission metrics								
Historic and current GHG emissions	■	■	■	■	■	■	■	■
Future GHG emissions projection	■	■	■	■	■		■	
Alignment assessment, including ITR	■	■	■					
Government commitment and policy metrics								
National Adaptation Plan	■		■	■				
Climate legislation			■			■		
Climate policy performance				■	■	■		■
Climate-related disclosures			■	■				
Carbon pricing			■			■		
Fossil fuel subsidies			■					
Energy metrics								
Energy use and intensity	■		■		■	■		■
Renewable energy trends and capacity	■		■		■	■		
Sectoral decomposition of energy generation or consumption			■					
Other metrics								
Just transition, equity, or fair share considerations			■	■		■		
Ecosystem vitality	■		■	■			■	
Environment and health	■					■	■	■
Education and human capital	■					■		
Innovation	■					■		■
Infrastructure and investments						■		

Note: Last updated in August 2024. GHG: Greenhouse gas. ITR: Implied temperature rise. LSEG: London Stock Exchange Group. ASCOR: Assessing Sovereign Climate-related Opportunities and Risks. CAT: Climate Action Tracker. CCPI: Climate Change Performance Index. ETI: Energy Transition Index. EPI: Environmental Performance Index. GFI: Green Future Index.
Source: Authors, based on publicly-available information of data providers, including (LSEG, 2024[49]; LSEG, 2024[50]).

2.3. Approaches to assess progress towards climate mitigation alignment for financial portfolios and institutions

Aggregating results across individual financial assets adds another layer of complexity as it requires weighing the contribution of different assets typically relating to different economic sectors, as well as adjusting for the potential double counting of emissions where relevant (PAT, 2020[6]). These issues become even more complex when considering aggregation across multiple asset classes (e.g., corporate-related equity and debt, sovereign bonds, real estate, and infrastructure) for which, as outlined in Section 2.2, methodologies and assumptions differ.

Despite these complexities, methodologies to assess the climate alignment of financial assets across asset classes have considered approaches to aggregate assessments to the level of financial portfolios held by investors and financial institutions (Subsection 2.3.1). However, existing methodologies and assessment providers do not tend to aggregate an alignment assessment into a single result at the level of a financial institution or financial jurisdiction yet. Such single aggregate assessment may not be desirable as they could obscure misaligned parts and the range of assumptions and complexities associated with the aim of a silver bullet assessment result.

For financial institutions a range of complementary metrics are being considered to assess progress towards net-zero commitments (Subsection 2.3.2). Alignment assessment methodologies at the level of financial jurisdictions are still very limited and, therefore, not yet included in the methodological review presented in this chapter. However, Chapter 3 does capture examples of available early estimates of data points relating to investments in activities respectively contributing to and undermining climate goals at the level of financial jurisdictions (Section 3.4) in addition to taking stock of those available at the level of financial institutions (Section 3.3).

2.3.1. Aggregate alignment assessments of financial portfolios

Providers of climate-alignment assessment methodologies are exploring approaches for aggregate asset-level assessments (Schwegler et al., 2022[17]; Institut Louis Bachelier et al., 2020[16]; CDP & WWF, 2020[51]; Thomä, Dupré and Hayne, 2018[24]; GFANZ, 2022[52]; PAT, 2020[6]). This primarily includes considering options to weigh the contribution of different assets for a given asset class both within a given economic sector (particularly relevant to inform active engagement strategies), and across different economic sectors (the respective assessment of which typically relies on sector-specific scenarios and metrics). Approaches to aggregate across multiple asset classes are not yet developed, both because of their significant complexity and given the risks of producing opaque and potentially misleading assessment results.

Currently, there is no clear dominant aggregation approach across climate-alignment assessment methodology providers for corporates, which use different approaches, sometimes tailored for different users of their methodology (Noels and Jachnik, 2022[3]). Approaches to aggregate alignment assessment results across assets within an asset class include:

- The *aggregated budget approach*: the over- or under-shoot of each asset is summed, either for total emissions of the entity, or the share of those emissions financed by the respective investor. In particular, the latter approach requires a complex comparison of the sum of "owned" projected GHG emissions against the sum of "owned" carbon budgets for the underlying holdings.
- The *weighted average approach*: the asset-level alignment metrics (e.g., Implied Temperature Rise metric) are weighted based on the relative weight of each entity in the portfolio. This weight can either be defined by the ownership stake of a financial institution for equity portfolios or the relative residual value of bond holdings for bond portfolios.
- The *portfolio-owned approach*: it combines the first and second approach by weighing asset-level alignment metrics by their respective proportion of the entity's emissions financed by the investor.

International-level collective assessment of progress against remaining global carbon budgets and towards the Paris Agreement temperature goal requires minimising double counting of GHG emission reductions and avoidance across actors, including investors and financial institutions. Within the investment and financial value chain, double counting of emissions can occur at multiple levels, namely between financial institutions co-financing the same entity or activity, between transactions within the same financial institutions, across different asset classes, as well as within the same asset class (PCAF, 2020[53]). Double-counting is problematic for portfolio-level assessments of climate alignment if GHG emissions that are counted more than once are interpreted as actual total emissions into the atmosphere, or if the double-counting distorts the alignment assessment result (Schwegler et al., 2022[17]). Approaches to adjust for double counting are still in the early stages of development (Portfolio Alignment Team, 2020[54]) and most methodologies, while acknowledging the need to address the issue, do not currently explicitly clarify whether and how they do so (Noels and Jachnik, 2022[3]).

2.3.2. Complementary metrics to assess financial institutions' progress to net-zero emissions

As highlighted in the previous subsection, a single alignment metric at the level of a financial institution is methodologically challenging to produce and likely to result in opaque and misleading results. Rather, assessing the climate consistency of financial institutions, including tracking progress towards their net-zero commitments, requires a clear set of complementary, credible, and comparable metrics (OECD, 2023[55]). Doing so can build on the increasing availability of a range of metrics at the level of individual asset classes, as highlighted by Table 2.5 for corporates and Table 2.7 for sovereigns.

Voluntary financial sector initiatives have attracted significant participation by financial institutions globally and influenced their practices to date, as further illustrated by available evidence in Chapter 3 Section 3.3. Such initiatives include the Glasgow Financial Alliance for Net Zero (GFANZ), which also oversees the UN-convened Net-Zero Asset Owner Alliance (NZAOA), the International Financial Reporting Standards Foundation's International Sustainability Standards Board (IFRS ISSB), which integrates the Task Force on Climate-related Financial Disclosures (TCFD), and the Institutional Investors Group on Climate Change (IIGCC). Voluntary initiatives support actions by market participants and can help develop good practices, as well as contribute to policies and regulations that encourage greater environmental integrity, transparency, and accountability.

These financial sector initiatives have developed frameworks that guide disclosure practices related to climate change actions or outcomes by financial institutions and investors. Their frameworks include the GFANZ Recommendations and Guidance on Financial Institution Net-Zero Transition Plans, the IFRS ISSB Sustainability Disclosure Standards, IIGCC Net Zero Investment Framework Implementation Guide, the NZAOA Target Setting Protocol, and the TCFD Recommendations. These frameworks have been developed with different audiences and aims in mind, from financial risk management to supporting a shift in investments to contribute to global net-zero goals. However, several of them cross-reference metrics and methodologies used in others, and build on other frameworks. Many frameworks have been developed with the aim of being living documents that integrate international developments and updates into account.

Guidance by such frameworks on information to be disclosed by financial institutions propose information points and metrics in relation to GHG emissions, portfolio composition, engagement, as well as strategy and governance. The overview of the guidance put forward by the selected frameworks across these four categories, as summarised in Table 2.8, highlights a high amount of information points, i.e., general descriptive disclosure on actions taken by financial institutions as well as on institutional knowledge and practices. In contrast, defining metrics involves specific measures, underpinned by methodological guidance and data requirements, thus leaving less room for different interpretations by a financial institution. Metrics typically measure actions and outcomes by financial institutions, resulting in quantifiable disclosure or measurable qualitative disclosure (e.g., yes, or no related binary data).

GHG emissions information points and metrics serve to capture progress on decarbonisation outcomes, which, in principle, should reflect the impact on real-economy GHG emissions of input actions in terms of portfolio management, engagement, and strategy. The frameworks largely propose information points and metrics assessed across three sub-categories, namely (1) historical or current emissions, (2) emission targets, and (3) alignment assessments using a recognised benchmark (including the Paris Agreement temperature goal), discussed in depth in Section 2.2.

Table 2.8. Climate mitigation information points and metrics proposed by voluntary frameworks

M*	Proposed metric with calculation method
M	Proposed metric
I	Proposed information
N	No information or metric proposed

	GFANZ	IFRS ISSB	IIGCC	NZAOA	TCFD
GHG emissions					
Historic and current GHG emissions	M	M*	M	M*	M*
GHG emission targets (short, medium, and long term)	M	M	M	M	I
Alignment assessment with a benchmark, inc. Paris Agreement	N	N	M	M*	M
Use of offsets (current and future)	N	I	N	N	N
Portfolio composition					
Portfolio share in low GHG assets and climate solutions	M	I	M*	M*	N
Portfolio share in assets consistent with net zero, or with targets based on an alignment assessment	M	N	M*	M	M
Portfolio share in carbon-intensive assets and assets exposed to transition risks and phase-out	M	M	M	N	M
Investment allocation practices driving GHG emission reductions	M	N	I	N	M
Overall portfolio composition and sector coverage	I	I	I	I	I
Other	M	M	I	N	M
Engagement					
General engagement/stewardship practices	M	I	M	I	I
Voting procedures and practices	M	M	I	I	N
Engagement escalation process	M	I	I	I	N
Collaborations and alliance engagements	M	N	I	I	N
Advocacy-based activities	M	N	I	I	N
Strategy and governance					
Remuneration linked to climate performance	M	M	N	N	M
Management/Board oversight and accountability	M	I	I	N	M
Integration of climate considerations in internal reporting and analytical processes	M	I	I	N	I
Integration of climate considerations in strategic decision-making and investment strategies	N	I	I	I	I
General strategy on climate goals and transition plans	N	I	I	I	I
Other	M	M	I	I	I

Note: M means the framework proposes at least 1 metric, I means the framework proposes at least one point of information but no metric. N means no information or metric is proposed by the frameworks.
Source: (OECD, 2023[55]), based on public reports from GFANZ, (2022[56]), Recommendations and Guidance on Financial Institution Net-zero Transition Plans; IFRS ISSB, (2023[39]), Sustainability Disclosure Standard: Climate-related Disclosures; IIGCC, (2021[57]), Net Zero Investment Framework, Institutional Investors Group on Climate Change; NZAOA, (2021[58]), Target Setting Protocol: Third Edition; TCFD, (2021[59]), Implementing the Recommendations of the Task Force on Climate-related Financial Disclosures.

The portfolio composition category serves to track the changes in a financial institution's investment or lending approach to change the composition of the portfolio. The frameworks concur that information points and metrics should be included on the portfolio share in low GHG emission assets and climate solutions, and assets that need to be phased-out but differ in how they express specific metrics. For instance, some frameworks refer to capital invested rather than portfolio shares. Frameworks propose a range of other information points and metrics, for instance, on the proportion of the portfolio with net-zero targets. They propose even more text-based information points with little or no overlap across frameworks, thus running the risk of a potential overburdening for reporting institutions.

Information points and metrics that support the effective tracking of engagement activities can help understand the extent to which steps are taken to support the reduction of clients' emissions and those of the economic actors underlying financial assets. While many information points are proposed by frameworks, metrics on engagement are very scarce. Frameworks mostly put forward information points relating to the overall and climate-specific engagement and stewardship practices of a financial institution, for instance, on how they identify and escalate engagement activities; engage in dialogue; present and vote on actions; and undertake phase-out engagement.

Strategy and governance information points and metrics could support an assessment of internal changes to a financial institution's strategy and shifts in internal processes to incentivise the net-zero transition. In this area, frameworks propose a large variety of information points on the integration of climate considerations in strategic decision-making and investment strategies, but very few concrete metrics.

2.4. Towards assessing the climate resilience alignment of finance

In response to rapidly increasing climate-related physical risks, a range of stakeholders are analysing physical climate risks to finance and related efforts to increase resilience to climate change. However, while there is a growing landscape of methodologies to integrate physical climate risks in traditional financial risk analysis, the operationalisation of the concept and assessments of alignment with climate resilience as a policy objective is still very limited, which also explains the lack of resilience data points in Chapter 3. This section provides an overview of developments in this area.

While financial risk and resilience alignment stem from different perspectives and aims, leading to differences in scope and results, they are interrelated and overlap in several analytical dimensions and data requirements (Mullan and Ranger, 2022[60]; UNEP FI, 2022[61]; Bernhofen and Ranger, 2023[62]). The evaluation of the climate resilience alignment of finance flows extends beyond risk analysis, comparing physical climate risks to climate resilience policy goals and reference points while taking into account adaptation actions by companies and the financial sector. This means not only identifying and quantifying risks, but also assessing how economic actors and financial sector participants contribute to reducing those risks in alignment with climate policy. Policymakers and the private sector could then also use such assessments to identify adaptation opportunities and where further public investment may be most needed for societal co-benefits. However, much more conceptual work in this area is needed.

As suggested in Noels et al. (2024[63]), which builds on existing approaches end emerging practices, assessing the climate resilience alignment of finance can involve five interrelated dimensions (Figure 2.7) Physical climate risk assessments for assets, entities and finance stocks and flows are analytical dimensions for both a financial risk analysis and a climate resilience alignment assessment dimensions 1 and 2). This is also the case of the dimension relating to analysing adaptation and resilience actions and strategies by financial system and economic actors (dimension 3). Assessing the alignment of finance with climate-resilient development, as called for in Article 2.1c of the Paris Agreement, further requires the availability and identification of relevant policy goals and targets (dimension 4). Bringing these dimensions together then allows an assessment of whether finance flows and stocks contribute or not to societies becoming more resilient to the impacts of climate change (dimension 5).

Figure 2.7. Methodological steps to assess the climate resilience-alignment of finance

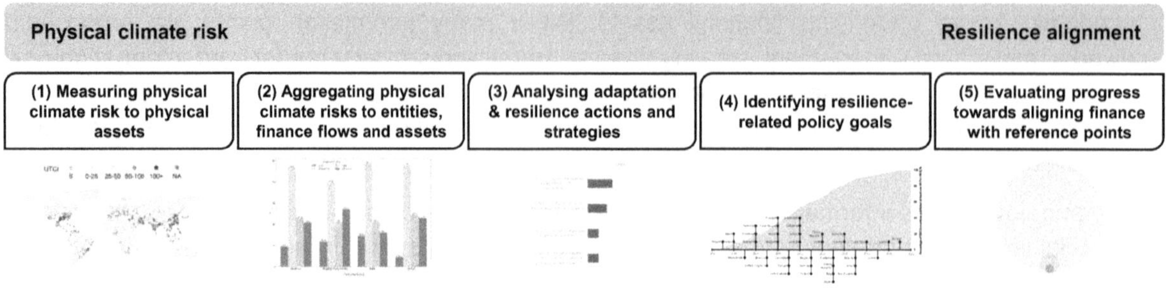

Source: (Noels et al., 2024[63]).

Overall, financial sector physical climate risk analyses and approaches are increasing. A range of commercial data providers provide different data solutions and analyses for different asset classes that can be used to assess physical climate risk for individual assets or financial portfolios. Financial institutions may further aggregate such assessments, and central banks may assess climate risks to the financial centres they oversee at a more aggregate level.

Methodologies to date have largely focussed on assessments of physical climate risks to corporate financial assets (Hain, Kölbel and Leippold, 2022[64]; UNEP FI, 2023[65]). In this context, some research has found that the different physical climate risk assessments lead to a very wide range of results for the same entity (Hain, Kölbel and Leippold, 2022[64]). Methodologies to assess physical climate risks to other large asset classes have, however, been explored for real estate and infrastructure (UNEP FI, 2023[66]; Coloia and Jansen, 2021[67]), as well as sovereign bonds (NGFS, 2024[68])

Challenges, however, remain for assessing climate change risks, such as the absence of comparable methodologies or set of metrics for assessing resilience to physical climate risks, as well as data availability constraints (Simpson et al., 2021[69]). These challenges similarly constrain climate resilience alignment assessments. There are, however, further challenges in the assessment of the climate resilience alignment of finance (Mullan and Ranger, 2022[60]). Notably, quantified adaptation goals remain elusive at the global level, owing to the context and location-specific nature of adaptation and resilience needs (Jeudy-Hugo and Charles, 2022[70]). Such goals and targets are needed at the national and subnational levels, where they, however, remain rare. more specifically, Noels et al. (2024[63]) highlight that:

- The geographical, sectoral, and temporal context of climate resilience alignment assessments influences the choice and prioritisation of climate-related hazards data and indicators. Although certain hazards, such as flooding and heatwaves, have been more impactful to date, the prevalence of climate-related hazards is heterogeneous across geographies. Hence, there is a need for high granularity in data and location-specific hazard prioritisation to capture risks accurately.
- There are a wide range of climate-related hazards and classifications. Existing climate risks analysis may refer to the same hazard differently and prioritise different hazard. Moreover, some existing methodologies combine acute and chronic climate related hazards, while others capture those in separate analysis. For climate alignment analysis, it may be practical initially to keep those separate as they require different adaptation responses.
- Data gaps for climate exposure and vulnerability at the asset level need to be filled. Relying solely on headquarters location data can significantly underestimate climate exposure. Many existing climate risk assessments only analyse climate exposure. Not adequately characterising vulnerability offers only a partial view of overall physical climate risk.
- Further developments of typologies and data for adaptation and resilience strategies are needed to inform both climate resilience-related financial risk and alignment assessments. These should cover

real-economy actors and financial institutions. Actions and strategies for reducing exposure are easier to identify as they require less information. Strategies to reduce vulnerability often rely on corporate disclosure, which is currently scarce.

- In contrast to climate change mitigation, there is a lack of clear quantitative global policy goals and reference point(s) on adaptation and resilience. Therefore, consistent with the context-specific nature of climate exposure and vulnerability, reference points at national and regional levels are critical for assessing adaptation and resilience alignment. In this context, adaptation relevant policies, goals and targets may be integrated into mainstream policies, such as worker policies, or as part of sustainability-related disclosure requirements.
- The final step in a climate resilience alignment assessment involves comparing the level of climate risk and the impact of adaptation actions on reducing that risk with relevant climate resilience policy goals. A metric for real-economy investments may relate to the share of activities consistent with National Adaptation Plans, while for financial system participants, this may relate to the share of assets under management aligned with climate resilience goals.

Due to the methodological and data challenges highlighted above, evidence on the alignment of finance with climate adaptation and resilience goals is very limited. This explains why the remaining chapters of this report on available estimates of financial flows and stocks (Chapter 3) and of climate-related financial sector policies and actions (Chapter 4) focus primarily on climate change mitigation.

In this context, it is, however, important to note that climate resilience alignment assessment of finance flows may in any case only partly be quantitative and require complementary types of indicators as some societal resilience goals are difficult to quantify. This lack of quantification is partly due to the insufficient progress in assessing such policies, and the policies themselves may not always be quantitatively formulated. Moreover, resilience alignment assessments may require examining how adaptation reduces exposure and vulnerability for each climate hazard individually.

Further, the climate resilience alignment of real-economy investments and financial system assets may further depend on wider actions, such as public investments in collective adaptation solutions and adaptation actions by other actors within the value chain. It is also dependent on advancements in climate change mitigation, which implies that adaptation goals remain moving targets. Moreover, there are limits to adaptation, especially under high-emission scenarios. This underscores the ongoing need for climate change mitigation efforts to limit global warming and prevent scenarios where adaptation and resilience alignment may no longer or only partly be feasible.

References

Allen, M. et al. (2022), "Indicate separate contributions of long-lived and short-lived greenhouse gases in emission targets", *npj Climate and Atmospheric Science*, Vol. 5/1, https://doi.org/10.1038/s41612-021-00226-2. [27]

ASCOR (2023), "ASCOR framework: methodology note", *Grantham Research Institute on Climate Change and the Environment, London School of Economics*, https://epi.yale.edu/downloads/2024-epi-executive-summary.pdf. [19]

Barrahhou, I., P. Ferreira and Y. Maalei (2023), *A Framework to Align Sovereign Bond Portfolios with Net Zero Trajectories*, https://papers.ssrn.com/sol3/papers.cfm?abstract_id=4515462. [48]

Battiston, S. et al. (2022), "The NACE – CPRS – IAM mapping: A tool to support climate risk analysis of financial portfolio using NGFS scenarios.", *SSRN Electronic Journal*, https://doi.org/10.2139/ssrn.4223606. [12]

Bernhofen, M. and N. Ranger (2023), *Aligning finance with adaptation and resilience goals: Targets and metrics for financial institutions: technical note*, https://www.cgfi.ac.uk/wp-content/uploads/2023/06/GRII_Adaptation_and_Resilience_Metrics_Note_June2023.pdf. [62]

Bingler, J., C. Colesanti Senni and P. Monnin (2021), *Climate Transition Risk Metrics: Understanding Convergence and Divergence across Firms and Providers*, https://doi.org/10.3929/ethz-b-000505345. [25]

CA100+ (2024), *Climate Action 100+ Net Zero Company Benchmark Version 2.1 Framework*, https://www.climateaction100.org/wp-content/uploads/2024/06/Net-Zero-Company-Benchmark-Version-2.1-Framework-v2.pdf. [42]

Calel, R. et al. (2021), *Do carbon offsets offset carbon? Centre for Climate Change Economics and Policy Working Paper 398/Grantham Research Institute on Climate Change and the Environment Working Paper 371. London: London School of Economics and Political Science*, https://www.lse.ac.uk/granthaminstitute/wp-content/uploads/2021/11/working-paper-371-Calel-et-al..pdf. [30]

CDP (2024), *CDP Full Corporate Questionnaire*, https://www.cdp.net/en/2024-disclosure/cdp-full-corporate-questionnaire. [41]

CDP & WWF (2020), *Temperature Rating Methodology: A temperature rating method for targets, corporates, and portfolios*, https://cdn.cdp.net/cdp-production/comfy/cms/files/files/000/003/741/original/Temperature_scoring_-_beta_methodology.pdf. [51]

CDP-WWF (2024), *CDP–WWF Temperature Scoring Methodology: A temperature scoring method for targets, companies, and portfolios*, https://cdn.cdp.net/cdp-production/comfy/cms/files/files/000/009/448/original/CDP%E2%80%93WWF_Temperature_Scoring_Methodology.pdf. [20]

Coloia, F. and D. Jansen (2021), *Flood risk and financial stability: Evidence from a stress test for the Netherlands. DNB Working Paper No. 730*, De Nederlandsche Bank, https://www.dnb.nl/en/publications/research-publications/working-paper-2021/730-flood-risk-and-financial-stability-evidence-from-a-stress-test-for-the-netherlands/. [67]

European Commission (2023), *A user guide to navigate the EU Taxonomy for sustainable activities*, https://ec.europa.eu/sustainable-finance-taxonomy/assets/documents/Taxonomy%20User%20Guide.pdf. [34]

Fankhauser, S. et al. (2021), "The meaning of net zero and how to get it right", *Nature Climate Change*, Vol. 12/1, pp. 15-21, https://doi.org/10.1038/s41558-021-01245-w. [29]

GFANZ (2022), *Measuring portfolio alignment: Enhancement, convergence, and adoption*, https://assets.bbhub.io/company/sites/63/2022/07/GFANZ-Portfolio-Alignment-Measurement-August2022.pdf. [52]

GFANZ (2022), *Recommendations and Guidance on Financial Institution Net-zero Transition Plans*, https://assets.bbhub.io/company/sites/63/2022/06/GFANZ_Recommendations-and-Guidance-on-Net-zero-Transition-Plans-for-the-Financial-Sector_June2022.pdf. [56]

Hain, L., J. Kölbel and M. Leippold (2022), “Let’s get physical: Comparing metrics of physical climate risk”, *Finance Research Letters*, Vol. 46, p. 102406, https://doi.org/10.1016/j.frl.2021.102406. [64]

Hertwich, E. and R. Wood (2018), “The growing importance of scope 3 greenhouse gas emissions from industry”, *Environmental Research Letters*, Vol. 13/10, p. 104013, https://iopscience.iop.org/article/10.1088/1748-9326/aae19a#erlaae19as3. [28]

IFRS ISSB (2023), *Sustainability Disclosure Standard: Climate-related Disclosures*, https://www.ifrs.org/content/dam/ifrs/publications/pdf-standards-issb/english/2023/issued/part-a/issb-2023-a-ifrs-s2-climate-related-disclosures.pdf?bypass=on. [39]

IIGCC (2021), *Net Zero Investment Framework, Institutional Investors Group on Climate Change*, https://www.iigcc.org/resource/net-zero-investment-framework-implementation-guide/. [57]

Institut Louis Bachelier (2024), *The alignment cookbook 2*, https://www.institutlouisbachelier.org/en/the-alignment-cookbook-2-2/. [5]

Institut Louis Bachelier et al. (2020), *The Alignment Cookbook - A Technical Review of Methodologies Assessing a Portfolio’s Alignment with Low-carbon Trajectories or Temperature Goal*, https://www.louisbachelier.org/wp-content/uploads/2020/10/cookbook.pdf. [16]

IPCC (2022), *Annex III: Scenarios and modelling methods*, Cambridge University Press, Cambridge, UK and New York, NY, USA, https://doi.org/10.1017/9781009157926.022. [11]

IPCC (2022), *Climate Change 2022: Mitigation of Climate Change*, https://www.ipcc.ch/report/ar6/wg3/ (accessed on 28 April 2022). [26]

IPSF (2022), *Common Ground Taxonomy – Climate Change Mitigation*, https://finance.ec.europa.eu/system/files/2022-06/220603-international-platform-sustainable-finance-common-ground-taxonomy-instruction-report_en.pdf. [35]

Jachnik, R. and A. Dobrinevski (2021), “Measuring the alignment of real economy investments with climate mitigation objectives: The United Kingdom’s buildings sector”, *OECD Environment Working Papers*, No. 172, OECD Publishing, Paris, https://doi.org/10.1787/8eccb72a-en. [4]

Jachnik, R., M. Mirabile and A. Dobrinevski (2019), “Tracking finance flows towards assessing their consistency with climate objectives”, *OECD Environment Working Papers*, No. 146, OECD Publishing, Paris, https://doi.org/10.1787/82cc3a4c-en. [1]

Jeudy-Hugo, S. and L. Charles (2022), “Translating outputs to outcomes under the global stocktake of the Paris Agreement”, *OECD/IEA Climate Change Expert Group Papers*, No. 2022/01, OECD Publishing, Paris, https://doi.org/10.1787/e06c61f0-en. [70]

Jeudy-Hugo, S., L. Lo Re and C. Falduto (2021), “Understanding countries’ net-zero emissions targets”, *OECD/IEA Climate Change Expert Group Papers*, No. 2021/03, OECD Publishing, Paris, https://doi.org/10.1787/8d25a20c-en. [33]

Kreibiehl, S. et al. (2022), “Investment and Finance”, in *Climate Change 2022: Mitigation of Climate Change*, Cambridge University Press, https://doi.org/10.1017/9781009157926.017. [2]

LSEG (2024), *FTSE Climate Risk Assessment Methodology v1.0*, https://www.lseg.com/content/dam/ftse-russell/en_us/documents/policy-documents/ftse-climate-risk-assessment-methodology.pdf. [49]

LSEG (2024), *Sustainable Sovereign Risk Methodology v1.1*, https://www.lseg.com/content/dam/ftse-russell/en_us/documents/policy-documents/sustainable-sovereign-risk-methodology.pdf. [50]

LSEG (2024), *Sustainable Sovereign Risk Methodology v1.1*, https://www.lseg.com/content/dam/ftse-russell/en_us/documents/policy-documents/sustainable-sovereign-risk-methodology.pdf. [44]

LSEG (2023), *The COP28 Net Zero Atlas*, https://www.lseg.com/content/dam/ftse-russell/en_us/documents/research/cop28-net-zero-atlas.pdf. [46]

LSEG (2021), *How to measure the temperature of sovereign assets*, https://www.lseg.com/content/dam/ftse-russell/en_us/documents/research/how-to-measure-temperature-sovereign-assets.pdf. [45]

McCollum, D. et al. (2018), "Energy investment needs for fulfilling the Paris Agreement and achieving the Sustainable Development Goals", *Nature Energy*, Vol. 3/7, pp. 589-599, https://doi.org/10.1038/s41560-018-0179-z. [7]

MSCI (2024), *Implied Temperature Rise Methodology*, MSCI ESG Research LLC, https://www.msci.com/documents/10199/7118a4c1-e446-ffa8-87f2-f4d6d2d07d36. [21]

Mullan, M. and N. Ranger (2022), "Climate-resilient finance and investment: Framing paper", *OECD Environment Working Papers*, No. 196, OECD Publishing, Paris, https://doi.org/10.1787/223ad3b9-en. [60]

National Treasury (2022), *South African Green Finance Taxonomy.* [36]

NGFS (2024), *Technical Document – Considering climate-related risks and transition impact in the sovereign investments of central banks*, https://www.ngfs.net/sites/default/files/media/2024/05/16/ngfs_technical_document_on_considering_climate-related_risks_and_transition_impact_in_the_sovereign_investments_of_central_banks_0.pdf. [68]

Noels, J. et al. (2024), "Towards assessing the alignment of finance with climate resilience goals: Exploring options, methodologies, data and metrics", *OECD Environment Working Papers*, No. 251, OECD Publishing, Paris, https://doi.org/10.1787/9446d65e-en. [63]

Noels, J. and R. Jachnik (2022), "Assessing the climate consistency of finance: Taking stock of methodologies and their links to climate mitigation policy objectives", *OECD Environment Working Papers*, No. 200, OECD Publishing, Paris, https://doi.org/10.1787/d12005e7-en. [3]

Noels, J. et al. (2023), "Climate change mitigation scenarios for financial sector target setting and alignment assessment: A stocktake and analysis of their Paris-consistency, practicality and assumptions", *OECD Environment Working Papers*, No. 223, OECD Publishing, Paris, https://doi.org/10.1787/bcd25b82-en. [8]

NZAOA (2021), *Inaugural 2025 Target Setting Protocol: U.N.-convened net-zero asset owner alliance monitoring reporting and verification track*, https://www.unepfi.org/wordpress/wp-content/uploads/2021/01/Alliance-Target-Setting-Protocol-2021.pdf. [58]

OECD (2023), "Assessing net-zero metrics for financial institutions: Supporting the monitoring of financial institutions' commitments", *OECD Business and Finance Policy Papers*, No. 37, OECD Publishing, Paris, https://doi.org/10.1787/dedcfe56-en. [55]

OECD (2022), *OECD Guidance on Transition Finance: Ensuring Credibility of Corporate Climate Transition Plans*, Green Finance and Investment, OECD Publishing, Paris, https://doi.org/10.1787/7c68a1ee-en. [43]

P.R. Shukla, J. (ed.) (2022), *Mitigation pathways compatible with long-term goals*, Cambridge University Press, Cambridge, UK and New York, NY, USA, https://doi.org/10.1017/9781009157926.005. [15]

PAT (2020), *Measuring Portfolio Alignment: Assessing the position of companies and portfolios on the path to net zero*, https://www.tcfdhub.org/wp-content/uploads/2020/10/PAT-Report-20201109-Final.pdf. [6]

PCAF (2020), *The global GHG accounting and reporting standard for the financial industry*, https://carbonaccountingfinancials.com/files/downloads/PCAF-Global-GHG-Standard.pdf. [53]

Portfolio Alignment Team (2020), *Measuring Portfolio Alignment: Assessing the position of companies and portfolios on the path to net zero*, https://www.tcfdhub.org/wp-content/uploads/2020/10/PAT-Report-20201109-Final.pdf. [54]

Pouille, C. et al. (2023), "Paris-consistent climate change mitigation scenarios: A framework for emissions pathway classification in line with global mitigation objectives", *OECD Environment Working Papers*, No. 222, OECD Publishing, Paris, https://doi.org/10.1787/0de87ef8-en. [10]

S&P (2024), *Trucost Paris Alignment Methodology*, https://portal.s1.spglobal.com/survey/documents/SPG_S1_Paris_Alignment_Methodology.pdf. [22]

SBTi (2024), *SBTi Corporate Net Zero Standard Version 1.2*, https://sciencebasedtargets.org/resources/files/Net-Zero-Standard.pdf. [40]

SBTi (2021), *SBTi Corporate Manual Version 2.0*, https://sciencebasedtargets.org/resources/files/SBTi-Corporate-Manual.pdf. [18]

Schleussner, C. et al. (2022), "An emission pathway classification reflecting the Paris Agreement climate objectives", *Communications Earth & Environment*, Vol. 3/1, https://doi.org/10.1038/s43247-022-00467-w. [9]

Schwegler, R. et al. (2022), *Portfolio Climate Alignment: Understanding unwanted disincentives when using climate alignment methodologies*, Swiss Federal Office for the Environment (FOEN), https://www.bafu.admin.ch/dam/bafu/de/dokumente/klima/externe-studien-berichte/Report_Portfolio%20Climate%20Alignment_Infras_HSG_22.06.2022.pdf.download.pdf/Report_Portfolio%20Climate%20Alignment_Infras_HSG_22.06.2022.pdf. [17]

Securities and Exchange Commission (2022), *The Enhancement and Standardization of Climate-Related Disclosures for Investors*, https://www.govinfo.gov/content/pkg/FR-2022-04-11/pdf/2022-06342.pdf. [37]

Simpson, N. et al. (2021), "A framework for complex climate change risk assessment", *One Earth*, Vol. 4/4, pp. 489-501, https://doi.org/10.1016/j.oneear.2021.03.005. [69]

TCFD (2021), *Implementing the Recommendations of the Task Force on Climate-related Financial Disclosures*, https://assets.bbhub.io/company/sites/60/2021/07/2021-TCFD-Implementing_Guidance.pdf. [59]

Teske, S. (ed.) (2022), *Achieving the Paris Climate Agreement Goals*, Springer International Publishing, Cham, https://doi.org/10.1007/978-3-030-99177-7. [13]

Thomä, J., S. Dupré and M. Hayne (2018), "A Taxonomy of Climate Accounting Principles for Financial Portfolios", *Sustainability*, Vol. 10/2, p. 328, https://doi.org/10.3390/su10020328. [24]

TPI (2024), *ASCOR Tool*, https://www.transitionpathwayinitiative.org/ascor. [47]

TPI (2023), *TPI's methodology report: Management Quality and Carbon Performance Version 5.0*, https://www.transitionpathwayinitiative.org/publications/uploads/2023-methodology-report-management-quality-and-carbon-performance-version-5-0.pdf. [23]

Transition Plan Taskforce (2023), *Disclosure Framework*, https://transitiontaskforce.net/wp-content/uploads/2023/10/TPT_Disclosure-framework-2023.pdf. [38]

UNEP FI (2023), *Climate Risks in the Real Estate Sector*, https://www.unepfi.org/wordpress/wp-content/uploads/2023/03/Real-Estate-Sector-Risks-Briefing.pdf. [66]

UNEP FI (2023), *The 2023 Climate Risk Landscape*, https://www.unepfi.org/themes/climate-change/2023-climate-risk-landscape/. [65]

UNEP FI (2022), *Adapting to a New Climate: An assessment of physical risk management and climate adaptation in banks and a proposal for accelerating climate resilient banking*, https://www.unepfi.org/wordpress/wp-content/uploads/2022/11/Adapting-to-a-New-Climate.pdf. [61]

UNEP FI & CICERO (2021), *Pathways to Paris: A practical guide to climate transition scenarios for financial professionals*, UN Environment Programme Finance Initiative, https://www.unepfi.org/industries/banking/pathways-to-paris/. [14]

Wetterberg, K., J. Ellis and L. Schneider (2024), "The interplay between voluntary and compliance carbon markets: Implications for environmental integrity", *OECD Environment Working Papers*, No. 244, OECD Publishing, Paris, https://doi.org/10.1787/500198e1-en. [31]

World Resources Institute & World Business Council for Sustainable evelopment (2004), *GHG Protocol Corporate Accounting and Reporting Standard*, https://ghgprotocol.org/sites/default/files/standards/ghg-protocol-revised.pdf. [32]

Notes

[1] CDR refers to anthropogenic activities removing CO_2 from the atmosphere and durably storing it (...) but excludes natural CO_2 uptake not directly caused by human activities.

[2] Scope 1 are direct emissions from owned or controlled assets, Scope 2 indirect emissions from the generation of purchased energy, and Scope 3 are indirect emissions from any other up- and down-stream activities related to the company's product (World Resources Institute & World Business Council for Sustainable evelopment, 2004[32]). These were defined via the GHG Protocol, a reference point for corporate level reporting and accounting.

3 Existing estimates on the degree of climate alignment of finance

Acknowledging remaining methodological and data gaps that currently prevent comprehensive alignment assessments, this chapter brings together best available, though still very partial, data and estimates of finance that can be considered as contributing to or undermining climate policy goals across different layers of finance. As climate alignment ultimately requires making all financial flows and stocks consistent with climate goals, such estimates are placed in the context of total volumes, for both finance stocks and flows. Apart from real-economy investments (capturing investment by all types of actors), the primary focus for other layers is on finance issued, underwritten, or held by private actors. Given the very limited data on climate change adaptation, the chapter focusses on mitigation-related evidence.

Key insights

- **Awaiting further methodological developments for comprehensive climate-alignment assessments, best-available, although partial, data on finance to activities contributing to or undermining climate goals must be placed in the context of total finance stocks and flows.** This needs to be done for all layers of finance, including real-economy investments, financial assets across asset classes, financial institutions, and financial jurisdictions.
- **Global real-economy investments going to activities clearly supporting climate change mitigation are growing but remain a small share of total investments.** Estimates for 2022 find investments in clean energy amounted to around USD 1.7 trillion compared to USD 1.5 trillion investments in fossil fuel supply, representing respectively just above and below 6% of total gross fixed capital formation (USD 26.4 trillion). However, more complete estimates of investments contributing to and undermining climate change mitigation are still missing.
- **For listed corporate equity, available estimates converge on a remaining low degree of alignment in sectors critical to the climate transition.** In 2022, listed corporate equity stocks in renewable electricity were estimated at USD 3.7 trillion and USD 9.6 trillion in fossil fuel supply, respectively representing 4% and 10% of global listed equity. There is also evidence of a continued need for improved ambition of emissions reduction targets to further align with climate goals, and of disclosure to support improved and more comprehensive alignment assessments.
- **While private corporate equity is a significant and growing asset class, it remains a key blind spot in terms of finance volumes going to activities supporting or undermining climate goals.** Available estimates find only USD 0.2 trillion (3%) out of a total of USD 7.6 trillion of private corporate equity stocks were going to climate-aligned activities in 2022. There are currently no estimates of private corporate equity financing activities undermining climate goals.
- **Within the corporate debt securities asset class, flows and stocks of green bonds remain lower than of carbon-intensive sector bonds, representing a small share of the total bond universe.** In 2022, green-labelled bond issuance (flows) reached USD 0.4 trillion, while carbon-intensive corporate debt security flows were estimated at USD 1.4 trillion, which corresponds to a third of non-financial debt issued. In terms of outstanding corporate bond stocks, green-labelled bonds and carbon-intensive bonds were USD 1.6 trillion and USD 1.7 trillion in 2023, respectively just above and below 5% of total outstanding corporate bonds.
- **Corporate loans represent another key blind spot in terms of data on transactions supporting and undermining climate goals.** Very partial and inconclusive evidence is available for green-labelled loans, while even less data was identified for carbon-intensive loans.
- **While identifying sovereign bonds that explicitly undermine climate goals is difficult, the scale of green-labelled sovereign bonds remains small.** Green-labelled bonds issued by the public sector in 2023 were only USD 0.25 trillion, a small share of total sovereign bond issuance.
- **Climate-related evidence for financial institutions and portfolios remains limited, despite the involvement in climate coalition of banks with over a third of global banking assets and institutional investors with over three-quarters of global assets under management.** Analysis of 1 100 large banks finds that they provided financing (flows) for nearly USD 1 trillion to fossil fuel supply in 2022, while USD 0.7 trillion went to low-carbon energy supply.
- **Efforts to generate evidence at the level of financial jurisdictions are ramping up but remain work in progress.** Updates to the System of National Accounts intend to include "green" breakdowns for debt securities, loans, equity, and investment fund shares, which would support such efforts, although not in relation to climate-misaligned finance.

Chapter 2 highlighted remaining challenges and gaps to comprehensively track the alignment of finance with climate policy goals. Acknowledging these challenges and gaps, this chapter compiles a selection of available data points and estimates that provide indications of the scale and share of investments and financing going respectively to activities contributing to or undermining climate goals, with a focus on climate change mitigation. Improvements in the availability, coverage, scale, and granularity of these data points and estimates over time will provide opportunities to develop actual alignment assessments involving a comparison with climate policy goals reference points and benchmarks.

This chapter presents available evidence across different levels of finance, starting with real-economy investments and considering different layers of the financial system (Figure 3.1[i]). This review focuses primarily on finance issued, underwritten, or held by private actors. It complements the multiple processes that already address the climate alignment of public finance, notably budgetary expenditures (IEA, 2023[1]; IEA, 2023[2]; OECD, 2024[3]) and international development finance (OECD, 2019[4]). In terms of geographical coverage, while tracking real-economy assets and corresponding investments can be contained within national boundaries, other layers typically involve a mixture of domestic and cross-border flows and stocks of investments and financing. For instance, financial institutions headquartered in a given financial centre will typically invest and hold assets in both that country and other jurisdictions (countries).

Figure 3.1. Different levels of aggregation for tracking climate-aligned finance

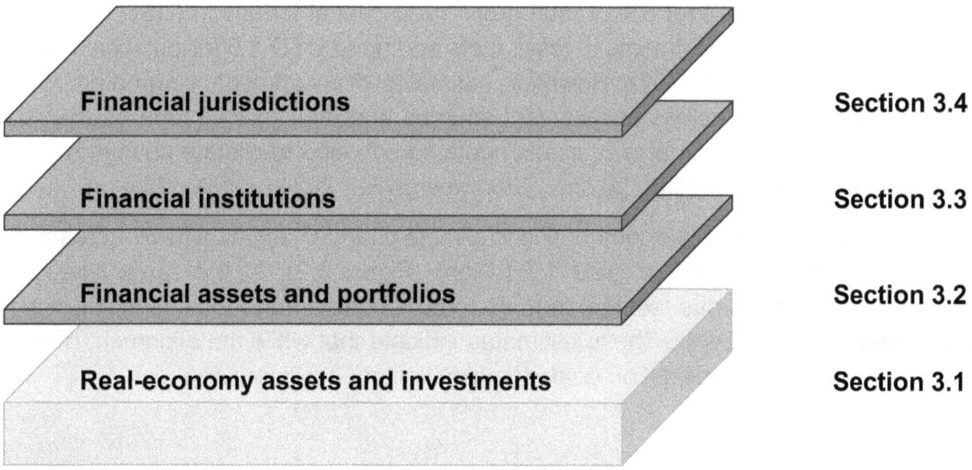

Source: Authors.

Within each of these layers, different initiatives and tracking exercises may define activities that contribute to or undermine climate goals slightly differently. In some cases, such estimates are based on categories of activities (projects or assets), technologies, or sub-sectors classifications. In other cases, finance stocks and flows are labelled as 'green' or climate-related based on voluntary labels or taxonomies providing definitions or guidance. The chapter clarifies where estimates across different parts of finance follow varying definitions or scopes.

Estimates of finance for activities that contribute to or undermine climate objectives may in themselves be partial. For example, while climate finance is relatively well tracked for international public sources and specific sub-sectors such as renewable energy, significant data gaps remain for domestic public finance and private sources and for sectors that involve smaller-scale activities (e.g., agriculture) (CPI, 2022[5]). Such gaps are typically even more acute for climate change adaptation than for climate change mitigation, as discussed in Chapter 2, which explains why only a few examples are included in this chapter. More generally, estimates of finance to activities that contribute to or undermine climate objectives tend to be less comprehensive for developing countries and unlisted companies (World Bank Group, IMF and OECD,

2023[6]). Notwithstanding these challenges and gaps, and with the aim to address the broader Article 2.1c goal to make all finance consistent with climate goals, the chapter places available figures in the context of total investments and financing flows and stocks as relevant.

3.1. Estimates of real-economy investments

A comprehensive analysis of the degree of (mis)alignment of real-economy investments does not yet exist, but pilot studies are being conducted at the sectoral level (Micale et al., 2020[7]) and country level (Jachnik and Dobrinevski, 2021[8]). Data points on real-economy investments contributing to or undermining climate change mitigation goals are mostly found at the sectoral level, and most prominently for the energy sector. In the absence of comprehensive evidence on the climate change mitigation alignment of all real-economy investments, these estimates can be compared to total real-economy investments, for which gross fixed capital formation[1] can be considered as an approximate benchmark for the order of magnitude of total real-economy investment flows (Jachnik, Mirabile and Dobrinevski, 2019[9]). By nature, gross fixed capital formation and other estimates presented in this section cover real-economy investments by both private and public actors (Box 3.1).

Estimated real-economy investments supporting climate change mitigation are growing and were larger than those in fossil fuels in 2022. In 2022, estimates indicate investments sin clean energy represented around USD 1.7 trillion, which is over 6% of total gross fixed capital formation (USD 26.4 trillion) in that year (Figure 3.2). Estimates of investments in fossil fuels add up to USD 1.5 trillion, which is nearly 6% of total gross fixed capital formation in 2022. However, estimates of investments supporting or undermining climate change mitigation differ across assessment sources and their exact scope of analysis and data access. For example, available estimates of investments contributing to climate change mitigation range from USD 1.3 to 1.7 trillion in 2022 (CPI, 2023[10]; BloombergNEF, 2024[11]; IEA, 2024[12]).

Real-economy investments in activities contributing to climate change mitigation have increased 45% since 2015 (from USD 1.1 trillion in 2015 to USD 1.7 trillion) (Figure 3.2). At the same time, the share of investments going to fossil fuels has reduced from 80 to 60% compared to total investment in fossil fuels and renewable energy (IEA, 2024[12]). These estimates indicate that while the alignment of real-economy investments with climate change mitigation goals remains limited, it is improving.

Figure 3.2. Estimates of global real-economy investments supporting or undermining climate mitigation

Layer: Real-economy assets and investments
Actor: Private and public

Theme: Mitigation
Type: Flows

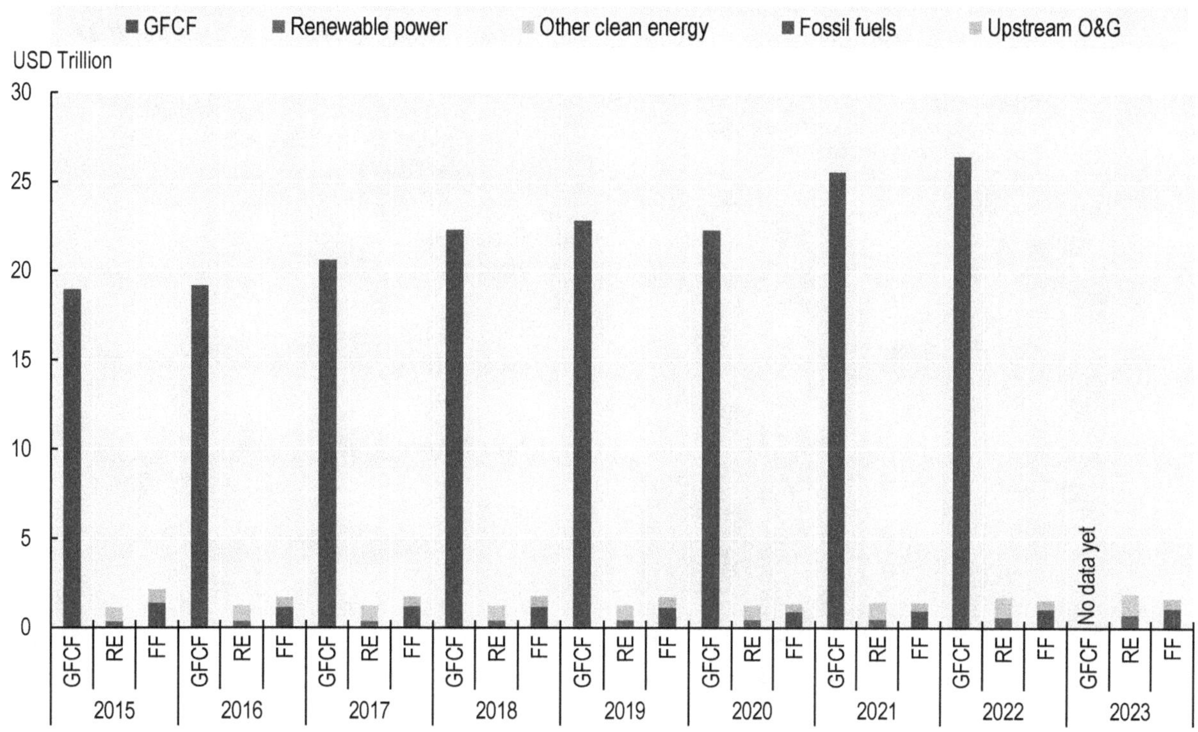

Note: GFCF is gross fixed capital formation. Renewable power relates to investments in power generation from renewables. Other clean energy refers to investments in energy efficiency and other end uses, electricity networks, storage, nuclear power generation, and clean fuels. Fossil fuels relates to investments in fossil fuel supply and power generation from coal, oil, and natural gas.
Source: Authors, based on (World Bank, n.d.[13]; IEA, 2024[12]).

Some sectors are shifting their investments towards climate-aligned activities slower than others. Focussing on capital expenditure by companies[2] across sectors provides further sectoral insights for real-economy investments by private actors. As of 2022, only about 1% of capital expenditure by oil and gas companies globally is going towards low-carbon activities (Figure 3.3, Panel A). While there is an increase compared to when the Paris Agreement was adopted, it remains a small fraction of total capital expenditure by those companies, and capital expenditure going to fossil fuel supply. Taking the example of green capital expenditure by manufacturing companies in Europe, transport and steel manufacturers have higher green capital expenditure shares than other manufacturing sectors such as chemical and food manufacturers (Figure 3.3, Panel B).

Figure 3.3. Sectoral estimates of real-economy investments supporting or undermining climate mitigation

Layer: Real-economy assets and investments
Actor: Private

Theme: Mitigation
Type: Flows

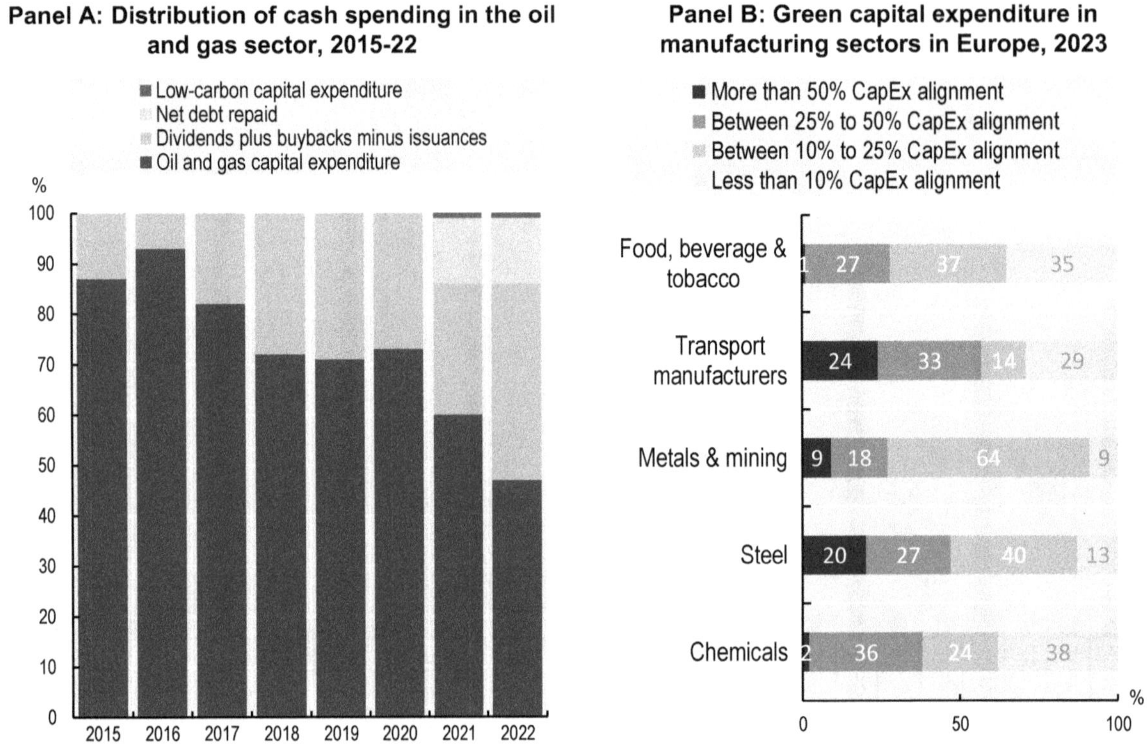

Note: For Panel B, CapEx alignment refers to the share of capital expenditure by companies in a given sector on areas aligned with their own corporate climate transition plans or sustainable finance taxonomy.
Source: Adapted from (IEA, 2023[14]) using S&P Capital IQ data for Panel A and from (CDP & Oliver Wyman, 2024[15]) for Panel B.

Volumes of real-economy investments in activities supporting and undermining climate change mitigation differ. Looking at total investments across geographies, high-income countries (85 countries with 39% of the world population) represented 54% of global gross fixed capital formation in 2022, middle-income countries (105 countries with 49% of the world population) represented 45% and low-income countries (26 countries with 12% of the world population) represented only 0.4% (Figure 3.4, Panel A). Investments in activities contributing to climate change mitigation can hence be expected to be smaller in, for example, Africa and Eurasia. While all regions have invested more in fossil fuels than renewables between 2015 and 2020, clean energy investments surpassed fossil fuel-related investments in 2022. For example, Asia Pacific and Europe invested more in clean energy than fossil fuel supply (Figure 3.4, Panel B). At the same time, Asia Pacific also invested the most in fossil fuel supply along with North America.

In the context of geographical disparities, it is important to recognise that the capacities of relatively less developed countries to invest in and finance climate action can be, to various degrees depending on the country, dependent on international climate finance provided and mobilised. This includes international climate finance provided and mobilised in the context of the existing annual USD 100 billion goal under the UNFCCC (which, as per (OECD, 2024[16]), was met for the first time in 2022), and its successor expected to be agreed at COP29 in November 2024 (see for instance (Falduto, Noels and Jachnik, 2024[17]).

Figure 3.4. Estimates of regional differences in real-economy investments

Panel A: Global gross fixed capital formation across region type, 2022

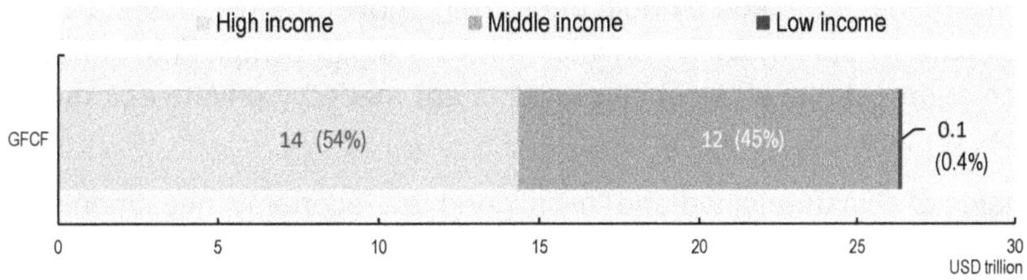

Layer: Real-economy assets and investments
Actor: Private

Theme: Mitigation
Type: Flows

Panel B: Investments in fossil fuel and renewable energy across regions, 2022

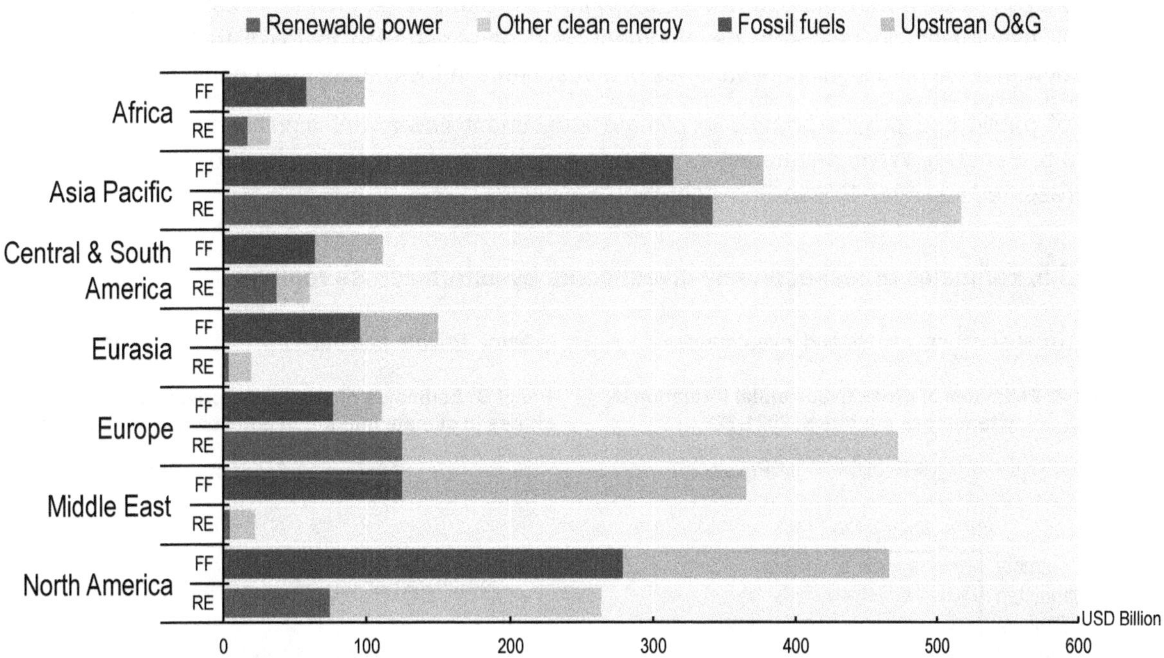

Note: Renewable power relates to investments in power generation from renewables. Other clean energy refers to investments in energy efficiency and other end uses, electricity networks, storage, nuclear power generations, and clean fuels. Fossil fuels relates to real-economy investments in fossil fuel supply and power generation from coal, oil, and natural gas.
Source: Authors based on (World Bank, 2024[18]) for Panel A and (IEA, 2024[12]) for Panel B.

Real-economy investments (by both private and public actors) in activities supporting climate action have mostly gone towards climate change mitigation, with much lower amounts going to climate change adaptation. In 2022, estimated investments in adaptation were USD 72 billion, up from just USD 42 billion in 2019 (CPI, 2023[10]). The historical focus on climate change mitigation reflects the need to reduce emissions, which would also reduce investments needed for adaptation. However, as mitigation efforts have been insufficient, adaptation investments need to increase, along with embedding resilience in all investments and avoiding investing in mal-adapted activities, for which there are currently no available estimates. With this in mind, initiatives for tracking and assessment of investments from a climate change resilience perspective need to be intensified, as motivated and detailed in Chapter 2, Section 2.4).

Box 3.1. Estimates of real-economy investments by private and public actors

Real-economy investments are made by both public (e.g., governments, national development banks, multilateral development banks) and private actors (e.g., companies, institutional investors, households). At an aggregate level, most investments are made by private actors, although there are regional differences (Figure 3.5, Panel A).

Connecting estimates of climate-aligned and -misaligned real-economy investments with actors can be challenging. Data presented in this section does not always allow to distinguish the actor type behind the investments. Available estimates of global real-economy investments in climate action indicate that public and private actors contribute almost equally to global investment flows (USD 640 and 625 billion respectively in 2021-22), but acknowledge significant gaps in coverage of, e.g., domestic public finance (CPI, 2023[10]). For investments in renewable energy specifically, private sector accounted for 69% in 2020 and 75% between 2013-20 cumulatively (IRENA, 2023[19]). However, public actors have played a crucial role in research, development, and demonstration in renewables, for which only 0.3% of investment by private actors in 2023 (IEA, 2024[12]). At the same time, private investment accounts for nearly all investments in research, development, and demonstration in fossil fuels (IEA, 2024[20]) consistent with remaining significant volumes of investments in fossil fuels more generally.

Shares of public and private finance in climate investment flows vary significantly across regions (Figure 3.5, Panel B). While private actors in North America and Europe account for nearly 80%, they only represented just over 10% in Sub-Saharan Africa in 2021-22.

Figure 3.5. Estimates of real-economy investments by actors across regions

Layer: Real-economy assets and investments   Actor: Private and public   Type: Flows

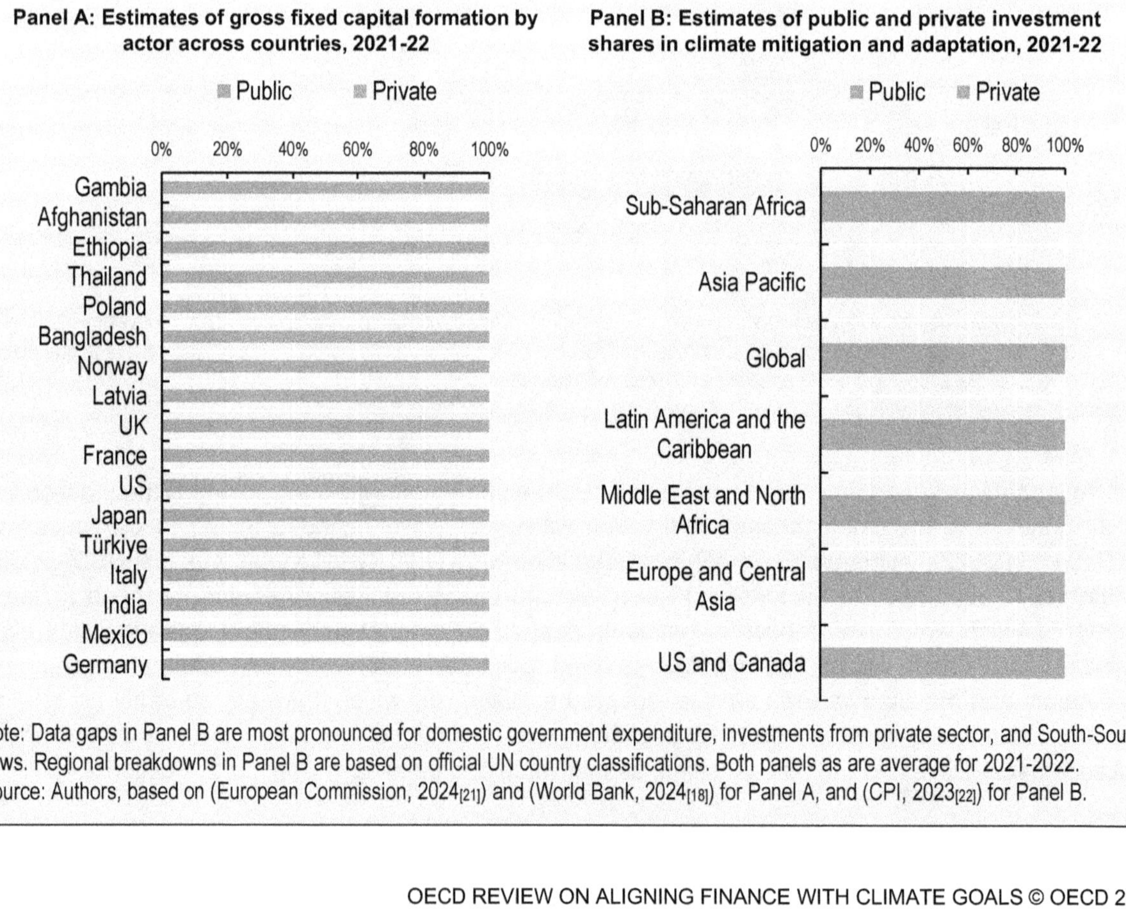

Note: Data gaps in Panel B are most pronounced for domestic government expenditure, investments from private sector, and South-South flows. Regional breakdowns in Panel B are based on official UN country classifications. Both panels as are average for 2021-2022.
Source: Authors, based on (European Commission, 2024[21]) and (World Bank, 2024[18]) for Panel A, and (CPI, 2023[22]) for Panel B.

3.2. Estimates across financial asset classes

The real-economy investments discussed in Section 3.1 can be financed through a range of financial instruments. Flows and stocks of financial assets are several times larger than flows and stocks of tangible fixed assets, which loosely speaking illustrates the financialisaton of the economy (Jachnik, Mirabile and Dobrinevski, 2019[9]). A significant amount of financial intermediation and secondary financial market activity is linked, on average, to each tangible fixed asset. In addition, the valuation of financial assets is influenced by secondary markets and their supply and demand dynamics.

Analysis of the financial sector requires looking into the specific types of financial instruments and asset classes that characterise the portfolios of investors and financial institutions. These include listed equity, unlisted equity, corporate debt securities (including corporate bonds), loans, sovereign bonds, real estate, and infrastructure (noting that investments in real estate and infrastructure typically take the form of equity, bonds, or other debt-related instruments).

Assessing progress towards the climate alignment of stocks (holdings) and flows (issuance) across different asset classes is also crucial as they tend to serve different purposes and complement each other. For example, primary equity markets enable early-stage companies to capitalise on future growth of climate solutions, while debt provides the majority of financing for established companies, such as in traditionally emissions-intensive sectors (Wilson and Caldecott, 2023[23]). Taking the US as an example, corporate bond issuance was ten times the issuance of equities in 2023 (SIFMA, 2024[24]). At the same time, the outstanding value of equities (which varies with market valuations) was over four times that of bonds. Similar trends can be observed for global finance flows in energy sectors (Figure 3.6).

Figure 3.6. Shares of equity, bonds, and loans in financing energy sectors

Layer: Financial assets and portfolios
Actor: Private

Theme: Mitigation
Type: Flows

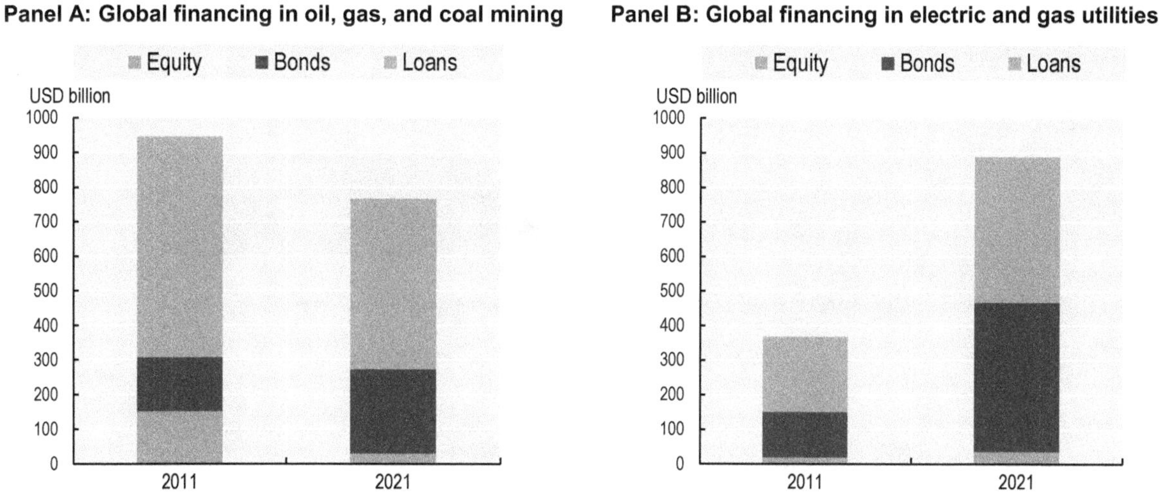

Source: Adapted from (Wilson and Caldecott, 2023[23]) based on LSEG data.

While all asset classes should be assessed to analyse progress towards Article 2.1c of the Paris Agreement in a comprehensive, as highlighted in Section 2.2 of Chapter 2, climate change-related assessment methodologies and data availability have developed more for some asset classes than others. The data points presented in this chapter for each asset class in relation to activities that contribute to or undermine climate goals also reflect such varying data availability. This in turn creates a risk that financing misaligned with climate objectives may be hidden in asset classes that are less well tracked.

3.2.1. Corporate equity

Available estimates find stocks of listed equity in low-carbon energy remain much lower than those in fossil fuel supply and total listed corporate equity (Figure 3.7, Panel A). In 2022, listed corporate equity in low-carbon energy supply was estimated at USD 3.7 trillion and USD 9.6 trillion in fossil fuel supply (BloombergNEF, 2024[25]). This represents, respectively, 4% and 10% of global equity valuation, which was at USD 101 trillion in 2022 (SIFMA, 2023[26]; WFE, n.d.[27]). Between 2021 and 2023, stocks of listed equity in fossil fuel supply have increased in value, while those in low-carbon energy decreased slightly (Figure 3.7, Panel B). Available estimates of the degree to which listed equity finances activities currently contributing to or undermining climate change mitigation are incomplete (Figure 3.7, Panel A).

Figure 3.7. Estimates of listed corporate equity in low- and high-GHG activities

Layer: Financial assets and portfolios
Actor: Private
Year: 2022

Theme: Mitigation
Type: Stock

Panel A: Global shares of listed equity stocks in low-carbon energy and fossil fuel supply in 2022

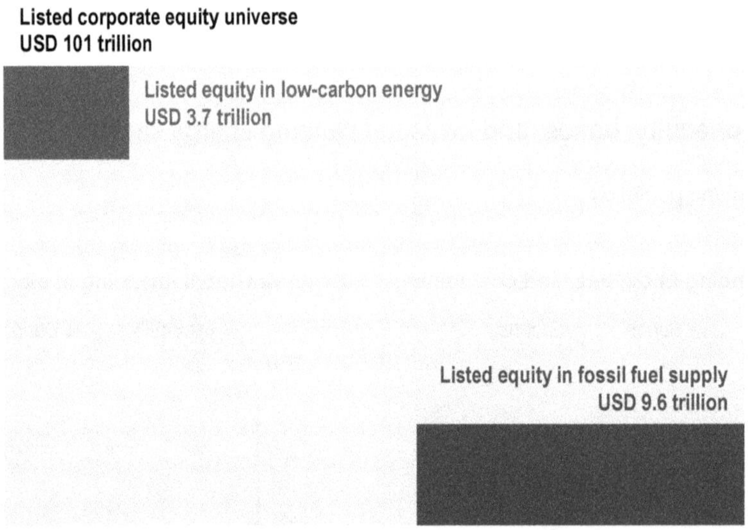

Panel B: Global shares of listed equity stocks in low-carbon energy and fossil fuel supply, 2021-23

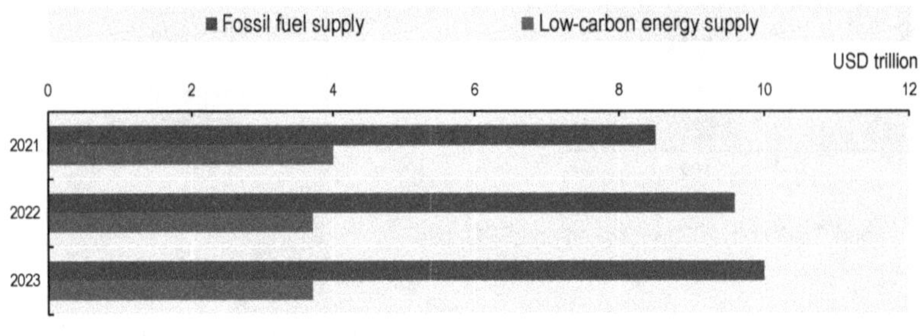

Note: Low-carbon energy supply includes stocks for low-carbon energy production sources (renewables, storage, biofuels and nuclear) and facilities manufacturing low-carbon energy equipment (equipment and services, such as modules, turbines, and components). Fossil fuel energy supply includes stocks for fossil-fuel-based sources of energy production (coal, oil and gas, and utilities' fossil-fuel power generation for electricity and heating/cooling, transportation, and refining businesses) and equipment to support such production (generators, boilers, parts and services).
Source: Authors, based on BloombergNEF and (SIFMA, 2023[26]) for Panel A and BloombergNEF for Panel B.

Listed corporate equity is one of a few asset classes for which actual climate-alignment assessments (i.e., analysis of finance against a reference point relating to climate policy goals, as outlined in Chapter 2) are available. Currently available alignment assessments, which consider current and targeted climate change mitigation performance based on different methodologies and indicators, converge on an aggregate misalignment and continued high levels of missing disclosure but vary significantly when looking at individual assets (as further discussed in Subsection 2.2.2 of Chapter 2) (Figure 3.7).

Current climate alignment assessments of listed corporate equity highlight a continued high degree of misalignment with long-term climate goals (Figure 3.8, Panel A). Where Figure 3.7 collects estimates of listed equity in activities with currently low- or high-emissions levels, Figure 3.8 shows a full climate alignment assessments based on current and targeted emissions levels. Such a focus on emissions targets allows for an assessment of activities that are in transition. However, it comes with methodological challenges, as explained in Chapter 2, as exemplified by the different aggregate results across providers. While Providers 1 and 2 assess almost the entire universe of listed equity, Provider 3 has a smaller sample size. The results of Provider 3 are, therefore, not as directly comparable with those the other providers. Climate-alignment results can also be shown by sector, showing some degree of agreement of less alignment of listed equity in the energy and materials sectors (Figure 3.8, Panel B).

Figure 3.8. Alignment assessments of climate targets of listed equity assets across providers

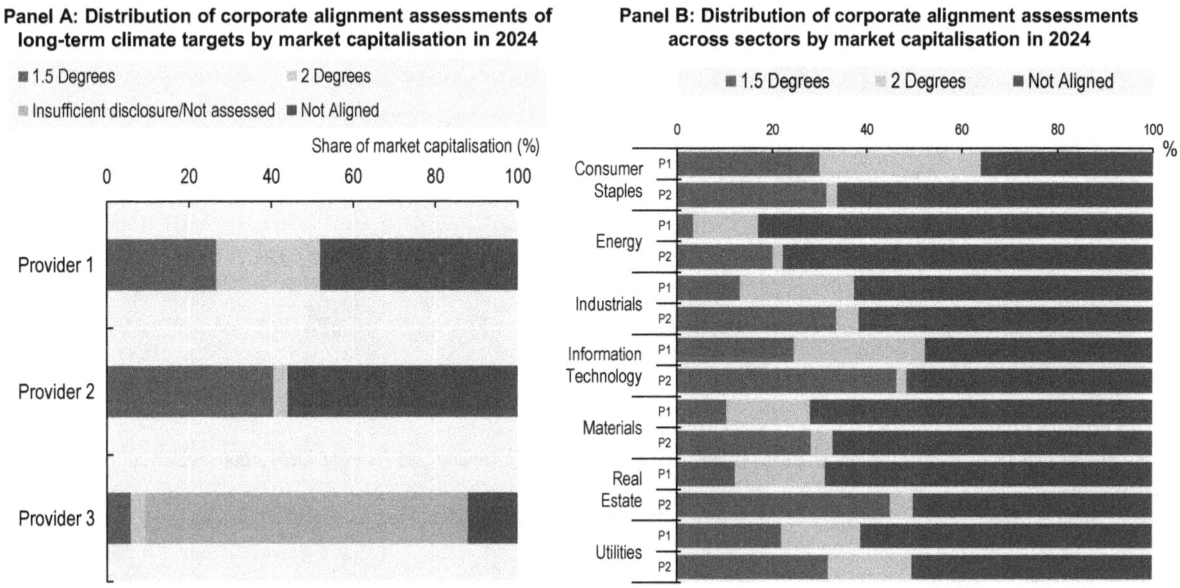

Note: Both panels include latest available alignment assessments as of August 2024 across three providers of alignment assessments. Such alignment assessments assess long-term climate targets as explained in Chapter 2. Sample sizes differ across providers, with around 13 000 companies in the sample universe of providers 1 (P1) and 2 (P2) and just over 1 000 companies for Provider 3.
Source: Authors, based on MSCI, S&P, and TPI data.

Private corporate equity remains a key blind spot, with very limited insights into how much it finances activities that support or undermine climate goals (Figure 3.9). While it is smaller in total size than listed equity, it is a growing asset class that plays a key role in financing real-economy investments. Total private equity was estimated at USD 8.25 trillion in 2023, up from USD 7.62 trillion in 2022 (Preqin, 2024[28]; McKinsey & Company, 2024[29]; Bain & Company, 2024[30]; McKinsey & Company, 2023[31]). Estimates of private equity contributing to climate change mitigation are scarce. Private equity or venture capital transactions in the global renewable electricity sector were estimated to have reached USD 0.014 trillion in 2022 (S&P, 2023[32]). Additionally, global private deal volumes in climate technologies reached USD 0.20 trillion in the same year (McKinsey & Company, 2023[31]). At the same time, there are no global estimates of private equity undermining climate goals. Moreover, some evidence suggests private equity continues to go more into fossil fuels than renewables (Private Equity Stakeholder Project, 2021[33]). Overall, the degree of current climate alignment remains unknown for 98% of private equity globally.

While there is no comprehensive assessment of differences of climate alignment across asset classes, examples across jurisdictions illustrate some degree of shifting financing from listed to unlisted companies in climate-relevant sectors. For example, listed domestic companies reduced their ownership of US electric power from 70% to 54% of total generation between 2005 and 2020, while private equity increased their ownership from 4% to 13% (Andonov and Rauh, 2024[34]). However, generally the decommissioning of coal-based power plants and scaling up of renewables has not differed significantly between those actors. Another example is coal power plants in Europe, where a large decline in public equity ownership was met by a sharp increase in private firms' ownership (Darmouni and Zhang, 2024[35]). This decline was not driven by public equity investors selling plants, but by their scaling down of plants quickly.

Figure 3.9. Estimates of (mis)alignment in private equity

Layer: Financial assets and portfolios
Actor: Private
Year: 2022

Theme: Mitigation
Type: Stock

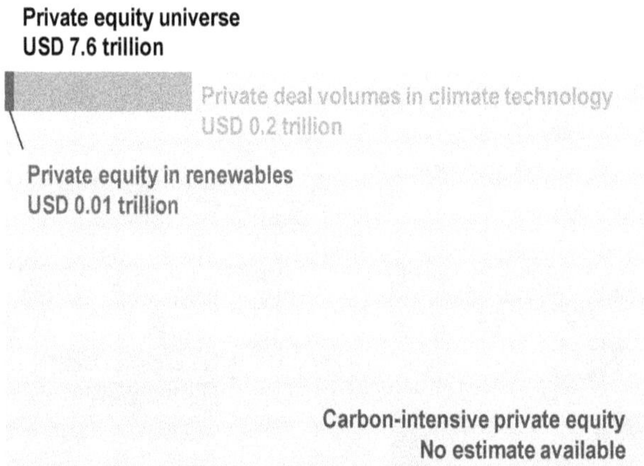

Note: Climate technology covers low-carbon technologies in a range of sectors including clean energy, low-carbon mobility, or sustainable food & agriculture.
Source: Authors, based on (S&P, 2023[32]) and (McKinsey & Company, 2023[31]) based on Preqin and PitchBook data.

3.2.2. Corporate debt

Moving from corporate equity to corporate debt securities, different sources provide partial estimates of low-GHG and GHG-intensive stocks and flows. Such efforts are focussed mostly on corporate bonds for which data is more widely available. Within this asset class, some assets are explicitly labelled as "green" based on existing voluntary labels or taxonomies in jurisdictions where those exist (as discussed in Subsection 4.2.1), which can serve as an approximation of finance supporting climate change mitigation goals. However, it should be noted that "green" labels cover a variety of activities beyond climate action, such as biodiversity conservation and wastewater management (OECD, 2024[36]), and further work needs to analyse their real decarbonisation impacts (Lam and Wurgler, 2024[37]). Other tracking exercises for corporate debt have considered the carbon-intensity of the sector to which issuers belong and the use of proceeds of the securities. Such estimates are not yet available for all types of debt securities, nor do they provide a comprehensive overview of the degree of (mis)alignment of debt stocks and flows.

Stocks of green corporate bonds are lower than of carbon-intensive corporate bonds and represent a small share of total bonds. At the end of 2023, global outstanding corporate bond debt reached USD 34 trillion, up from around USD 25 trillion a decade earlier (OECD, 2024[36]). In the same year, outstanding green-labelled corporate bonds amounted to USD 1.6 trillion, representing just under 5% of the corporate bond universe (Figure 3.10, Panel A). Available estimates of outstanding carbon-intensive corporate bonds find a total of USD 1.7 trillion outstanding as of June 2023 (LSEG, 2024[38]), representing just over 5% of the corporate bond universe (Figure 3.10, Panel A).

Considering total outstanding carbon-intensive corporate debt securities more broadly, including bonds, notes, commercial paper, and other corporate debt securities, points to large amounts flowing to GHG-intensive sectors. In 2023, outstanding carbon-intensive corporate debt securities add up to USD 5.5 trillion (LSEG, 2024[38]). Currently, 38% of that debt is owed by private companies, 35% by listed companies, and 27% by state-owned enterprises, highlighting the importance of tracking financing of non-listed companies, as already discussed in the previous subsection on private equity. Considering all corporate debt issued between 2000 and 2023 (both currently active and inactive debt), carbon-intensive debt securities represented 35% of total corporate debt securities between that period (LSEG, 2024[38]).

Green-labelled bond issuance (flows) is, however, on a rising trend, increasing from USD 0.02 trillion issued in 2015 to USD 0.36 trillion in 2023 (Figure 3.10, Panel B). Such issuance is split almost equally between non-financial and financial corporates. Green-labelled corporate bonds are mostly financing projects in alternative energy, energy efficiency and green buildings (Mastouri, Shah and Pandey, 2023[39]). Green-labelled corporate bonds represented on average 92% of sustainable corporate bonds prior to 2020 (OECD, 2024[36]).

Issuance of debt securities (flows) by carbon-intensive non-financial corporate sectors, on the other hand, has remained a significant part of corporate debt security flows, staying around USD 1.38 trillion issued in 2022, which corresponds to about a third of corporate debt issued in 2022 (LSEG, 2024[38]). While most of these debt securities are issued in advanced countries, emerging and developing countries are representing an increasing share. Between 2000 and 2022, the share of carbon-intensive debt volumes issued from emerging and developing countries increased from 4% to 41% (LSEG, 2024[38]).

It is important to note that a range of companies in carbon-intensive sectors have started to issue green-labelled bonds to support their transition to net-zero emissions (Figure 3.10, Panel C). An estimated 7% of new debt securities issued by carbon-intensive sectors in 2022 were structured as green-labelled bonds. An estimated additional 1% related bonds not labelled as green but financing low-carbon activities such as electric vehicles production and renewable energy generation (LSEG, 2024[38]). These green-labelled and 'de facto green' bonds were mainly concentrated in electric utilities and car manufacturing sectors.

Although corporate loans are a relatively big asset class and are critical to financing activities of both large and small companies, data and estimates are scarce, whether relating to the total size of the asset class or volumes relating to activities contributing or undermining climate goals. In 2021, fossil fuel sectors financed themselves 53% through loans, 43% through bonds, and only 4% through equities. On the other hand, green-labelled loan flows remain low in absolute terms, despite a significant relative increase over the past years. Issuance of green loans moved from USD 0.02 trillion in 2020 to USD 0.20 trillion in 2023 (Environmental Finance, n.d.[40]). Green loans are more concentrated in the energy and utilities sectors than green bonds, with 84% of green loans issued by those sectors (Dursun-de Neef, Ongena and Tsonkova, 2023[41]).

Figure 3.10. Estimates of (mis)alignment in corporate debt

Layer: Financial assets and portfolios
Actor: Private

Theme: Mitigation and adaptation
Type: Stock and flows

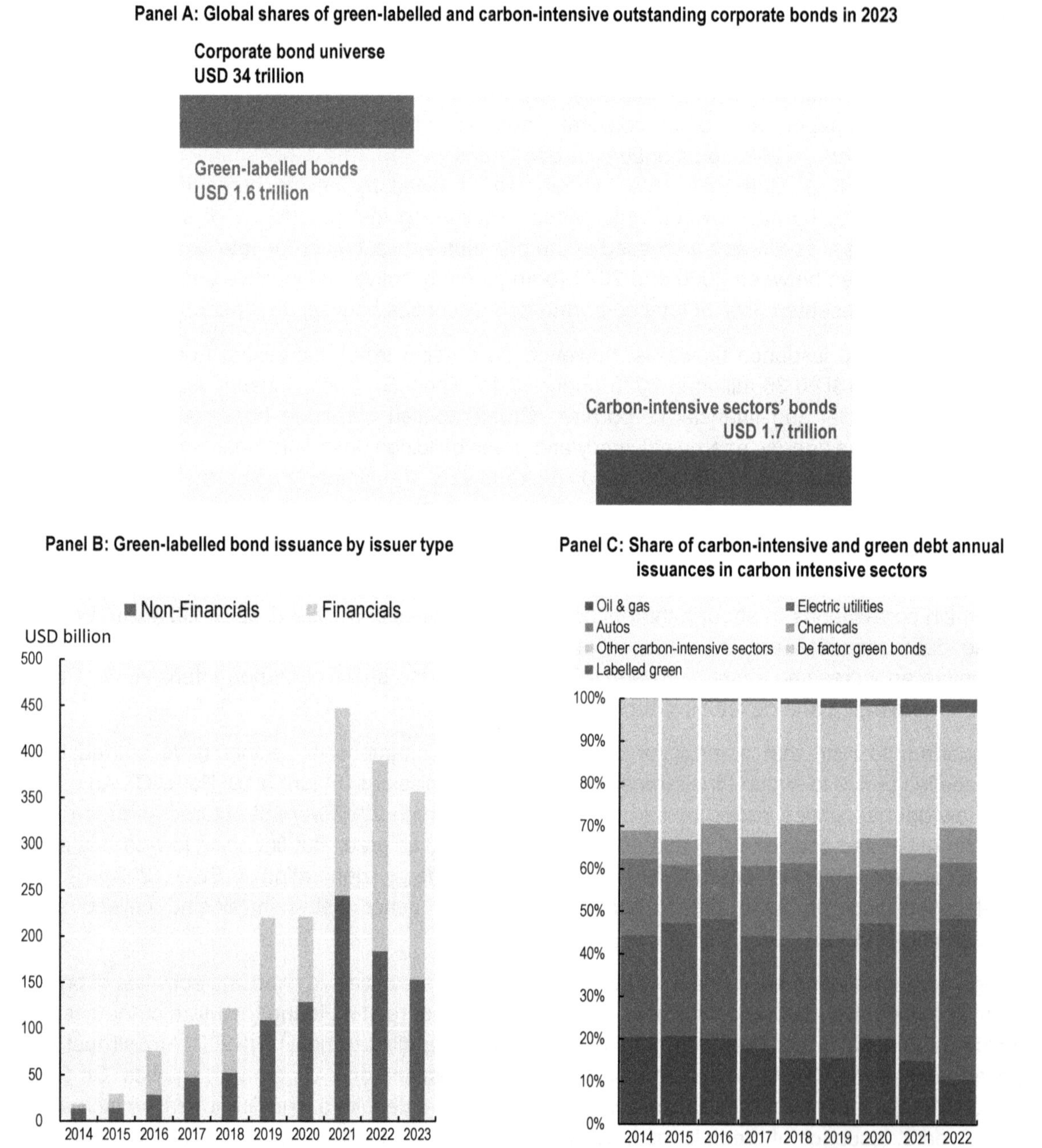

Note: Green-labelled bonds are based on use of proceeds going towards projects in renewable energy, clean transportation, biodiversity conservation, and wastewater management. Carbon-intensive sectors are identified based on granular sector activities identified as carbon intensive within the energy, materials, industrial and transport sectors, based on LSEG's Reference data Business Classification. Panel C includes active and inactive corporate debt issued between 2000 and June 2023.
Source: Authors, based on (LSEG, 2024[38]; OECD, 2024[36]) for Panel A, (OECD, 2024[36]) for Panel B, and (LSEG, 2024[38]) for Panel C.

3.2.3. Sovereign bonds

Moving from more corporate-related asset classes to government-related financial assets, global outstanding sovereign bonds are valued at USD 64 trillion, double the stock of corporate bonds (OECD, 2024[36]). As discussed in Chapter 2, different approaches to assess climate-alignment are needed than for corporates and methodological developments are underway. In the meantime, while estimates of sovereign bonds that explicitly undermine climate goals are missing, estimates of sovereign bonds explicitly supporting climate goals can be based on government-issued bonds labelled as green.

Figure 3.11. Estimates of (mis)alignment in sovereign bonds

Layer: Financial assets and portfolios
Actor: Public issuer and mixed subscriber

Theme: Mitigation and adaptation
Type: Stock and flows

Panel A: Estimates of green and total outstanding sovereign bonds, 2023

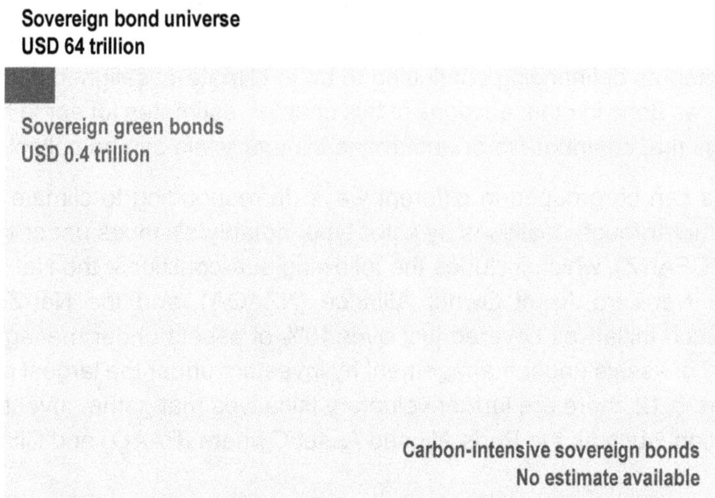

Panel B: Official sector green-labelled bond issuance by issuer, 2014-23

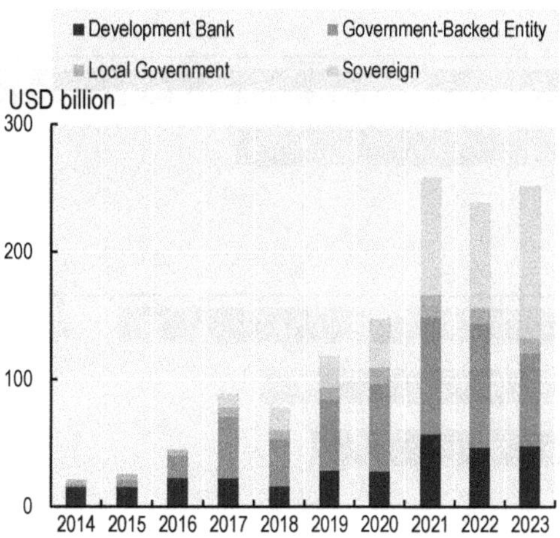

Note: Green-labelled bonds are based on use of proceeds going towards projects in renewable energy, clean transportation, biodiversity conservation, and wastewater management.
Source: Authors, based on (OECD, 2024[36]) and (Climate Bonds Initiative, 2024[42]).

Although sovereign bonds are a big asset class, volumes of green-labelled sovereign bonds are small. Outstanding green-labelled bonds (stocks) by official actors (including sovereigns, local and government-backed entities, as well as multilateral institutions) in 2023 were estimated at USD 1.29 trillion, out of which USD 0.39 trillion in green sovereign bonds (Figure 3.11, Panel A). The volume of annual green-labelled bond issuances (flows) by the public sector increased significantly between 2014 and 2021, but then plateaued around USD 0.25 trillion in 2023 (Figure 3.11, Panel B).

3.3. Estimates for different categories of investors and financial institutions

The climate alignment of finance can next be assessed at the level of investors and financial institutions, and the extent to which they are aligning their portfolios with climate policy goals. Such aggregate assessments can be highly complex as investors and financial institutions can have diversified portfolio structures across asset classes, including but not limited to the ones for which estimates are presented in the previous section. Analysing such structures thus requires both detailed, often proprietary data, as well as methodological assumptions to aggregate results across business lines and assets, which in turn can lead to more opaque and less robust results that could notably hide, within aggregate portfolio assessments, large amounts of financing continuing to go to climate-misaligned activities (see Chapter 2, Section 2.3). However, as done in other sections of this chapter, estimates for some financial sector actors' investments in activities that contribute to or undermine climate goals can be collected.

Financial sector actors can be grouped in different ways. In responding to climate change, the financial sector has come together through coalitions by actor type, notably alliances under the Glasgow Financial Alliance for Net Zero (GFANZ), which includes the following sub-coalitions: the Net Zero Asset Managers Initiative (NZAM), the Net-Zero Asset Owner Alliance (NZAOA), and the Net-Zero Banking Alliance (NZBA). As of 2024, such initiatives covered just over 40% of assets under management in the banking sector, and nearly 70% of assets under management by investors under the largest coalition (Figure 3.12). As highlighted in Figure 3.12, there are further voluntary initiatives that gather investors for the purpose of stimulating climate action, such as the Paris Aligned Asset Owners (PAAO) and Climate Action 100+.

Figure 3.12. Assets under management by climate-related banking and investor coalitions

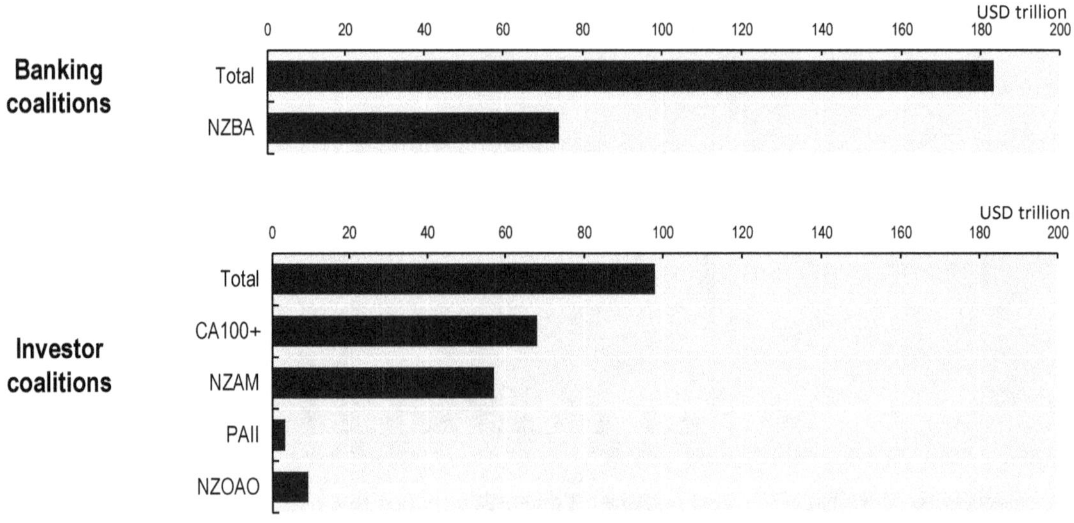

Note: Total assets under management values for banking and investors are for 2023. Assets under management of initiatives are the latest values available as of August 2024. NZBA is the Net-Zero Banking Alliance. CA100+ is Climate Action 100+. NZAM is the Net Zero Asset Managers Initiative. PAII is the Paris Aligned Asset Owners. NZAOA is the Net-Zero Asset Owner Alliance.

Source: Authors, updated from (UNFCCC SCF, 2022[43]; UNFCCC, 2022[44]).

While adherence to such coalitions typically reflects investors' and financial institutions' commitments to climate actions, they do not represent a measure of contribution to climate goals, which requires looking at holdings (stocks) and new investment (flows), which the remainder of this section partly does, as well as actions such as engagement, managed divestment and exclusion, and portfolio construction practices, which are addressed in Section 4.3 of Chapter 4.

3.3.1. Banks

Bank-facilitated financing (which includes both direct lending and underwriting) continues to flow more towards fossil fuel than low-carbon energy supply. In 2022, total assets of commercial banks worldwide (stocks) added up to USD 183 trillion (FSB, 2023[45]). Analysis of 1 100 large banks finds that they provided financing (flows) for nearly USD 1 trillion to fossil fuel supply in 2022, while USD 0.7 trillion went to low-carbon energy supply (Figure 3.13, Panel A). Compared to 2021, the ratio of financing to low-carbon energy compared to fossil fuel energy remained stable, in the context of an overall decrease in financing for energy supply activities. Besides direct financing, banks play a critical role in facilitating large financing transactions via underwriting, a process through which, on behalf of a client, they raise capital from investors in the form of debt or equity. In 2022, banks that are part of the NZBA collectively underwrote USD 0.52 trillion of fossil fuel supply financing (representing 54% of all fossil-fuel financing), compared to USD 0.46 trillion of low-carbon energy supply financing (representing 63% of all low-carbon energy supply financing) (BloombergNEF, 2023[46]).

In terms of geographical differences, volumes of bank-facilitated financing were higher in Europe and Latin America than in North America and China, where financing volumes to fossil fuel energy supply are also the largest. In 2022, bank-facilitated financing to low-carbon energy, by issuing region of risk, was USD 0.208 trillion in Europe, followed by USD 0.207 trillion in North America and USD 0.166 trillion in China (Figure 3.13, Panel B). On the other hand, bank-facilitated financing to fossil fuel supply reached USD 0.406 trillion and USD 0.298 trillion in North America and China had the highest respectively, whereas in Europe, financing to fossil fuel supply only represented a third of low-carbon energy financing. Across regions, bank-facilitated financing for low-carbon energy supply exceeded that for fossil fuel energy supply only in Europe and Latin America, which have a low-carbon to fossil fuel energy supply financing ratio of 2.81 and 1.05 respectively. These trends are generally consistent when considering regions based on bank headquarters locations (BloombergNEF, 2023[46]).

Figure 3.13. Estimates of banks financing fossil fuels and green projects

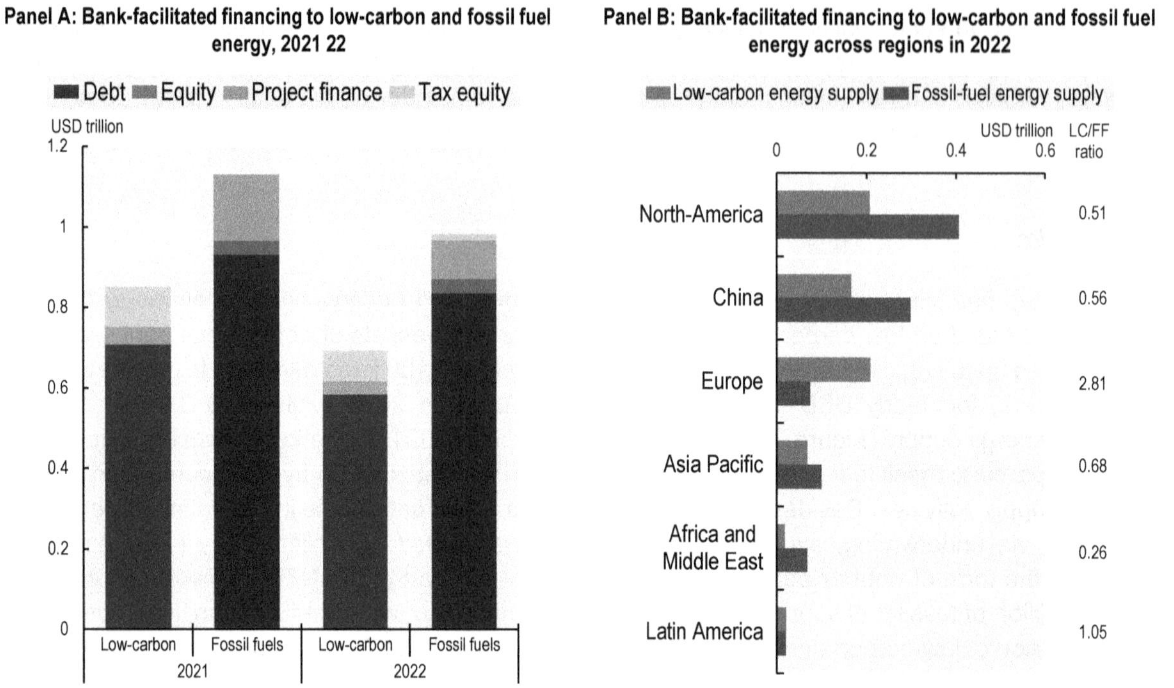

Note: Both panels include financing through equity, bonds, loans, project finance and tax equity by 1 100 large banks. In Panel B, the location of the capital raising entities is defined by the region of risk. In Panel B, LC is short for low-carbon energy supply financing, and FF for fossil fuel energy supply financing by banks. Low-carbon energy supply includes financing related to low-carbon sources of energy production (including renewables, storage, biofuels and nuclear) and the development of plants/facilities manufacturing low-carbon energy equipment (including equipment and services, such as modules, turbines, and components). Fossil fuel energy supply includes financing related to fossil-fuel-based sources of energy production (including coal, oil and gas, and utilities' fossil-fuel power generation for electricity and heating/cooling, as well as transportation and refining businesses) and the equipment used to support power generation from fossil-fuel-based sources (including equipment, parts and services, such as generators and boilers).
Source: (BloombergNEF, 2023[46]).

3.3.2. Institutional investors

Institutional investors are a diverse set of financial sector actors, including pension funds, sovereign wealth funds, insurance companies, asset managers, endowments among others. Different tracking exercises may focus on different actors or the range of different assets they hold. Currently, however, only partial or anecdotal estimates are available across some actors, where some point estimates do not necessarily get updated in more recent years. Hence, the data points presented below rely on examples for assets under management by pension funds, asset managers, and investment funds, as well as infrastructure investments across institutional investors.

Taking the example of pension funds, several earlier studies highlighted historically significant holdings in fossil fuel sectors, but more recent estimates are not yet available. For example, a study dating back to 2017 based on 2015 data estimated that 7% of the equity portion of pension funds in Europe was in fossil fuels (Battiston et al., 2017[47]). In contrast, another study from 2018 found that only 1% of the assets managed by the world's largest 100 pension funds were invested in low-carbon solutions (ShareAction, 2018[48]). More recently, an international survey of 75 large pension funds and 13 sovereign wealth funds, which in total managed USD 10.8 trillion (USD 4 trillion and USD 6.8 trillion respectively) in assets in 2021, found that nearly all funds had less than 10% of assets in green assets (OECD, 2022[49]).

Looking at asset managers, 55 having disclosed to CDP in 2023 reported USD 1.72 trillion in assets under management going towards fossil fuel activities (CDP, 2023[50]). Other analysis finds that the largest 40 asset managers each have around 2% of their assets under management in oil and gas companies (Carbon Tracker, 2023[51]). Few estimates are available on assets under management going towards activities contributing to climate goals.

Investment funds' holdings (stocks) show that only a very limited share of their total equity and bond investments goes to companies involved in carbon solutions (OECD, 2023[52]). Considering the broader category of sustainable funds for which data is more readily available, assets under management by investment funds in sustainable funds only accounted for 6.2% of total assets under management by investment funds in 2022 (Figure 3.14, Panel A). However, assets under management by investment funds in sustainable funds increased by 600% over the last decade, highlighting the potential capital to be leveraged. Only 6% of sustainable funds went to emerging markets, which is less than the overall average of 11% across all types of funds held by investment funds (Lepers and De Crescenzio, 2024[53]). Focusing specifically on "green" assets, defined as securities of companies involved in carbon solutions (renewable energy, transport, buildings, efficiency), they amount to USD 3.8 trillion invested globally by investment funds as of 2022, representing 8% of total global assets under management (OECD, 2023[52]). Zooming in on funds specialised in green (defined as funds with more than 25% of their portfolio invested in green assets), their green investments are heavily skewed towards the US (almost 70%). China is by far the next largest investment destination. Overall, emerging markets represent only 13.6% of total green investment by 'green' funds in the sample, and less than 1% excluding China (Figure 3.14, Panel B).

Figure 3.14. Sustainable and green investments by investment funds

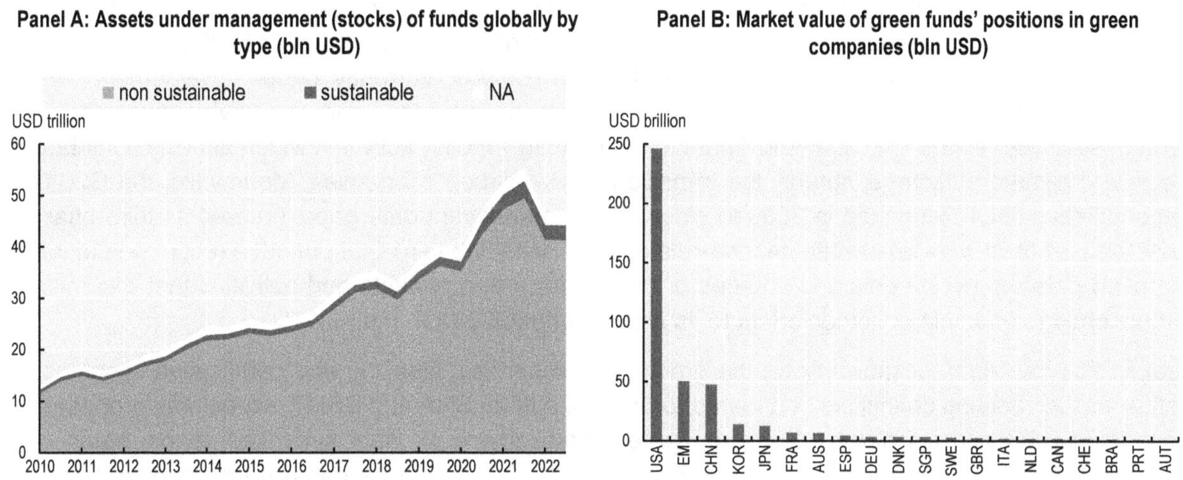

Note: For Panel A, the sustainable classification is based on name and prospectus. For Panel B, "Green" funds are defined as funds with more than 25% of green assets, where "green" assets are defined using the metric by Morningstar "% of the revenue from involvement in carbon solutions", which captures the key sectors involved in climate transition, including renewable energy, transport, buildings, and energy efficiency. EM refers to emerging markets.
Source: (OECD, 2023[52]).

Taking the example of infrastructure, a relatively smaller asset class within institutional investors' portfolios, in 2020, they held an estimated USD 1.04 trillion worth of infrastructure assets, of which USD only 0.3 trillion were identified as investments in green infrastructure (OECD, 2020[54]). Asset owners represented most of these investments through unlisted funds and project-level equity or debt, while asset managers predominantly used securitised products. Most of these investments were made within the jurisdictions of the investors, with very limited shares crossing borders, consistent with more general home bias documented in white and grey literature institutional investors (OECD, 2024[55]).

3.4. Insights at the level of financial jurisdictions

Assessments at the level of jurisdictions can bring together perspectives from the real economy, financial assets, and financial institutions addressed in the three previous sections. As such, while the financial sector is transnational, available evidence of climate alignment or misalignment at the level of financial jurisdictions can inform policymakers about actions they can undertake to influence investors and financial institutions incorporated within their jurisdictions towards enhancing the degree of climate alignment.

The System of National Accounts (SNA) is the international standard for compiling national accounts, which are a key source of official macroeconomic statistics. Countries use the SNA framework to collect and collate data to produce sets of accounts, including national financial accounts and balance sheets, which record transactions and balances (financial assets and liabilities) between resident institutional units and between resident institutional units and the rest of the world. The transactions and balances are organised according to financial instrument categories, including debt securities, loans, equity, and investment fund shares (discussed in Sections 3.2 and 3.3), as well as currency and deposits, financial derivatives and employee stock options, and other accounts payable/receivable (UN, EC, OECD, IMF & World Bank, 2009[56]). Sub-categories exist for each financial instrument, which for debt, securities and loans include whether they are short- or long-term, and for equities whether they are listed or unlisted. Financial transactions and balances are recorded for different sectors of the economy, notably non-financial corporates, financial corporates, general government, and households.

The financial accounts and balance sheets in the 2008 SNA do not include any subcategory or dimension relating to sustainable, green, or climate-related transactions. However, the 2025 SNA and its sister publication, the seventh Balance of Payments Manual (BPM7), currently under development, aim to provide expanded information on the interplay between the economy and the environment, including through statistics related to sustainable finance that quantify funding activities which actively contribute to green and climate outcomes, notably the transition to low-carbon economies. Meanwhile, the G20 Data Gaps Initiative (DGI), launched in 2009 to close the policy-relevant data gaps, entered its third phase in 2022. As part of its work on climate change-related data gaps, the third DGI put out a recommendation for improved data on investments and sources of finance for green projects and activities that can mitigate climate change and help countries adapt to its implications (G20 DGI, n.d.[57]).

Against this backdrop, acknowledging the growth in taxonomies, labelling and certification schemes, as well as further working definitions and market practices, a 2025 SNA and BPM7 issues note proposes the creation of ESG and, as a subset of that, "green" breakdowns for debt securities, loans, equity, and investment fund shares (Barahona, Girón and Tebrake, 2024[58]), to be compiled as part of countries' financial accounts and balance sheets, balance of payments and international investment positions. Such developments have the potential to result in a significant improvement in terms of scope and coverage of evidence compared to currently available estimates as presented in this chapter. Notably, under the third DGI, most G20 countries as well as several additional jurisdictions, have made self-commitments to start transmitting data for "green debt securities" by the end of 2025 or 2027 (G20 DGI, n.d.[59]).

While data on these green financial instruments in the context of the System of National Accounts will only be compiled from 2025, initiatives across jurisdictions provide preliminary information for these instruments. In particular, several central banks have collected and aggregated data on green finance, so far mostly focussed on green bonds. Across a selection of jurisdictions, estimates show an increasing share of green bonds compared to total bond issuance in those jurisdictions. In the Eurozone, for example, green bond issuance accounted for 6% of total bond issuances in 2023 (Figure 3.15, Panel A). Over the same period, data by the Reserve Bank of Australia (RBA) shows that green bonds accounted for only

0.6% of the bond universe in Australia, up from 0.1% in 2015 (Figure 3.15, Panel B). Use of proceeds from Australian green bonds, issued between 2014 and 2023, mostly financed clean transport projects, followed by energy efficiency and green construction/buildings (Armour, Hunt and Lwin, 2023[60])).

In contrast to green bonds, initiatives to estimate green loans, green equity, and green investment fund shares are much more limited across jurisdictions. These efforts are not yet done uniformly across jurisdictions and financial asset classes, and current data points may follow different scopes, approaches, and metrics, as well as have different data limitations. Even green bonds face the lack of a global uniform and clear definition, as they are often identified based on a range of labelling schemes that rely on information relating to the use of proceeds. Hence, only relatively anecdotal evidence was found based on what different central banks have published so far.

Data and estimates at the level of jurisdictions of the size of finance undermining climate goals are even less available. Some initiatives do assess exposure of financial portfolios to carbon-intensive sectors. Some central banks publish such information in the context of financial risk analysis, including on the effect of climate policy and different transition scenarios on financial institutions' equity valuations (e.g., (Bank of Canada, 2021[61])) and bank losses (e.g., (Bank of England, 2022[62])). Overall, the challenge remains that comparisons across jurisdictions are limited as different scopes, metrics, and approaches are used.

Figure 3.15. Estimates of green bonds in financial jurisdictions

Layer: Financial jurisdictions
Actor: Mixed

Theme: Mitigation
Type: Flows

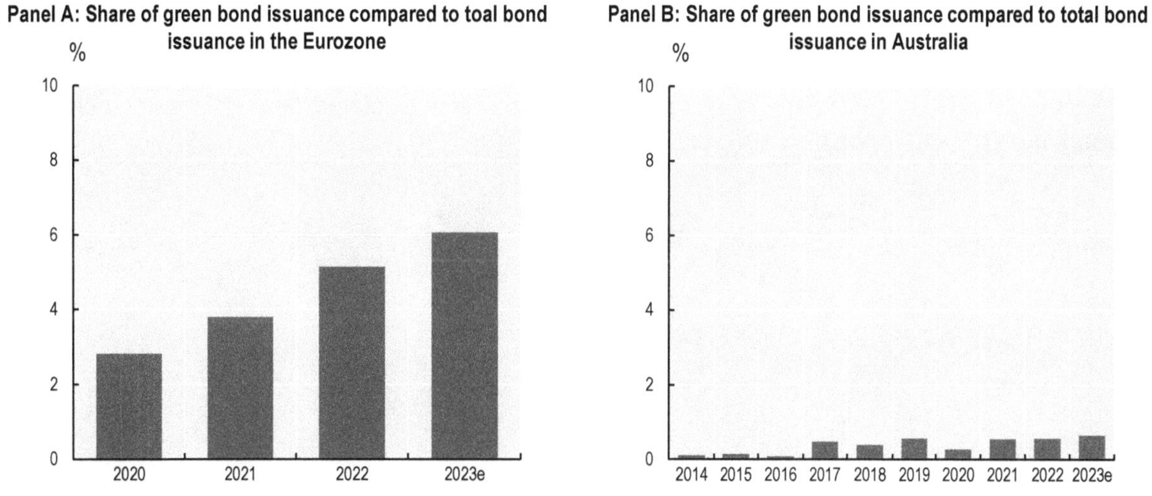

Note: Values for 2023 are preliminary, not yet covering the fourth quarter for the Eurozone and not yet covering the second half for Australia.
Source: Authors from (ECB, 2024[63]; Reserve Bank of Australia, 2023[64]).

In the limited jurisdictions for which initial evidence was found, estimates of both low-carbon and carbon-intensive activities in equity and bond portfolios indicate continuing higher stocks in carbon-intensive activities. For example, in Switzerland, as of 2022, equity stocks in low-carbon activities and carbon-intensive activities in selected sectors were estimated at 3% and 5% respectively, while the equivalent figures for bonds were 2.5% and 5% respectively (Figure 3.16, Panels A and B). Equity portfolios have a larger share in the power sector, while bond portfolios have a larger share in fossil fuel supply. Low-carbon power accounts for sizeable proportions of both equity and bond portfolio exposures, though bond portfolios have minimal exposure to low-carbon automotives. Since 2020, fossil fuel shares in portfolios (stocks) held across Swiss financial institutions have fallen, decreasing from 2-4% to 1% for equities and from 3-5% to 3% in bonds (PACTA, 2022[65]).

At the level of financial jurisdictions, estimates of low-carbon and carbon-intensive activities across asset classes show some variance across types of financial institutions. Continuing the example for Switzerland, banks tend to hold more carbon-intensive automotive equities, while asset managers have the largest holdings of low-carbon power across equities and bonds (Figure 3.16, Panels A and B). In Colombia, for example, insurers have equity and bond portfolio exposure to fossil fuel extraction of 3% and 5% respectively – double that of insurers in Switzerland (PACTA, 2023[66]). Notably, bond portfolio exposure to hydropower is almost 10% among Colombian insurers and 6% for Peruvian pension funds – both figures substantially above the global market. In Peru, equity exposures to fossil fuel extraction and high-carbon power sectors are only a half and a third respectively, compared to the global market (PACTA, 2023[67]).

Zooming in on bank portfolios, initial sample estimates at the level of financial jurisdictions find significant degrees of misalignment. In the Eurozone, the credit portfolios of 90% of banks, out of 95 included in the sample, were misaligned with the benchmark decarbonisation scenario in 2022. With regards to sectoral exposures, euro area banks have the highest credit exposures to the power and automotive sectors, which are also the most misaligned (Figure 3.16, Panel C). Conversely, the steel sector had the largest number of aligned banks in the study. There is also significant disparity within sectors, where, for example, euro area automotives showed an accelerated shift towards electric vehicles and phasing out of internal combustion engine cars (ECB, 2024[68])). Another example from Korea finds bank holdings of loans, bonds, and stocks in 2021 comprised of 16.5% exposure to carbon-intensive sectors (Bank of Korea, 2021[69]). Within the banking industry, specialised banks had the largest exposure to carbon-intensive sectors. In contrast, commercial banks had the smallest exposure (Figure 3.16, Panel D). Across all bank types, portfolio investments are concentrated in sectors with a medium level of carbon intensity.

While data and estimates on low-carbon and carbon-intensive finance at the level of financial centres remain limited, the case studies and trial data presented here can be complemented with analysis of climate-related financial sector policies in jurisdictions. Analytical efforts are underway to analyse this for some jurisdictions (e.g., (Hoffmann et al., 2022[70])). Such climate-related financial sector policies are discussed more broadly in the next chapter.

Figure 3.16. Estimates of low- and high-carbon portfolio shares in financial jurisdictions

Layer: Financial jurisdictions
Actor: Mixed

Theme: Mitigation
Type: Flows

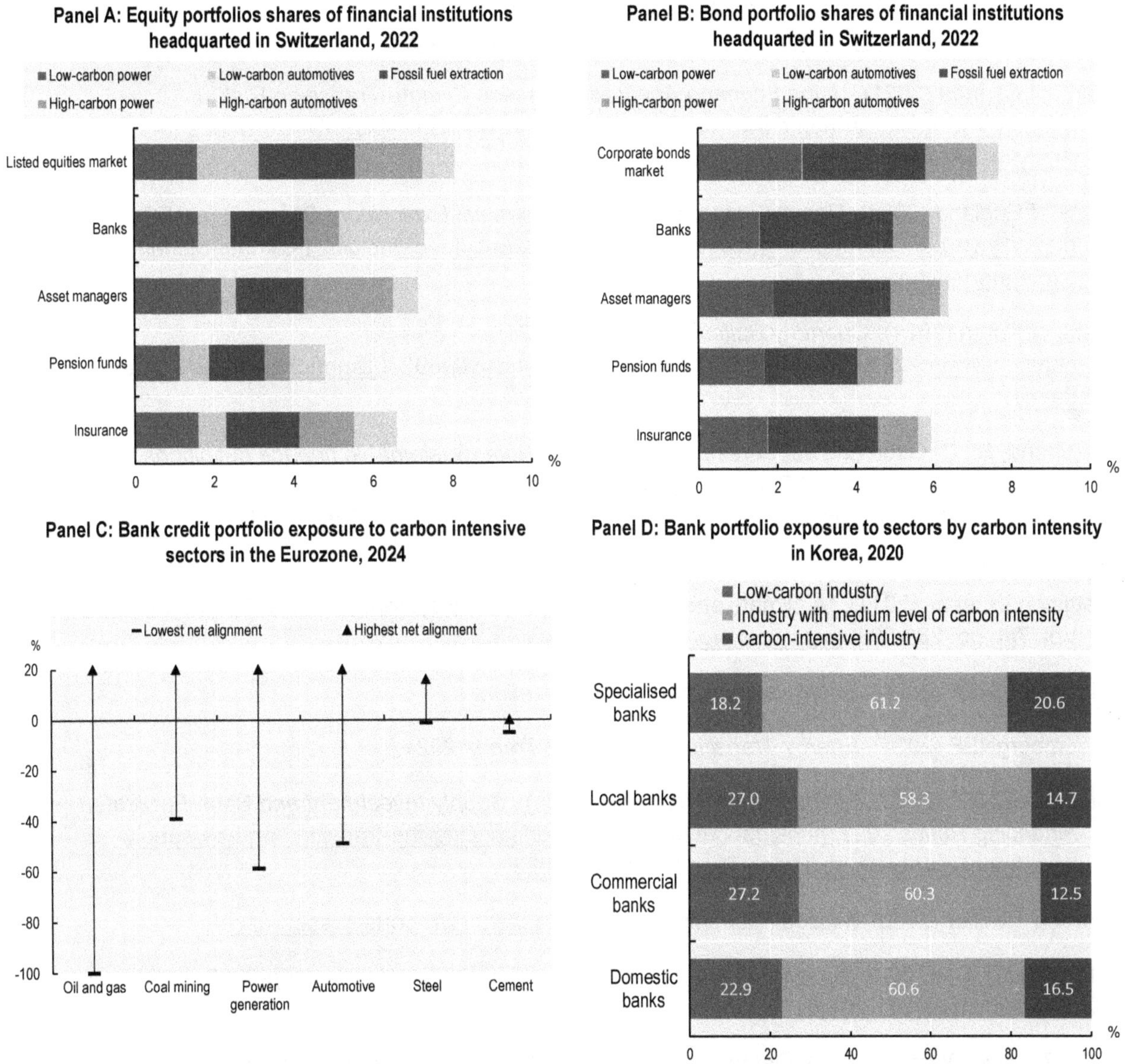

Note: For Panels A, B, and C, production data is collected at the physical asset level and consolidated up the corporate ownership tree, from subsidiaries to parent companies. In Panel C, the net alignment is computed using the IEA NZE 2050 decarbonisation pathway. Net alignment higher than 20% is reduced to 20%, and net alignment lower than -100% is raised to -100% for visualisation purposes.
Source: (PACTA, 2022[65]; ECB, 2024[68]; Bank of Korea, 2021[69]). PACTA analysis is based on data from Asset Impact.

References

Andonov, A. and J. Rauh (2024), *The Shifting Finance of Electricity Generation*, Stanford University Graduate School of Business Research Paper No. 4287123, https://doi.org/10.2139/ssrn.4287123. [34]

Armour, C., D. Hunt and J. Lwin (2023), *Green and Sustainable Finance in Australia*, https://www.rba.gov.au/publications/bulletin/2023/sep/green-and-sustainable-finance-in-australia.html. [60]

Bain & Company (2024), *Global Private Equity Report 2024*, https://www.bain.com/insights/topics/global-private-equity-report/. [30]

Bank of Canada (2021), *Using Scenario Analysis to Assess Climate Transition Risk*, https://www.bankofcanada.ca/wp-content/uploads/2021/11/BoC-OSFI-Using-Scenario-Analysis-to-Assess-Climate-Transition-Risk.pdf. [61]

Bank of England (2022), *Results of the 2021 Climate Biennial Exploratory Scenario (CBES)*, https://www.bankofengland.co.uk/stress-testing/2022/results-of-the-2021-climate-biennial-exploratory-scenario. [62]

Bank of Korea (2021), *Quarterly Bulletin(December 2021)*, https://www.bok.or.kr/eng/bbs/E0000829/view.do?nttId=10069260&menuNo=400216&pageIndex=1. [69]

Barahona, S., C. Girón and J. Tebrake (2024), *Issues Note: Sustainable finance definitions in the 2025 SNA and Balance of Payments Manual 7*, https://unstats.un.org/unsd/nationalaccount/aeg/2024/M25/M25_2_Sustainable_Finance_Definitions.pdf. [58]

Battiston, S. et al. (2017), "A climate stress-test of the financial system", *Nature Climate Change*, Vol. 7/4, pp. 283-288, https://doi.org/10.1038/nclimate3255. [47]

BloombergNEF (2024), *Energy supply market capitalization*. [25]

BloombergNEF (2024), *Energy Transition Investment Trends 2024*. [11]

BloombergNEF (2023), *Financing the Transition: Energy Supply Investment and Bank-Facilitated Financing Ratios 2022*, https://about.bnef.com/blog/financing-the-transition-energy-supply-investment-and-bank-facilitated-financing-ratios-2022/. [46]

Carbon Tracker (2023), *Missed Pitch*, https://carbontracker.org/reports/missed-pitch/. [51]

CDP (2023), *CDP 2023 disclosure data*, https://www.cdp.net/en/companies/cdp-2023-disclosure-data-factsheet#2023trends. [50]

CDP & Oliver Wyman (2024), *Get the money moving: Meeting the European corporate transition challenge*, https://www.cdp.net/en/research/cdp-europe-reports/cdp-europe-report. [15]

Climate Bonds Initiative (2024), *Interactive Data Platform*, https://www.climatebonds.net/market/data/ (accessed on 20 July 2024). [42]

CPI (2023), *Global Landscape of Climate Finance 2023*, https://www.climatepolicyinitiative.org/publication/global-landscape-of-climate-finance-2023. [10]

CPI (2023), *Global Landscape of Climate Finance 2023*, Climate Policy Initiative, https://www.climatepolicyinitiative.org/publication/global-landscape-of-climate-finance-2023/. [22]

CPI (2022), *Tracking Investments in Climate Resilient Infrastructure*, https://www.climatepolicyinitiative.org/publication/tracking-investments-in-climate-resilient-infrastructure/. [5]

Darmouni, O. and Y. Zhang (2024), *Brown Capital (Re)Allocation*, https://doi.org/10.2139/ssrn.4796331. [35]

Dursun-de Neef, Ö., S. Ongena and G. Tsonkova (2023), *Green Versus Sustainable Loans: The Impact on Firms' ESG Performance*, Swiss Finance Institute Research Paper No. 22-42, https://doi.org/10.2139/ssrn.4115692. [41]

ECB (2024), *Climate change-related statistical indicators*, https://www.ecb.europa.eu/pub/pdf/scpsps/ecb.sps48~e3fd21dd5a.en.pdf. [63]

ECB (2024), *Risks from misalignment of banks' financing with the EU climate objectives: Assessment of the alignment of the European banking sector*, https://www.bankingsupervision.europa.eu/ecb/pub/pdf/ssm.bankingsectoralignmentreport202401~49c6513e71.en.pdf. [68]

Environmental Finance (n.d.), *Environmental Finance Data*, https://efdata.org/ (accessed on 2 August 2024). [40]

European Commission (2024), *Download annual data set of the macro-economic database AMECO*, https://economy-finance.ec.europa.eu/economic-research-and-databases/economic-databases/ameco-database/download-annual-data-set-macro-economic-database-ameco_en. [21]

Falduto, C., J. Noels and R. Jachnik (2024), "The New Collective Quantified Goal on climate finance: Options for reflecting the role of different sources, actors, and qualitative considerations", *OECD/IEA Climate Change Expert Group Papers*, No. 2024/02, OECD Publishing, Paris, https://doi.org/10.1787/7b28309b-en. [17]

FSB (2023), *Global monitoring report on non-bank financial intermediation 2023*, https://www.fsb.org/2023/12/global-monitoring-report-on-non-bank-financial-intermediation-2023/. [45]

G20 DGI (n.d.), *DGI-3 Recommendation 4*, https://www.imf.org/en/Data/Statistics/working-group-on-securities-databases/dgi-3-recommendation-4 (accessed on 27 August 2024). [59]

G20 DGI (n.d.), *DGI-3 Recommendations*, https://www.imf.org/en/News/Seminars/Conferences/DGI/g20-dgi-recommendations#rec3-4 (accessed on 27 August 2024). [57]

Hoffmann, C. et al. (2022), *Consistency case study: actions supporting Article 2.1c of the Paris Agreement in Germany*, ClimateWorks Foundation and ODI., https://www.germanwatch.org/en/87667. [70]

IEA (2024), *Energy Technology RD&D Budgets*, https://www.iea.org/data-and-statistics/data-product/energy-technology-rd-and-d-budget-database-2. [20]

IEA (2024), *World Energy Investment 2024*, https://www.iea.org/reports/world-energy-investment-2024. [12]

IEA (2023), *Government Energy Spending Tracker*, https://www.iea.org/reports/government-energy-spending-tracker-2. [1]

IEA (2023), *Government Energy Spending Tracker: Policy Database*, https://www.iea.org/data-and-statistics/data-tools/government-energy-spending-tracker-policy-database. [2]

IEA (2023), *World Energy Investment 2023*, IEA, https://www.iea.org/reports/world-energy-investment-2023. [14]

IRENA (2023), *Global Landscape of Renewable Energy Finance, 2023*, https://www.irena.org/-/media/Files/IRENA/Agency/Publication/2023/Feb/IRENA_CPI_Global_RE_finance_2023.pdf?rev=8668440314f34e588647d3994d94a785. [19]

Jachnik, R. and A. Dobrinevski (2021), "Measuring the alignment of real economy investments with climate mitigation objectives: The United Kingdom's buildings sector", *OECD Environment Working Papers*, No. 172, OECD Publishing, Paris, https://doi.org/10.1787/8eccb72a-en. [8]

Jachnik, R., M. Mirabile and A. Dobrinevski (2019), "Tracking finance flows towards assessing their consistency with climate objectives", *OECD Environment Working Papers*, No. 146, OECD Publishing, Paris, https://doi.org/10.1787/82cc3a4c-en. [9]

Lam, P. and J. Wurgler (2024), *Green Bonds: New Label, Same Projects*, National Bureau of Economic Research, Cambridge, MA, https://doi.org/10.3386/w32960. [37]

Lepers, E. and A. De Crescenzio (2024), *What Drives Capital to Green Companies in Emerging Markets:Evidence from Investment Funds*, https://doi.org/10.2139/ssrn.4822081. [53]

LSEG (2024), *Tracing carbon-intensive debt: Identifying and calibrating climate eisks in corporate fixed income*, London Stock Exchange Group, https://www.lseg.com/en/insights/tracing-carbon-intensive-debt-identifying-climate-risks-fixed-income. [38]

Mastouri, A., B. Shah and V. Pandey (2023), *How Sovereigns Have Changed the Green-Bond Market*, MSCI, https://www.msci.com/www/blog-posts/how-sovereigns-have-changed-the/03778801668. [39]

McKinsey & Company (2024), *McKinsey Global Private Markets Review 2024: Private markets in a slower era*, https://www.mckinsey.com/industries/private-capital/our-insights/mckinseys-private-markets-annual-review. [29]

McKinsey & Company (2023), *McKinsey Global Private Markets Review: Private markets turn down the volume*, https://www.mckinsey.com/industries/private-capital/our-insights/mckinseys-private-markets-annual-review-2023/. [31]

Micale, V. et al. (2020), *Paris Misaligned: An Assessment of Global Power Sector Investment*, Climate Policy Initiative, https://www.climatepolicyinitiative.org/publication/paris-misaligned/ (accessed on 2 February 2021). [7]

OECD (2024), *Annual investment by asset and institutional sector*, https://data-explorer.oecd.org/vis?lc=en&tm=gfcf&pg=0&snb=6&df[ds]=dsDisseminateFinalDMZ&df[id]=DSD_NASEC10%40DF_TABLE14_GFCF&df[ag]=OECD.SDD.NAD&df[vs]=1.1&dq=A.MEX....P51G.....V..&lom=LASTNPERIODS&lo=5&to[TIME_PERIOD]=false. [72]

OECD (2024), *Climate Finance Provided and Mobilised by Developed Countries in 2013-2022*, Climate Finance and the USD 100 Billion Goal, OECD Publishing, Paris, https://doi.org/10.1787/19150727-en. [16]

OECD (2024), "Cross-border investment into low-carbon infrastructure: An empirical glance", *OECD Working Papers on International Investment*, No. 2024/1, OECD Publishing, Paris, https://doi.org/10.1787/e82ee163-en. [55]

OECD (2024), *Global Debt Report 2024: Bond Markets in a High-Debt Environment*, OECD Publishing, Paris, https://doi.org/10.1787/91844ea2-en. [36]

OECD (2024), *Green Budgeting in OECD Countries 2024*, OECD Publishing, Paris, https://doi.org/10.1787/9aea61f0-en. [3]

OECD (2023), "Towards Orderly Green Transntion: Investment Requirements and Managing Risks to Capital Flows", *OECD Business and Finance Policy Papers*, No. 57, OECD Publishing, Paris, https://doi.org/10.1787/24520e7e-en. [52]

OECD (2022), *Long-term investing of large pension funds and public pension reserve funds 2022*, OECD Publishing, Paris, https://doi.org/10.1787/809eff56-en. [49]

OECD (2020), *Green Infrastructure in the Decade for Delivery: Assessing Institutional Investment*, Green Finance and Investment, OECD Publishing, Paris, https://doi.org/10.1787/f51f9256-en. [54]

OECD (2019), *Aligning Development Co-operation and Climate Action: The Only Way Forward*, The Development Dimension, OECD Publishing, Paris, https://doi.org/10.1787/5099ad91-en. [4]

OECD (n.d.), *Investment (GFCF)*, https://www.oecd.org/en/data/indicators/investment-gfcf.html. [71]

PACTA (2023), *Assessing Readiness for the Low-Carbon Transition: Climate scenario analysis of Peruvian pension fund investment portfolios*, https://pacta.rmi.org/wp-content/uploads/2023/06/assessing_readiness_for_the_low_carbon_transition.pdf. [67]

PACTA (2023), *From Bogotá to Paris? Measuring the climate alignment of Colombian insurance companies' portfolios*, https://pacta.rmi.org/wp-content/uploads/2023/06/from_bogota_to_paris.pdf. [66]

PACTA (2022), *Aiming Higher: Measuring progress on the climate goal alignment & climate actions of Swiss financial institutions*, https://www.google.com/url?sa=t&rct=j&q=&esrc=s&source=web&cd=&cad=rja&uact=8&ved=2ahUKEwiT0O691bCJAxUXVaQEHRrEGkoQFnoECBYQAQ&url=https%3A%2F%2Fwww.bafu.admin.ch%2Fdam%2Fbafu%2Fen%2Fdokumente%2Fklima%2Fexterne-studien-berichte%2Fpacta-climate-test-switzer. [65]

Preqin (2024), *Preqin 2024 Global Report: Private Debt*, https://www.preqin.com/insights/global-reports/2024-private-debt. [28]

Private Equity Stakeholder Project (2021), *Private equity propels the climate crisis: The risks of shadowy industry's massive exposure to oil, gas and coal*, https://pestakeholder.org/wp-content/uploads/2021/10/PESP_SpecialReport_ClimateCrisis_Oct2021_Final.pdf. [33]

Reserve Bank of Australia (2023), , https://www.rba.gov.au/publications/bulletin/2023/sep/green-and-sustainable-finance-in-australia.html. [64]

S&P (2023), *Value of private equity-backed renewable investments hits 5-year high of $14.6B*, https://www.spglobal.com/marketintelligence/en/news-insights/latest-news-headlines/value-of-private-equity-backed-renewable-investments-hits-5-year-high-of-14-6b-79595438. [32]

ShareAction (2018), *Pensions in a changing climate*, https://cdn2.assets-servd.host/shareaction-api/production/resources/reports/AODP-PensionsChangingClimate.pdf. [48]

SIFMA (2024), *Capital Markets Fact Book, 2024*, https://www.sifma.org/resources/research/fact-book/. [24]

SIFMA (2023), *2023 Capital Markets Fact Book*, https://www.sifma.org/resources/research/fact-book/. [26]

UN, EC, OECD, IMF & World Bank (2009), *System of National Accounts*, https://unstats.un.org/unsd/nationalaccount/docs/SNA2008.pdf. [56]

UNFCCC (2022), *Standing Committee on finance (SCF): Launch of flagship report for COP27*, https://unfccc.int/sites/default/files/resource/SCF_COP27_Side-event_11Nov_Reportslidepack.pdf. [44]

UNFCCC SCF (2022), *Fifth Biennial Assessment and Overview of Climate Finance Flows*, https://unfccc.int/sites/default/files/resource/J0156_UNFCCC%20BA5_2022_Report_v4%5B52%5D.pdf. [43]

WFE (n.d.), *WFE Statistics Database*, https://www.world-exchanges.org/our-work/statistics. [27]

Wilson, C. and B. Caldecott (2023), "Investigating the role of passive funds in carbon-intensive capital markets: Evidence from U.S. bonds", *Ecological Economics*, Vol. 209, p. 107792, https://doi.org/10.1016/j.ecolecon.2023.107792. [23]

World Bank (2024), *Gross fixed capital formation (current US$)*, https://data.worldbank.org/indicator/NE.GDI.FTOT.CD. [18]

World Bank (n.d.), *Gross fixed capital formation (current US$)*, https://data.worldbank.org/indicator/NE.GDI.FTOT.CD (accessed on 29 June 2024). [13]

World Bank Group, IMF and OECD (2023), *Activating Alignment: Applying the G20 Principles for Sustainable Finance Alignment with a Focus on Climate Change Mitigation*, World Bank, https://www.imf.org/external/np/g20/091323.htm. [6]

Notes

[1] Gross fixed capital formation (GFCF), also called "investment", is defined as the acquisition of produced assets by companies, governments, and households (including purchases of second-hand assets), and the production of such assets by producers for their own use, minus disposals (OECD, n.d.[71]). GFCF also covers intangible assets, which represents 1% to 30% of the total depending on the country but does not cover a large share of household spending on equipment (Jachnik, Mirabile and Dobrinevski, 2019[9]).

[2] Companies represented 60.4% of gross fixed capital formation across OECD countries in 2022, while governments represented 15.9% and households 23.6% (OECD, 2024[72]).

4 Emerging evidence of the role of financial policies and actions in influencing the climate alignment of finance

This chapter first recalls the range of real-economy public policies that may drive alignment or misalignment of finance with the Paris Agreement. It then focusses on financial sector policies, taking stock of existing typologies and best-available evidence on the degree of integration of climate-related considerations as well as on the expected or observed effects in relation to financial and climate policy goals. Additionally, the chapter briefly summarises available evidence on a selection of climate-related actions taken by investors and financial institutions.

Key insights

- **Real-economy policies remain crucial levers to influence the attractiveness of investments in activities contributing to or undermining climate goals.** Governments have relied more on climate-related economic policies, but other types of climate-related policies, such as regulatory, government investment and consumption, voluntary approaches, and information, have increased more in recent years. At the same time, existing policies continue to provide incentives for emissions-intensive economic activities and investments, both domestically and internationally, such as fossil fuel subsidies and investment treaties.
- **Financial sector policies have financial and price stability, and market integrity and efficiency, as primary objectives but can also influence climate outcomes.** Such influence can result from existing core financial sector policies or, depending on mandates of relevant authorities, from financial sector policies integrating climate considerations. By 2023, 81 countries worldwide and the EU had adopted financial sector policies integrating climate considerations, up from 43 countries in 2015 when the Paris Agreement was adopted. Over 450 such policies have been adopted since 2000.
- **Climate-related financial sector policies have mainly taken the form of transparency and information policies, with the aim to enhance market transparency and, in some cases, enable other climate-related policies and actions in the financial sector.** By 2023, supervisory and regulatory authorities or ministries in 77 countries and the EU had established such policies. 55 countries adopted disclosure policies and 70 countries adopted climate-related finance guidelines, such as taxonomies. Climate-related disclosure by financial and non-financial corporates has improved, but many gaps remain in terms of data accessibility, interoperability, and completeness for complementary metrics. Scarce evidence on real-economy impacts finds decreases in emissions-intensive finance volumes but mixed effects on emissions reductions.
- **In light of growing climate-related risks to the financial system, prudential policies across jurisdictions increasingly integrate those risks into policies aimed at maintaining financial stability.** Climate-related prudential policies, relating to risk management and supervision, market discipline, and the level and quality of capital, had been adopted in 41 jurisdictions by 2023, mainly by central banks. Understanding of the effects of climate-related prudential policies is primarily based on conceptual analysis and assumptions. Limited research finds mixed effects and trade-offs between core financial and climate policy objectives, especially for policies related to the level and quality of capital. Limited conceptual research expects potential positive effects across policy objectives for climate-related large exposure policies and some leverage and risk management and supervision policies, although effects may be small.
- **As the main aim of monetary policy is to maintain price stability, the degree to which it can consider climate change varies across jurisdictions, with few examples of adoption of climate-related considerations.** While conceptual research expects strong trade-offs between pricing and climate objectives, theoretical and empirical evidence are missing.
- **Financial market participants increasingly implement climate-related actions, primarily through engagement, divestment and exclusion, and portfolio construction practices.** Initial evidence finds that non-financial corporates respond to environmental preferences of investors, but it remains to be proven whether these responses result in emission reductions. Emerging research indicates that divestment and exclusions can have mixed effects, while the effects of climate-related portfolio construction practices are not tracked yet.

Aligning finance with climate policy goals requires an ecosystem of climate-aligned policies and actions incentivising financing and investments towards activities aligned with climate goals. A wide variety of interventions can be tailored to climate-related considerations by public and private actors (UNFCCC SCF, 2023[1]), a selection of which are summarised in Figure 4.1. While climate-related considerations can relate to both climate change mitigation and adaptation, the focus in this chapter is mainly on mitigation, seeing the current challenges in resilience assessments discussed in Chapter 2.

Figure 4.1. Public and private interventions that may influence climate alignment of finance

Real-economy policies	Financial sector policies	Private financial sector actions
Economic policies	Transparency and information policies	Engagement
Regulatory policies	Prudential policies	Divestment and exclusion
Government investment and consumption	Credit allocation	Tilting
Voluntary approaches	Monetary policies	Other portfolio construction practices
Information policies		
Section 4.1	Section 4.2	Section 4.3

Note: This is a non-exhaustive overview of types of public and private interventions that may influence the climate alignment of finance.
Source: Authors, based on (OECD, Forthcoming[2]) subject to further changes, and own research.

Aligning policies with climate goals across real-economy and financial sector policy areas, which are inherently linked, is a prerequisite for aligning finance with climate goals. Financing and investment decisions are still hampered by different policy uncertainties and disincentives (OECD, 2023[3]). Additionally, climate policy can be made more effective if policymakers with portfolios situated outside the traditional climate agenda can revisit the most misaligned policy instruments in their domains (OECD, 2015[4]). However, there may be both synergies and trade-offs with current core objectives and mandates of such policymakers. For example, as further addressed in Section 4.2, financial sector policies' primary objectives are financial and price stability, market efficiency and transparency.

The Paris Agreement temperature goal, as well as ambitious greenhouse gas emissions reduction and net-zero targets across countries have sent a policy message to private sector actors to integrate climate considerations in their actions. In some cases, the private sector has also moved ahead in the absence of or beyond the ambition of existing climate-related policies. As for policymakers, private financial sector actors may also be faced with synergies or trade-offs between different financial and societal objectives.

4.1. Overview of real-economy policies influencing climate alignment in finance

Governments may use a range of policy instruments and interventions to stimulate climate-aligned actions, notably by the private sector (companies and households), which can influence the alignment of real-economy investments and underlying financing with climate goals. Building on existing analytical frameworks in this area, policy instruments influencing climate change outcomes can be grouped into five major categories: (1) economic policies, (2) regulatory policies, (3) government investment and consumption, (4) voluntary approaches, and (5) information policies (OECD, Forthcoming[2]; Nachtigall et al., 2022[5]; Dubash et al., 2022[6]; OECD, 2008[7]). Importantly, some policies may have a primary purpose other than climate action, such as industrial development. Generally, the use of these instruments can affect the attractiveness of private investment in activities they target.

Figure 4.2. Real-economy policies that may influence the climate alignment of finance

Real-economy policies				
Economic policies	**Regulatory policies**	**Government investment and consumption**	**Voluntary approaches**	**Information policies**
Subsidies	Performance standards	Public investment	Voluntary targets	Capacity building and awareness
Taxes	Technology standards	Public procurement	Voluntary trading systems	Disclosure requirements
Trading systems	Framework standards	Public appraisal	Voluntary information systems	

Note: This is a non-exhaustive overview of real-economy public policy interventions that may influence the climate alignment of finance. The grey boxes provide examples of types of policies under policy areas.
Source: Authors, based on (OECD, Forthcoming[2]) subject to further changes.

Countries rely on different mixes of policies and instruments for climate change mitigation (Stechemesser et al., 2024[8]). Trends in the use of each type is changing over time (Nachtigall et al., 2022[5]; OECD, 2024[9]; OECD, 2023[10]). While efforts and data collection to track the reliance on the five categories are underway, relatively more comprehensive evidence is currently available for three broader policy groups: market-based policies (which is broadly the same as economic policies, i.e., (1) above), non-market-based policies (which broadly covers the other four categories (2-5)), and other policies (which include high-level policy documents with targets such as NDCs and infrastructure plans). Historically, policymakers relied more on market-based or economic policies (Figure 4.3, Panel A). More recently, non-market-based policies have been increasingly adopted by countries to mitigate climate change.

Economic policies can change the investment incentives for aligned and misaligned activities. The most used economic climate-related policies include subsidies, taxes, and fees (OECD, 2024[9]). Governments may use subsidies to attract private investments in climate solutions and rely on carbon taxes to discourage investments in carbon-intensive activities. Currently, carbon prices cover nearly a quarter of global emissions. As of 2023, 75 carbon taxes and emissions trading schemes are in operation worldwide, including in nearly all OECD countries (World Bank, 2024[11]). Several studies have found that carbon pricing tends to increase total investments by firms in abatement technologies such as installations of heat recovery solutions (Venmans, Ellis and Nachtigall, 2020[12]). Market-based climate policies, more broadly, can also reduce the negative effects of financing constraints (Costa et al., 2024[13]).

Regulatory policies directly restrict or mandate specific activities and hence related investments. Regulatory climate-related policies are increasingly relied upon. Some regulatory instruments, such as minimum energy performance standards (MEPS) for appliances and fuel efficiency standards for passenger cars, have been implemented and updated since the 1990s (OECD, 2023[10]). More recently other standards, such as building energy codes and MEPS for electric motors, are increasingly being adopted. Bans and phase-out requirements for some fossil fuel assets and equipment are increasingly used in some countries to shift consumption and production decisions (OECD, 2023[10]). These technology standards help mainstream low-carbon technologies by prohibiting the sale of conventional technologies based on fossil fuels (a ban) or prohibiting the use of the respective fossil-based technology altogether (a phase-out). Such policies support redirecting investments towards the production and diffusion of more sustainable alternatives (Trencher et al., 2022[14]).

Figure 4.3. Adoption of climate change-related real-economy policy instruments

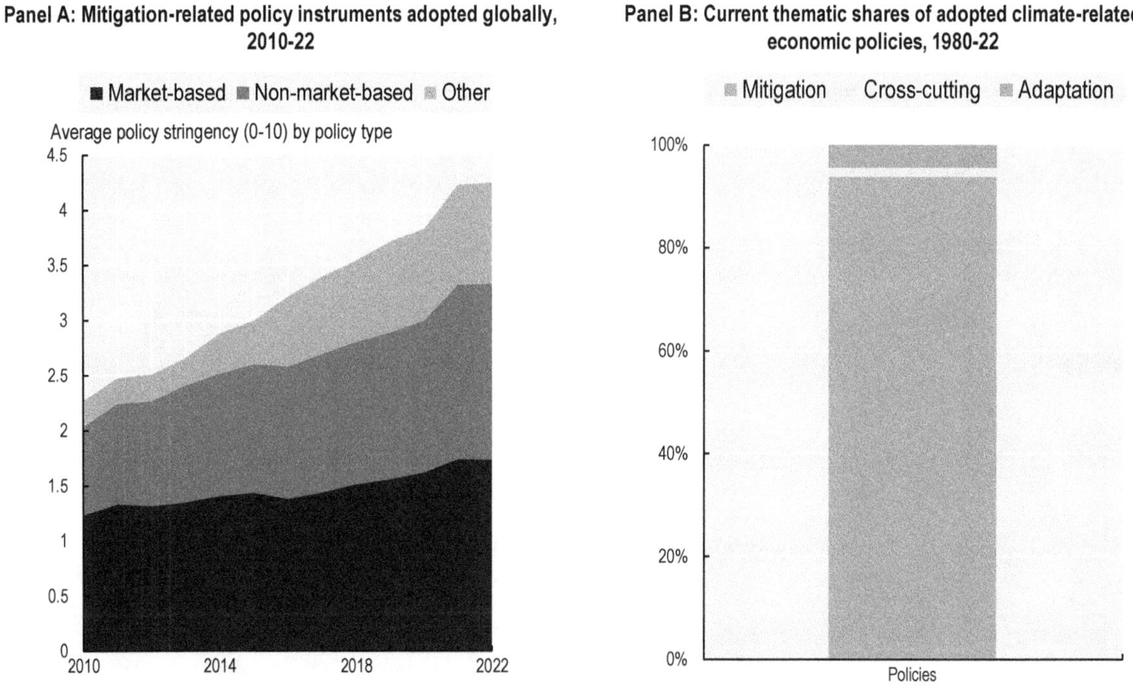

Note: In Panel A, other instruments include targets, international cooperation, governance, and climate data.
Source: Authors, based on (Nachtigall et al., 2022[5]; OECD, 2024[9]; Chhun et al., 2024[15]).

A range of other policies can further contribute to creating a domestic enabling environment for more climate-aligned and less misaligned investments. Information policies such as corporate disclosure requirements are commonly relied-upon policies across countries (and addressed in Subsection 4.2.1). Real-economy information-related policies also refer to national targets and roadmaps, capacity-building activities, government-funded certification (Bhandary, Gallagher and Zhang, 2021[16]), expert groups (Steffen, 2021[17]), and consumer education (WWF & Frankfurt School of Finance & Management, 2019[18]). Government-backed frameworks and schemes can also result in private-sector voluntary approaches and actions to mitigate climate change. For example, the OECD Guidelines for Multinational Enterprises on Responsible Business Conduct are internationally agreed standards with expectations for companies to understand and respond to climate impacts associated with their own activities (OECD, 2023[19]), and are thus also referred to in Section 4.3.

Direct public investment, financing, and consumption also play an important role (OECD, Forthcoming[2]). Public investments by governments and subnational authorities, as well as financing provided by official agencies, institutions and banks that can take the form of grants, lending, equity investments, guarantees and insurances can contribute directly to the implementation of climate-aligned projects, activities, and solutions, as well as has the potential to help mobilise and incentivise significant volumes of private finance for climate-aligned investments. Many initiatives are underway, addressing for instance the greening of public budgets (OECD, 2024[20]), or alignment with the Paris Agreement of international development finance (OECD, 2019[21]) and of development finance institutions.

A set of domestic economic policies providing continued support to and incentives for greenhouse gas emission-intensive economic activities and investments, however, remains in place, thus impeding and delaying the alignment of finance with climate goals. This notably includes fossil fuel subsidies (IEA, 2023[22]), which negatively affect the relative risk-return profile of climate-aligned investments such as in renewable energy (Ang, Röttgers and Burli, 2017[23]). In 2022, the fiscal cost of global support for fossil fuels amounted to USD 1.48 trillion, nearly double the average over the past decade (Figure 4.4). This jump in 2022 was, however, largely due to government measures (such as new support for coal production and consumption) to offset exceptionally high energy prices, driven in part by Russia's war of aggression against Ukraine (OECD, 2023[24]). Some additional analysis also estimates implicit subsidies, from undercharging for environmental costs and foregone consumption taxes, which could amount to USD 5.7 trillion (Black et al., 2023[25]). Explicit and implicit fossil fuel subsidies combined represented around 7% of global GDP in 2022 (IMF, 2023[26]).

Figure 4.4. Fiscal cost of support measures for fossil fuels

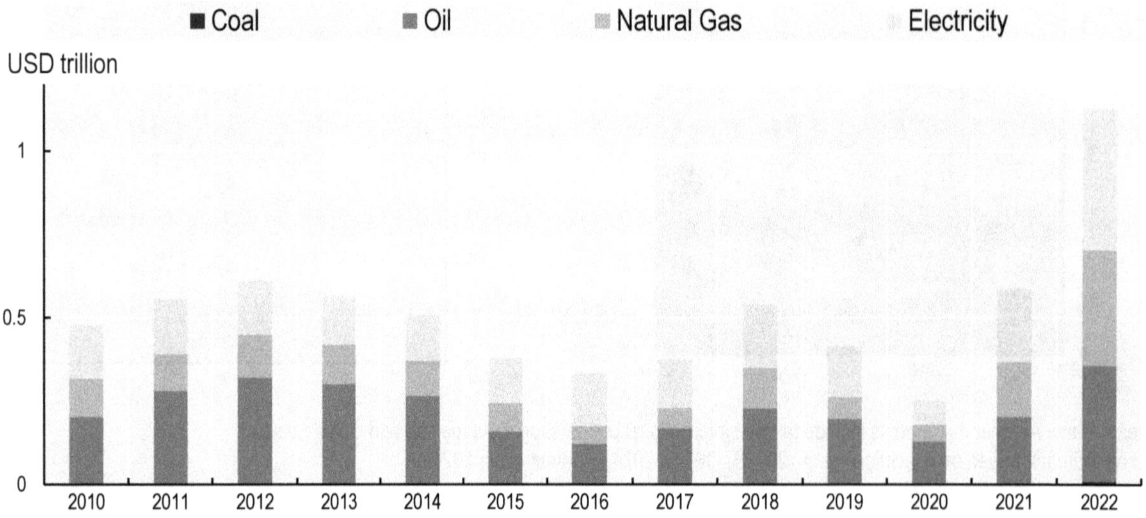

Note: The OECD-IEA combined estimate covers 82 countries. Fiscal cost of support for the fuel "Electricity" is derived from measures providing support for electricity generation or consumption.
Source: (OECD, 2023[24]; IEA, 2023[27]).

Policy instruments are much less frequent for climate change adaptation than for mitigation, and only limited evidence of their effects on investments is available. As of 2023, the OECD Pine Database included 90 adaptation-related policies implemented in 21 OECD member countries (Figure 4.3). Adaptation-related subsidies or tax breaks to developers and homeowners can encourage investments in climate-resilient infrastructure, for instance through stricter building practices to withstand extreme weather events. Adaptation-related regulations and standards ensure project holders incorporate resilience considerations into new investments (OECD, 2023[28]). Direct regulations, plans, and capacity building are found to be most effective and transformational (The Global Adaptation Mapping Initiative Team, 2021[29]). An example includes wildfire standards as part of building codes, which increase resilience-aligned investments in infrastructure (Baylis and Boomhower, 2021[30]).

Government policies can further influence international public and private investment flows to accelerate the net-zero transition and ensure they do not increase the vulnerability or fragility of systems (OECD, 2023[31]). Over the past decades, foreign direct investments in low-income countries have, at an aggregate level, been associated with increases in greenhouse gas emissions intensities in beneficiary countries (Wang et al., 2023[32]). Specific policies and enabling conditions can attract foreign direct investment contributing to the achievement of climate goals, including (i) governance, (ii) regulation, and (iii) targeted support measures (OECD, 2023[31]; OECD, 2022[33]). In addition, bilateral and multilateral public investments can crowd in private investments (OECD, 2023[34]). However, the magnitude of the effect is smaller for flows to and in EMDEs than in advanced economies (Haščič et al., 2015[35]).

Investment treaties (including provisions within broader trade agreements) are another important part of the policy framework influencing the climate alignment of finance (Gaukrodger, 2022[36]). These treaties typically protect investments by providing benefits in the event of a range of government actions, including expropriation, discrimination, or even lawful government actions. An investor can claim compensation, including potential lost profits if the government violates the treaty. While investment treaties generally do not impose climate-related requirements on investors, they often provide benefits to carbon-intensive activities. For example, about 10% of existing global fossil fuel production benefits from the treaties, while planned new oil and gas projects that will benefit from these treaties as they currently exist have been estimated to have an expected net present value between USD 60 and 234 billion (Tienhaara et al., 2022[37]). Investment treaty benefits not only incentivise investment but also affect government incentives to take climate action. Litigation and financial risks for governments under the treaties are substantial, with damages claims averaging over USD 700 million. At the same time, beneficiary investors do not have obligations under the treaties. The largest claims and awards involve fossil fuels. Such litigation and financial risks could delay climate action and need to be addressed by governments.

4.2. Financial sector public policies influencing climate alignment

Any analysis of financial sector policies' influence on the climate alignment of finance must acknowledge the core objectives of such policies. They oversee and guide the functioning of the financial system towards ensuring its stability, integrity, and efficiency. The core official entities implementing these policies are central banks, supervisory and regulatory authorities, and ministries (financial ministries in particular). Importantly, the exact mandates of these policymakers differ across jurisdictions.

Traditionally, financial sector policies did not consider climate change-related concerns. However, as the collective understanding of climate risks grows and the impacts of climate change intensify, climate risks are increasingly understood as being financially material (ECB, 2024[38]; FSB, 2023[39]; Stiroh, 2022[40]; FSB, 2022[41]; Bank of England, 2022[42]; Dikau and Volz, 2021[43]). Such risks to financial sectors, institutions, portfolios and assets arise from a misalignment of underlying economic activities and actors with a low-carbon pathway and resilient development (Dikau et al., 2024[44]).

Policymakers have started to consider climate-related considerations in financial sector policymaking. On the one hand, existing financial sector policies may have unintended consequences on climate goals. On the other hand, tailored financial sector policies can be adopted to address climate risks, which this report refers to as climate-related financial sector policies.

The climate-related financial sector policy data, which informs all of Section 4.2 was collected using a structured, multi-step approach to create a comprehensive database of climate-related financial policies spanning 2000 to 2023 (D'Orazio, 2023[45]). Relevant policies were identified by systematically retrieving official documents from the websites and databases of central banks, financial regulators, ministries, and banking associations. The search utilised specific keywords related to climate finance and financial regulation to ensure comprehensive coverage. The gathered documents were carefully read, validated, and cross-checked to ensure accuracy and completeness to avoid duplication and errors. The complete methodology is presented in (D'Orazio and Thole, 2022[46]; D'Orazio, 2023[47]).

Climate-related financial sector policies have been increasingly adopted since the Paris Agreement. By 2023, 81 countries (37%) and the EU had adopted at least one such policy (Figure 4.5, Panel A), up from 43 countries in 2015. Of those, 43 were advanced economies (AEs) and 38 emerging and developing economies (EMDEs), including 33 OECD member countries and all G20 jurisdictions. These can relate to climate change mitigation and/or resilience. Most existing climate-related financial sector policies directly or indirectly relate to climate-related transition and physical risks, designed to support core objectives of safeguarding the stability and functioning of the financial system. However, they may still have an impact on the degree of alignment of finance with climate goals despite such outcome not being their objective.

Climate-related financial sector policies have been adopted by a range of policymakers (Figure 4.5, Panel B). As of 2023, governments (ministries) are responsible for 30% of these policies, supervisory and regulatory authorities for 26%, central banks for 28%, and stock exchanges and securities exchanges 9%. The remainder of policies were adopted by a combination of these policymakers. The mandates of each type of policymakers and the extent to which it can integrate climate change considerations vary across jurisdictions. This is notably the case for central banks (Dikau and Volz, 2021[43]). Notwithstanding these variations, and as illustrated and discussed in the remainder of this section, some policies are more likely to be adopted by certain authorities than others (D'Orazio, 2023[47]; World Bank, 2021[48]).

Financial sector policies that are designed with climate considerations in mind can cover different policy areas. While there are different ways to group such policies, and some may fulfil multiple purposes, they can be grouped in four common policy areas (D'Orazio and Thole, 2022[46]; D'Orazio, 2023[45]; D'Orazio, 2023[47]; Steffen, 2021[17]; Bhandary, Gallagher and Zhang, 2021[16]; Krogstrup and Oman, 2019[49]).

Climate-related transparency and information policies: Generally, they support the efficiency and integrity of financial systems. Tailored climate-related policies in this policy area can create further transparency and increase the accessibility of climate-related information, with the aim of strengthening the foundation for well-informed financial decisions (Steffen, 2021[17]; WWF & Frankfurt School of Finance & Management, 2019[18]). Over the past few decades, these are by far the most relied-upon types of climate-related financial sector policies (Figure 4.5, Panel C). Governments, primarily finance or environmental ministries, are the most common authorities to launch disclosure requirements, followed by supervisory and regulatory authorities.

Climate-related prudential policies: Prudential policies are typically implemented to support the stability of the financial system. Climate-related prudential policies aim to address risks posed by climate change to the stability of the financial system by integrating climate-related risks more thoroughly in prudential policy frameworks (D'Orazio and Thole, 2022[46]; D'Orazio and Popoyan, 2019[50]). Such policies have been mostly implemented by central banks, consistent with their broader mandates to safeguard the stability of the financial system (Figure 4.5, Panel C).

Climate-related credit allocation policies: They typically support certain economic development objectives by influencing the flow of credit to specific sectors. Climate-related credit allocation policies directly promote climate-related credit measures and investments (D'Orazio, 2023[47]). Such policies can be adopted by a range of policymakers, including governments, but have mainly been adopted by central banks (Figure 4.5, Panel C).

Climate-related monetary policies: Their primary aim is to maintain price stability in the economy. Climate-related monetary policies generally aim to better reflect climate risk in standard monetary policy instruments such as the collateral framework and the central bank portfolio, or even introduce additional green quantitative easing (Krogstrup and Oman, 2019[49]; Steffen, 2021[17]). No consistent data is currently collected on such policies, likely because they remain relatively limited.

Figure 4.5. Climate-related financial sector policies adopted globally across policy areas

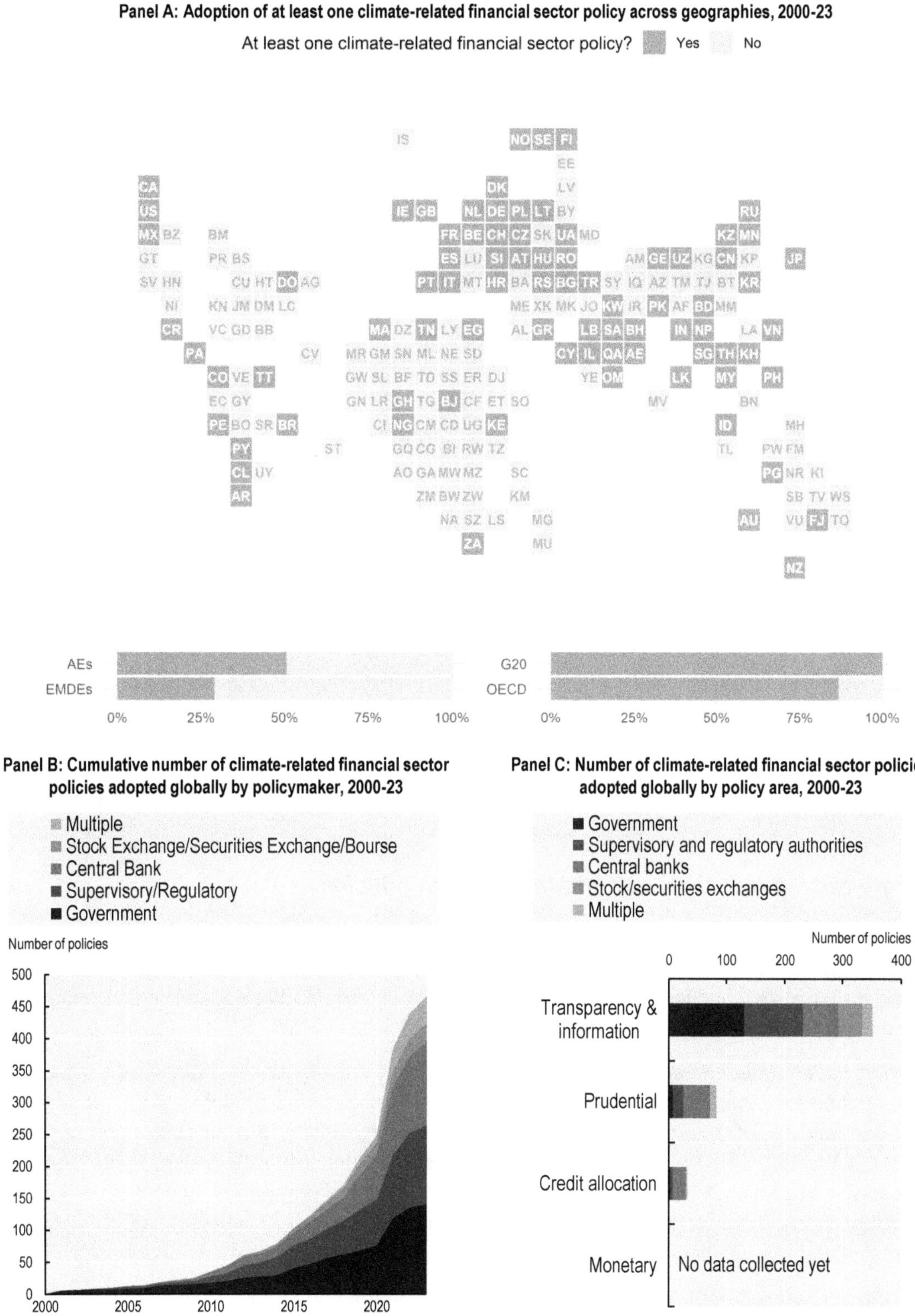

Note: Data for monetary policies are not currently consistently collected. Climate-related disclosure requirements for banks are counted under transparency and information policies in Panel C. AEs is advanced economies, based on the high-income country classification of the World Bank. EMDEs is emerging markets and developing economies, based on the World Bank classification for upper middle income, lower middle income, and low-income countries.
Source: Authors, based on (D'Orazio, 2023[45]) and updated data.

Some policy measures can fall under multiple policy areas. Notably, disclosure requirements for banks (3% of total climate-related financial sector policies by 2023). In this chapter, they are primarily analysed in the section to climate-related transparency and information policies, but they also qualify as climate-related prudential policies. Additionally, there may be policies relevant to the financial sector that currently fall outside the scope of this analysis. For example, regulation could be developed with respect to ESG rating activities, as has been done in the EU (European Parliament, 2024[51]).

Figure 4.6. Financial sector policies that may influence the climate alignment of finance

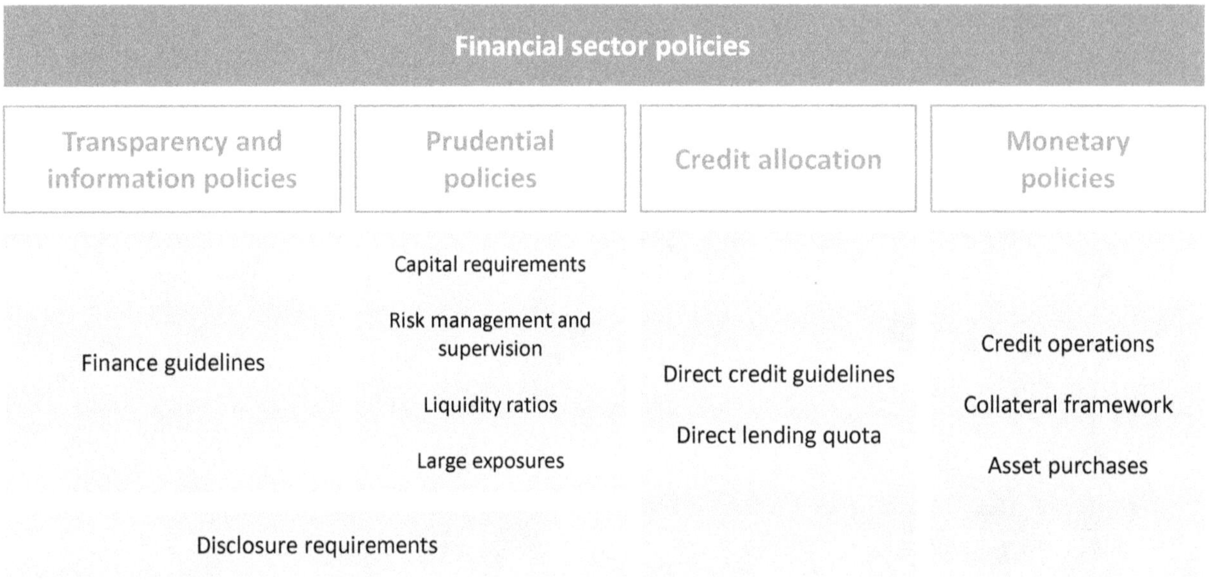

Note: This is a non-exhaustive overview of financial sector public policy interventions that may influence the climate alignment of finance. The grey boxes provide examples of types of policies under policy areas.
Source: Authors, based on (D'Orazio and Thole, 2022[46]; D'Orazio, 2023[45]; D'Orazio, 2023[47]; Steffen, 2021[17]; Bhandary, Gallagher and Zhang, 2021[16]; Krogstrup and Oman, 2019[49]).

4.2.1. Climate-related transparency and information policies

Transparency and information policies within the financial sector policy domain can be implemented to enhance the comparability of financing decisions, supporting the efficient functioning of the financial system. Some transparency and information policies also help inform market supervision, supporting the stability of the financial system.

In this context, climate-related transparency and information policies can serve multiple purposes and often provide a foundation for other climate-related financial sector policies and practices. They contribute to improved understanding of climate performance, reduced information asymmetries and increased comparability (NGFS, 2021[52]). This can enable financial sector players to reflect climate preferences in investment decisions (Section 4.3), as well as inform asset purchase programmes by central banks if they choose to tilt their portfolios towards better climate performers (explained in Subsection 4.2.3). Climate-related information can also be needed for climate-related prudential policy (the focus of Subsection 4.2.2).

Over the past two decades, climate-related transparency and information policies have grown significantly, and even more so since the adoption of the Paris Agreement. Between 2015 and 2023, they more than quadrupled, from 75 to 351 policies. By 2023, 77 countries and the EU had adopted at least one such policy (Figure 4.7, Panel A). This encompasses 42 AEs and 35 EMDEs, including 33 OECD member countries and all G20 countries. Across jurisdictions, there are differences in their stringency and level of bindingness, from purely voluntary to fully mandatory.

Figure 4.7. Adoption of climate-related transparency and information policies

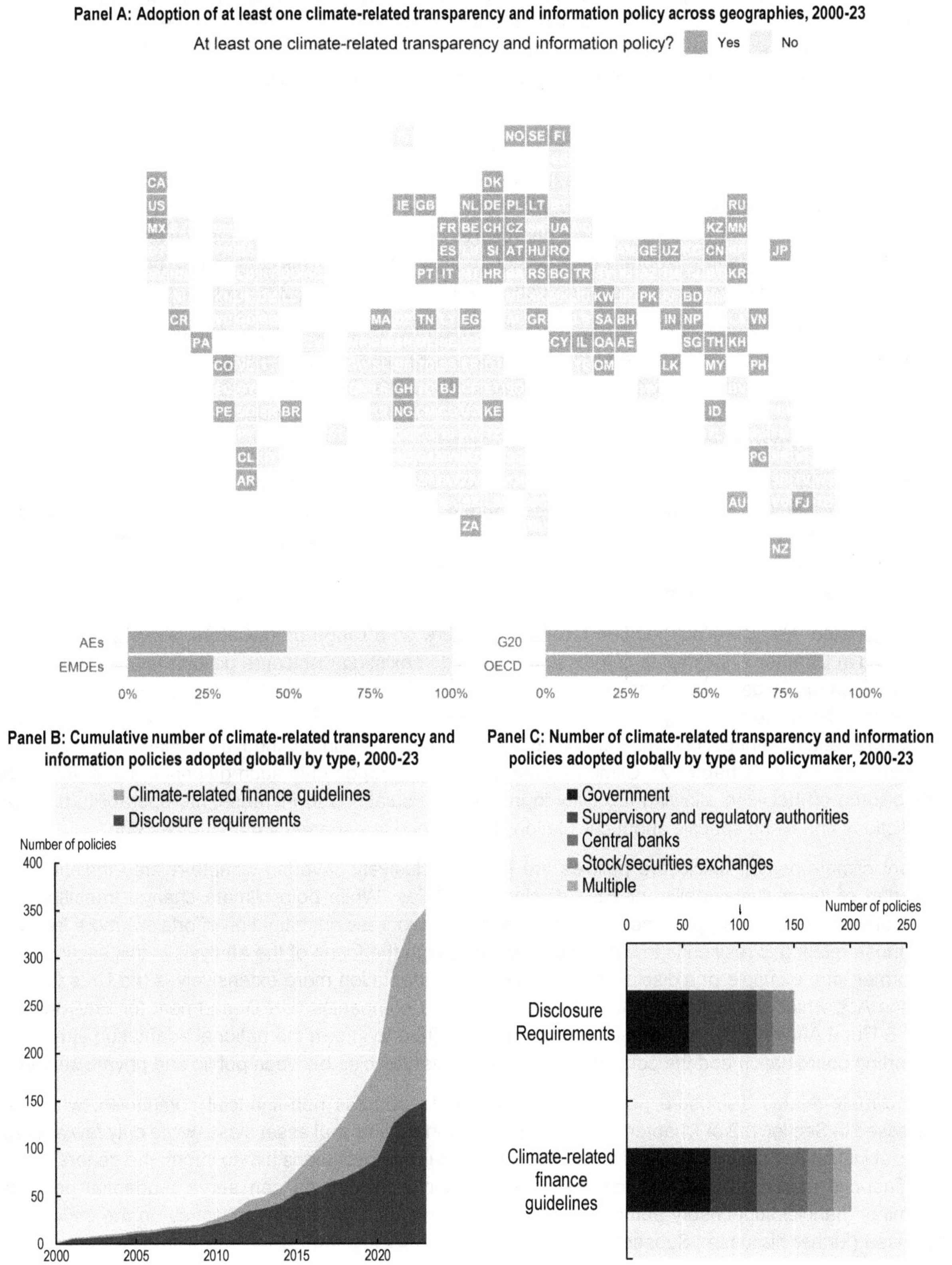

Note: AEs is advanced economies, based on the high-income country classification of the World Bank. EMDEs is emerging markets and developing economies, based on the World Bank classification for upper middle income, lower middle income, and low-income countries.

Source: Authors based on (D'Orazio, 2023[45]) and updated data.

Climate-related transparency and information policies can take different forms, notably disclosure requirements and financial guidelines (which include taxonomies and labelling policies). Climate-related disclosure requirements were the most common type of policy in this policy area until 2020 (Figure 4.7, Panel B). Between 2020 and 2023, climate-related finance guideline policies doubled.

Climate-related disclosure policies

Acknowledging differences in mandates across policymakers and jurisdictions, disclosure requirements aim to provide transparency, support market efficiency, and prevent information asymmetries or greenwashing claims. For example, regular disclosures on greenhouse gas emissions allow investors and other stakeholders to monitor progress on emission reduction targets. This could allow for capital allocation that considers greenhouse gas emission reductions (Monasterolo et al., 2017[53]).

Climate-related disclosure policies are widely relied upon. As of 2023, climate-related disclosure policies had been adopted in 55 countries and the EU (Figure 4.8). This encompasses 33 AEs and 22 EMDEs, including 28 OECD member countries and 17 G20 jurisdictions. There is a concentration of such policies in Europe, as well as in parts of the Americas and Asia-Pacific. Climate-related disclosure requirements adopted by policymakers in EMDEs remain more limited.

As of 2023, 40% of climate-related disclosure policies had been adopted by supervisory and regulatory authorities, and 37% by government ministries (Figure 4.7, Panel B). This is consistent with their mandates to ensure market efficiency, including through the availability of robust information and with the aim to address greenwashing issues. Central banks were behind 10% of such policies, and stock or securities exchanges 12%, while less than 1% were issued by a combination of policymakers.

Climate-related disclosure policies can require disclosure on a range of indicators, some of which were discussed in Chapter 2. Examples of indicators required in existing disclosure policies include Scope 1, 2 and 3 greenhouse gas emissions, climate targets, climate risks, transition plans, climate resilience strategies, climate-related engagement, or (for financial institutions) results of climate stress tests. Disclosure requirement policies may also be complemented by voluntary industry guidance on disclosure (as also discussed in Chapter 2). Climate-related indicators proposed in such guidance and policies can face a trade-off between allowing flexibility in indicator calculations to increase interoperability between jurisdictions and being specific about calculations to enhance transparency (OECD, 2023[54]).

Current climate-related disclosure policies are either exclusively covering climate-related indicators, or form part of wider sustainability or ESG disclosure policies. While both climate change transition and physical risks are covered, proposed indicators to assess progress on mitigation efforts are more frequent than those relating to resilience to climate change. Although the focus of the analysis in this section is on the former, one example of a disclosure policy covering adaptation more extensively is the UK's Climate Change Act, which mandates adaptation reports by listed companies (UK Department for Environment, Food & Rural Affairs, 2021[55]). These reports were designed to inform the national adaptation strategies, supporting coordination and the consideration of interdependencies between public and private sectors.

Most climate-related disclosure policies adopted to date address non-financial companies, which, as addressed in Section 3.2 of Chapter 3, represent an important financial asset class, while only few address financial institutions or both. While disclosures by non-financial institutions aim to inform the general public and financial market participants, disclosures by financial institutions can serve prudential goals by informing financial supervisory authorities, which can base their prudential initiatives on the information disclosed (further discussed Subsection 4.2.2).

Figure 4.8. Adoption of climate-related disclosure policies

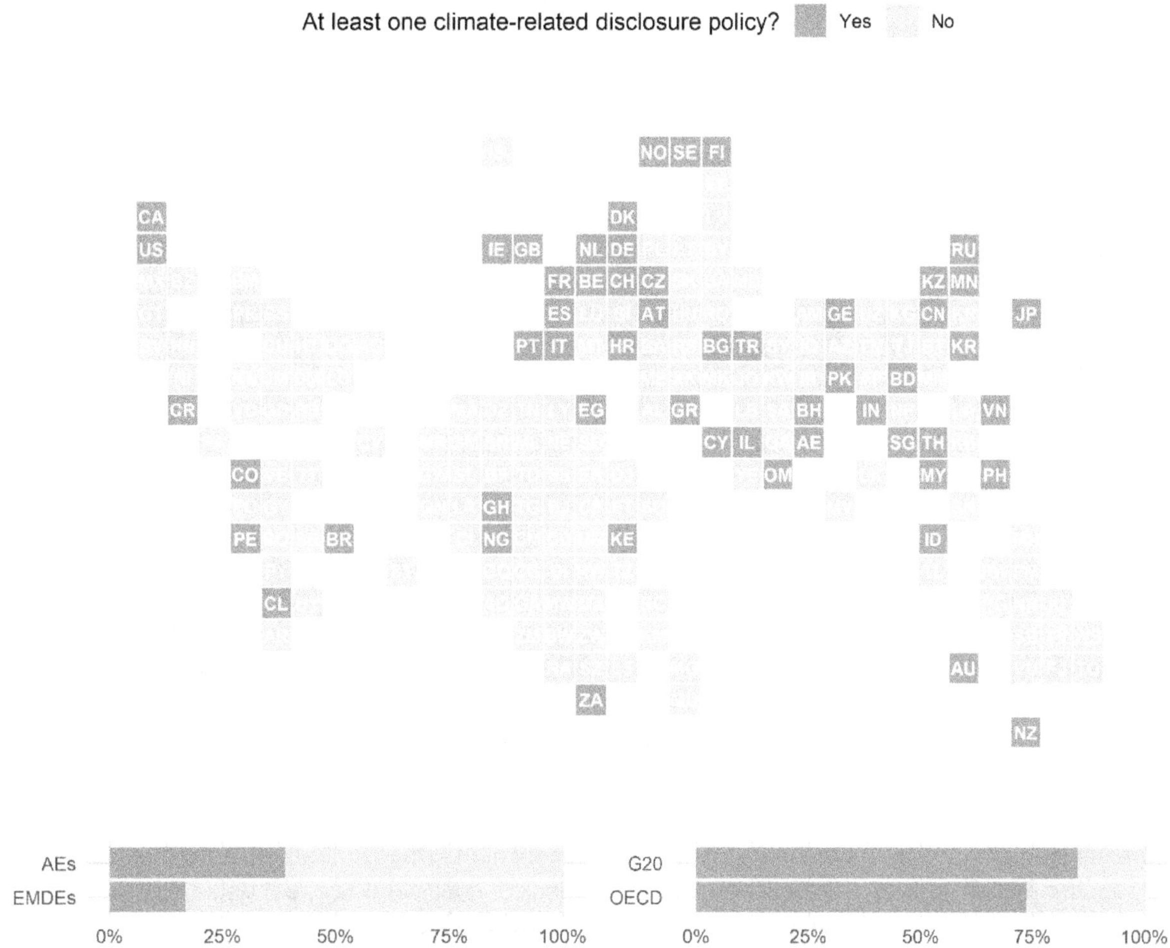

Note: AEs is advanced economies, based on the high-income country classification of the World Bank. EMDEs is emerging markets and developing economies, based on the World Bank classification for upper middle income, lower middle income, and low-income countries.
Source: Authors based on (D'Orazio, 2023[45]) and updated data.

Looking at the effects of these policy developments, climate-related disclosure practices by non-financial and financial companies have been improving. Notably, disclosure of simple GHG emissions-based indicators has become relatively well available globally. Companies representing 77% of market capitalisation disclosed Scope 1 and 2 emissions and 60% Scope 3 emissions disclosure in 2022 (Figure 4.9). While this is in great part due to the implementation of disclosure public policies in this area, in some cases, companies already disclosed (at least partly) on a voluntary basis, which may reduce the effect from and additionality of mandatory disclosure policies and requirements.

Despite increases in climate-related disclosure and reporting, many gaps remain. In 2022, climate-related information was available for less than 20% of listed companies that, however, represent 77% of market capitalisation, indicating a size bias in disclosure (Figure 4.9). Moreover, research for a smaller sample of companies finds that only half of companies disclosing any Scope 3 emissions disclose Scope 3 emissions data needed for informing robust assessments, including emissions associated with the use of produced products is typically not reported (LSEG, 2024[56]). Additionally, disclosure of emissions in EMDEs is overall lower than in advanced economies.

Figure 4.9. Current state of climate-related disclosure by non-financial and financial companies

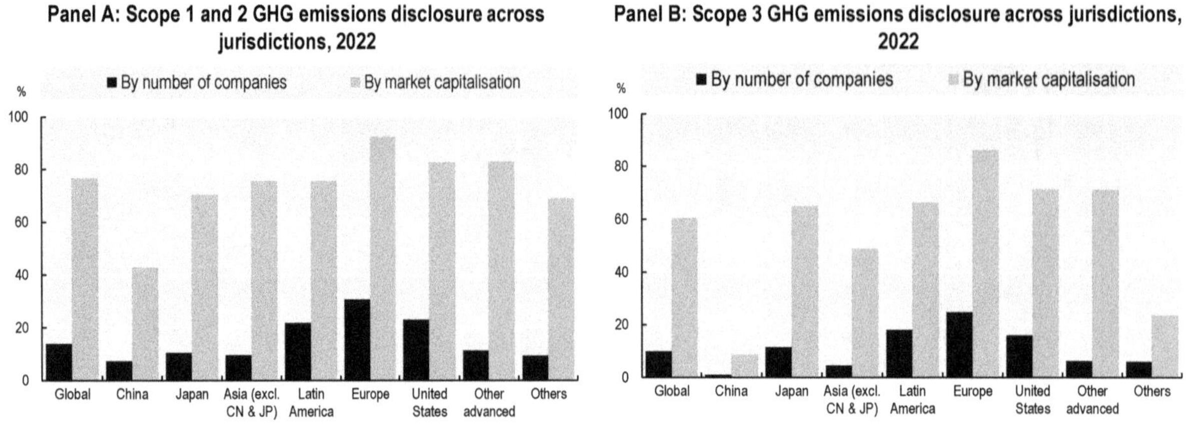

Note: This analysis includes 43 970 listed companies globally with a total market capitalisation of USD 98 trillion.
Source: (OECD, 2024[57]).

Further, disclosure on non-emissions-based indicators relevant to assessing climate risks and performance tend to be more limited. For example, very few of the largest financial institutions disclose information related to portfolio construction, engagement and governance practices, which, as discussed in Chapter 2, Subsection 2.3.2, are relevant for assessing progress towards their climate performance and net-zero commitments (OECD, 2023[54]). Some of these gaps will at least partially be resolved over the next few years due to new mandatory disclosure requirements (Box 4.1).

Assessments of the effects of climate-related disclosure policies in relation to climate goals are scarce and face inherent data challenges. A lack of reference data on Scope 1, 2, and 3 greenhouse gas emissions before the start of mandatory disclosure complicates impact assessments. Further, current research often only includes Scope 1 and 2 CO_2 emissions due to the lack of consistent Scope 3 data (e.g., (Shi, Bu and Xue, 2021[58])). Besides, few studies analyse the effects of disclosures for asset classes beyond listed equity, although there is evidence that debt, for example, plays an important role for financing emission reducing projects (Emambakhsh et al., 2022[59]).

Enhanced climate-related disclosure alone cannot be expected to reduce emissions, but can enable investors and financial institutions to act based on increased transparency. As further discussed in Section 4.3, such actions include engagement with investees, as well as portfolio management to reduce exposure to emissions-intensive assets and increase the share of climate solutions. Besides informing their investors and creditors, the data gathered and reported by non-financial companies also allows them to take action in relation to their operations, for example, to identify opportunities for energy saving either for reducing production costs or because they interpret mandatory climate disclosures as a signal for more rigid real-economy or financial policies to come (He, Xu and Shi, 2023[60]).

Box 4.1. Expected increase in climate-related disclosure under mandatory policies

Climate-related data disclosure by companies is critical to inform climate-related decisions and actions in the financial sector. Analysis by the Net-Zero Data Public Utility, a global initiative providing a centralised repository of company-level climate data that is transparent and freely accessible, finds that the potential number of companies covered by climate-related disclosure requirements is expected to triple by 2030 to over 120 000 (Figure 4.10). Moreover, while a significant share of companies disclosing climate-related data are doing so on a voluntary basis, the share of companies disclosing information in response to recent and upcoming mandatory climate-related disclosure requirements is foreseen to increase rapidly and at scale by 2030.

Despite the rise of mandatory climate-related disclosure policies, corporate climate-related data could remain difficult to access, limiting its effectiveness. Of the nearly 40 000 companies covered by mandatory disclosure requirements as of 2024, less than 7 000 (17%) are in easily discoverable locations and accessible formats (Figure 4.10). Digital tagging of climate data is expected to ramp up from 2026 onwards resulting in an improvement of the accessibility of these disclosures in company reports. In the European Union, for example, over 40 000 companies are set to be reporting under the EU Corporate Sustainability Reporting Directive (SCRD) with digital tagging by 2026, once the digital reporting mandate is adopted into the European Single Electronic Format regulation. Official repositories, which improve the ability to explore and analyse data, are expected to significantly expand their coverage. Based on the current trajectory of announced disclosure regulations, over 50% of disclosures from companies covered by existing or expected disclosure requirements will be digitally tagged and located in official repository by 2030, while, unless further action is taken, over 40% will remain non-machine readable and/or located outside of official repositories.

Figure 4.10. Expected company coverage of climate-related disclosure requirements

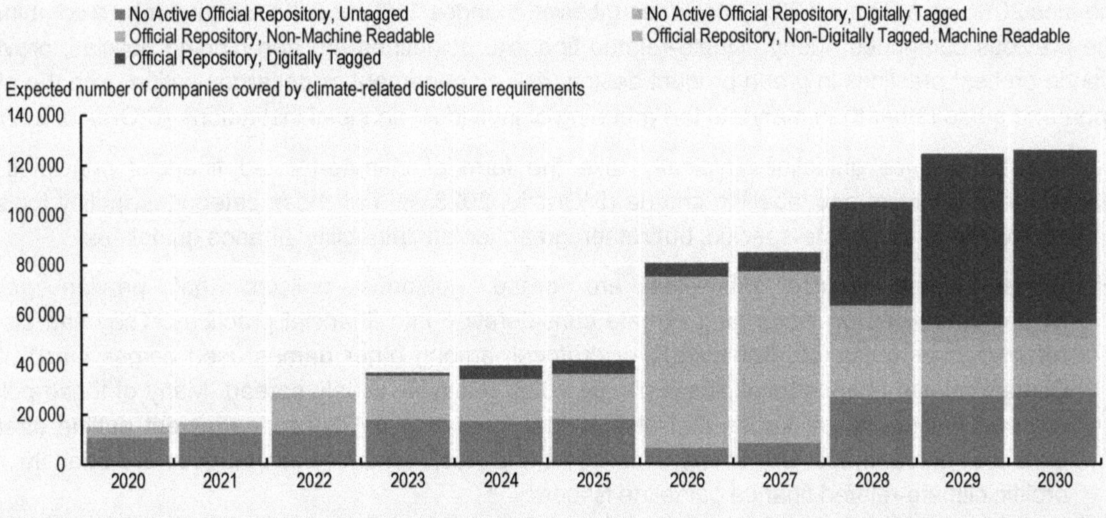

Note: Covered companies refer to the upper bound of the estimated number of companies covered by requirements relating to disclosure of company-level GHG emissions, including those still in consultation periods not yet officially finalized and comply-or-explain. "No Active Official Repository, Digitally Tagged" reflects the tagging of EU Corporate Sustainability Reporting Directive disclosures (assuming tagging mandate is adapted into European Single Electronic Format regulation for 2026) prior to the existence of European Single Access Point. Company disclosures not held in an official repository may still be extractable. Machine readable data refers to structured data that can be automatically read and processed by a computer (e.g., xml, json, csv). Digitally tagged refers to the act of applying machine-readable labels that align with a digital taxonomy to enable data to be read automatically.
Source: Net-Zero Data Public Utility.

In all cases, the effects of disclosure policies on GHG emissions would be mostly indirect, and tracing effects on actual real-economy decarbonisation is difficult. Thus, existing literature in this field mostly focuses either on the effects of disclosure by financial institutions on inflows into their funds, or the effects of corporate disclosure on their funding opportunities and very sparsely effects of corporate disclosure on their emissions. Initial evidence finds decreases in emissions-intensive finance volumes and mixed effects on emissions reductions due to mandated corporate disclosure:

- On the one hand, examples from the UK and the US find that mandatory disclosure led to a decrease of approximately 8% in Scope 1 and 2 GHG emissions (Downar et al., 2021[61]; Tomar, 2024[62]). On the other hand, other studies have found limited or no effects of disclosure on emissions but acknowledge important data and design limitations (Zhang and Liu, 2020[63]).
- Mandatory consolidated and high quality disclosure that can stimulate and support active investor interest was assessed as more impactful in the UK (DEFRA, 2010[64]; Sullivan and Gouldson, 2012[65]; Cong, Freedman and Park, 2020[66]). For example, UK firms already disclosing emissions at the installation level drastically reduced emissions after the introduction of disclosure requirements at the corporate level (Downar et al., 2021[61]).
- A recent study by the central bank of France found that mandatory climate disclosure regulations introduced in France have contributed to French investors curbing their investments in fossil fuel companies by 40% (Mésonnier and Nguyen, 2021[67]).
- Asset owners and managers in EMDEs cite the lack of information about corporates' emissions or transition as a key deterrent to transition investments in such jurisdictions (WEF, 2022[68]).

Climate-related finance guidelines

Climate-related finance guidelines are widely adopted by different policymakers across jurisdictions (Figure 4.7). By 2023, such guidelines had been adopted in 70 countries and the EU. This encompasses 36 AEs and 34 EMDEs, including 30 OECD member countries and all G20 jurisdictions. As of 2023, government ministries had adopted 37% of climate-related finance guidelines, supervisory and regulatory authorities 20%, central banks 23%, stock/securities exchanges 11%, and the remainder by a combination of the previous categories. Many climate-related financial guidelines are non-binding policies, providing guidance on best practices in green product design, risk management or decarbonisation, with the aim to support and guide rather than mandate the greening of individual financial institutions (D'Orazio, 2023[69]).

Climate-related finance guidelines typically take the form of climate-related financial principles and guidance, or taxonomies and labelling criteria (D'Orazio, 2023[69]). For these categories, policy tools are often not referred to as climate-specific, but rather 'green' or 'sustainability' finance guidelines.

- Climate-related finance principles are broad guidance policies that provide general recommendations on integrating climate consideration into financial practices. They can also be referred to as guidance, framework, or protocol, among other names used across jurisdictions. Climate-related finance principles were, by 2023, relatively widely spread. Many of these policies are part of broader packages that also include guidance on risk management outline strategic principles or roadmaps. Government ministries and stock/securities exchanges have been the most prolific climate-related finance guideline issuers.
- Climate-related taxonomies classify activities, for example, as green, transition relevant, or supporting adaptation (Tandon, 2021[70]). Climate-related labelling guidance outline requirements to name a financial product as 'climate' or 'green'. Taxonomies and labelling guidance relate to disclosure requirements (see previous subsection) when disclosed information is an input to the classification process or when the disclosure of taxonomy alignment is required for labelling financial products. Such labels are often the basis of currently available evidence of finance going to activities that support climate goals (as shown in Chapter 3). Since the adoption of the Paris

Agreement, sustainable and green taxonomies have been increasingly developed, remaining mostly voluntary. Currently, around 75% of AEs, but less than 10% of EMDEs have a sustainable or green finance taxonomy (World Bank, 2024[71]). Green bond frameworks can be established independently from taxonomies or build on them or other disclosure requirements. Some jurisdictions have also adopted more general labelling, naming and communication guidelines to clarify the intent and strategies of financial products beyond green bonds, such as green funds.

Literature on the effects of climate-related guidelines on volumes of investments and financing for activities contributing to climate goals, and on GHG emissions reductions is scarce. Due to the broad nature of climate-related finance principles, identifying and tracing impact channels may not be possible. Such principles may also frame or be adopted together with other policies, making it difficult to isolate the effect on emissions from such principles policies individually (D'Orazio and Dirks, 2021[72]).

Overall, the aim of, and thus expectation from, such policies is that they improve the credibility and transparency of activities or financial assets supporting climate actions, allowing investors to choose products reflecting their preferences. In other areas, such as food labels, labelling containing greenhouse gas emissions or climate-related information has been shown to significantly alter consumption choices towards less emission-intensive and more environmentally friendly products (Muller, Lacroix and Ruffieux, 2019[73]; Camilleri et al., 2018[74]). For the financial sector, current analysis points to greater inflows into funds labelled as more sustainable (Becker, Martin and Walter, 2022[75]; Scherer and Hasaj, 2023[76]). The additionality of the policy effect is, however, difficult to demonstrate as such policies may respond to investor demand as well as redirect finance from self-labelled funds to funds labelled according to the policy. While climate-related taxonomies and green bond frameworks may increase flows to funds using such labels, there is currently no evidence that they influence emissions reductions. For the time being, econometric studies of the effects on decarbonisation face data availability challenges, as many taxonomies and frameworks have only been recently adopted.

4.2.2. Climate-related prudential policies

Prudential policy mainly aims to maintain financial stability. Financial stability is understood as the capacity of a financial system to absorb severe shocks and maintain the provision of financial services (Tamez, Weenink and Yoshinaga, 2024[77]). Microprudential regulation is concerned with the financial health of individual institutions, while macroprudential regulation addresses risks to financial stability at an aggregate level as a result of the combined effects of financial institutions' behaviour.

As climate change can affect the value of physical and financial assets to an extent that threatens financial stability, policymakers need to integrate climate risks into existing prudential policy frameworks (NGFS, 2020[78]; Tamez, Emre and Gullo, 2024[79]). At micro level, climate risks affect individual banks. Such risks need to be integrated into their risk assessments and disclosures (Smoleńska and van 't Klooster, 2022[80]; BIS, 2022[81]; NGFS, 2020[78]). At macro level, the impacts of climate change and related policies on all economic activities are increasingly highlighted as a systemic risk to the financial system (FSB, 2022[82]), requiring the aggregate effects of financial institutions' exposure and vulnerability to climate-related risks need to be integrated into macroprudential policies (Grill, Popescu and Rancoita, 2024[83]).

Traditional prudential policies can have unintended consequences on climate goals. For instance, there is some evidence that incumbent GHG emissions-intensive assets and underlying finance benefits from the current prudential framework (Gasparini et al., 2024[84]; D'Orazio and Popoyan, 2019[50]), notably by undervaluing the risks associated with such assets (Campiglio, 2016[85]). Moreover, prudential reforms following the 2008 global financial crisis have introduced short-term risk management requirements, in order to address the vulnerabilities at the root of this crisis, such as frequent reporting in banking (Kraft, Vashishtha and Venkatachalam, 2017[86]) or liquidity coverage requirements for financial institutions (Ameli et al., 2019[87]). In addition, some medium-term requirements have also been introduced to encourage banking institutions to ensure stable funding conditions at a longer horizon. However, those requirements may not always be tailored to favour investments in climate solutions, which are often in need of high upfront capital and long-term financing, are less liquid as well as perceived as riskier (WEF, 2013[88]; Narbel, 2013[89]; Gersbach and Rochet, 2012[90]; Thanassoulis, 2014[91]; Ang, Röttgers and Burli, 2017[23]). Further documented side effects of the current prudential framework include the potential to disincentivise cross-border lending to EMDEs (Linehan, 2024[92]; Attridge, Getzel and Gregory, 2024[93]), in particular for infrastructure projects and SMEs (Beck, 2018[94]).

Degree of adoption of climate-related prudential policies

The integration of climate change-related risks into prudential policies can relate to different dimensions of the Basel III framework. This framework is an internationally agreed set of measures that aims to strengthen the regulation, supervision, and risk management of banks (BIS, n.d.[95]) . The Basel III framework has three pillars relating to capital (broadly covering minimum capital requirements (Pillar 1), risk management and supervision (Pillar 2), and market discipline (Pillar 3)), as well as policies relating to liquidity and large exposures (BIS, n.d.[96]).

Individual climate-related prudential policy instruments can cover various aspects of the Basel III framework, and primarily include:

- Capital-related policies:
    - Capital requirements aim to ensure that credit institutions[1], particularly banks, have enough capital to absorb losses and continue operating during periods of financial stress, which can result from the effects of sudden economic shocks on banks. Climate-related capital requirements would thus focus on adjusting capital adequacy ratios of banks according to the level of exposure and vulnerability of their portfolio to climate-related risks and impacts (D'Orazio and Popoyan, 2019[50]). This can be done through adjusting capital adequacy ratios with so-called green supporting or brown penalising factors, adjusting capital requirements for specific sectors highly exposed to climate-related risks or that can benefit from the climate transition, and adjusting counter-cyclical and systemic risk buffers (originally introduced to mitigate the effects of system-wide economic shocks).
    - Risk management and supervision policies aim to ensure that financial institutions effectively manage risks to prevent excessive risk-taking that could threaten their stability and the broader financial system. This can result in holding more capital if additional risks are identified. Climate-related risk management and supervision policies aim to enhance financial system stability through regulating banks' identification and management of climate-related risks. This mainly includes expanding conventional risk management practices, integrating climate risks in stress tests, adjusting requirements for the quality and level of capital, or specifying lending limits (Bhandary, Gallagher and Zhang, 2021[16]; WWF & Frankfurt School of Finance & Management, 2019[18]).
    - Market discipline policies aim to enhance the transparency and accountability of financial institutions, notably to encourage prudent behaviour. Climate-related market discipline mainly refers to climate-related disclosure policies for banks. Climate-related micro-prudential policies can support the integration of climate risks for individual banks into their disclosures (Smoleńska and van 't Klooster, 2022[80]; BIS, 2022[81]; NGFS, 2020[78]). As Subsection 4.2.1 already addressed disclosure policies, they will not be explained again here but will still be counted in aggregate prudential policy statistics in Figure 4.11.
- Liquidity-related policies are designed to ensure that financial institutions maintain sufficient liquid assets to meet their short-term obligations and continue operating during periods of stress. Similar to capital requirements, liquidity requirements can be adjusted to better reflect climate related risks to banks' operations (Baranović et al., 2021[97]; D'Orazio and Popoyan, 2019[50]).

- Large exposure-related policies aim to limit the concentration of risk by ensuring that financial institutions do not have excessive exposure to a single counterparty or group of related counterparties. Policymakers could restrict the share of banks' portfolios that are exposed to particularly high climate-related risks (Miller and Dikau, 2022[98]) to limit their vulnerability to shocks. Similar exposure restrictions already exist for other risks.

Climate-related prudential policies have mostly been implemented for capital-related policies (Figure 4.11, Panel B). By 2023, 41 countries and the EU had developed climate-related capital-related policies (Figure 4.11, Panel C). This encompasses 20 AEs and 21 EMDEs, including 18 OECD member countries and 12 G20 jurisdictions. Consistent data collection on climate-related liquidity policies and lending limits through large exposure policies does not yet exist, likely because such policies are rare.

Within climate-related capital-related prudential policies, climate-related risk management and supervision policies are most common, often combined with related disclosure policies for financial institutions. Policymakers, mainly central banks, have particularly relied more on enhanced supervisory reviews (relating to Basel III Pillar 2) for climate-related prudential policy. Looking at sub-categories of climate-related risk management and supervision policies:

- Adoption of climate-related prudential policies enhancing minimum capital and leverage requirements for banks (relating to Basel III Pillar 1) has been scarce. As of 2023, only one country had adopted a capital adequacy requirement with a green supporting factor. Hungary's central bank introduced green preferential capital requirements in 2020, focusing on projects with energy savings and renewable energy components (Magyar Nemzeti Bank, 2022[99]). No country has currently adopted capital adequacy requirements with a brown penalising factor, with the aim to increase capital requirements for investments in high-emitting activities (Krogstrup and Oman, 2019[49]).
- Climate stress tests have been, to date, the most common climate-related risk management and supervision policies adopted or piloted. By 2023, banking authorities (notably central banks) had conducted a climate risk assessment, such as climate stress tests, in around 80% of AEs and 20% of EMDEs (World Bank, 2024[71]). Climate stress tests can evaluate risks based on the balance sheets of individual institutions or on a macroeconomic level based on aggregate exposures (Baudino and Svoronos, 2021[100]). Ideally, they provide both supervisors and participating banks with information on how to adapt operations to cope with likely scenarios. Climate stress tests generally aim to understand and test the resilience of banks in several climate scenarios, with the NGFS scenarios being the most prominent framework (Dunz et al., 2021[101]). Several EMDEs have generated tailored scenarios to their particularly high vulnerability to physical climate risks, such as from droughts or typhoons (World Bank, 2024[71]). Most literature focuses on outlining methods and applying them, highlighting the importance of smooth and immediate transition induced by policies to avoid adverse impacts on financial stability (Jung, Engle and Berner, 2023[102]; Allen et al., 2020[103]; Battiston et al., 2017[104]; Baudino and Svoronos, 2021[100]; Dunz et al., 2021[101]).

Figure 4.11. Adoption of climate-related prudential policies

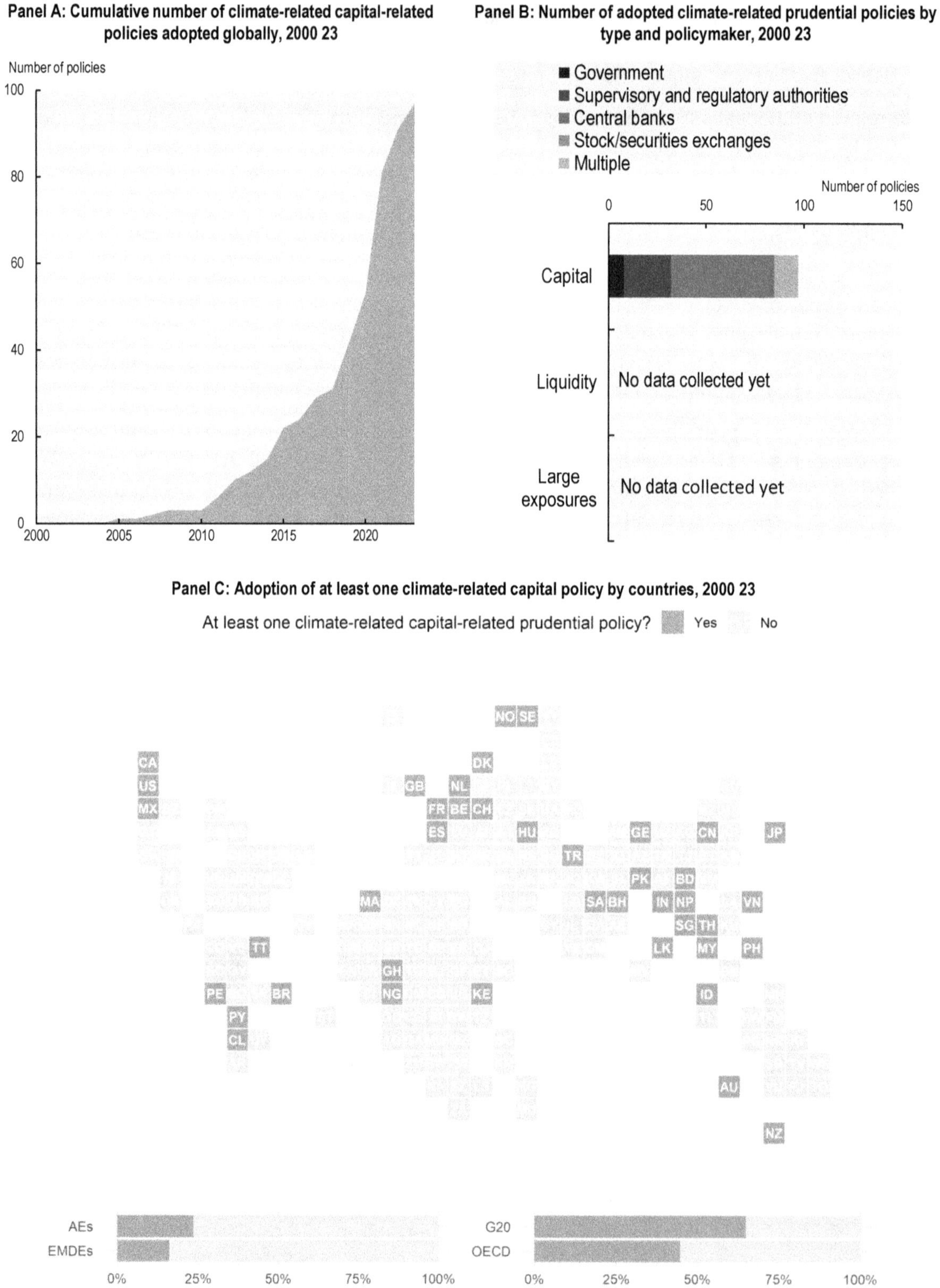

Note: AEs is advanced economies, based on the high-income country classification of the World Bank. EMDEs is emerging markets and developing economies, based on the World Bank classification for upper middle income, lower middle income, and low-income countries.
Source: Authors based on (D'Orazio, 2023[45]) and updated data.

- A limited number of countries have considered amending Internal Capital Adequacy Assessment. For example, Brazilian policymakers issued an amended Internal Capital Adequacy Assessment Procedure (ICAAP), in which their central bank required the explicit integration of climate (environmental) risks in banks' assessments of capital requirements (Banco Central do Brasil, 2011[105]). In the UK, the Bank of England has also provided guidance for banks to consider climate-related financial risks as part of their ICAAP (Bank of England, 2019[106]). The EU plans to enable supervisory authorities to adjust capital requirements including systemic risk buffers when financial institutions fail to adequately integrate climate risk into their operations starting in 2025 (Council of the European Union, 2021[107]).
- Some countries have included climate considerations in other risk management and supervision policies. For example, Philippines' Sustainable Finance Framework defines climate risk management as a responsibility of senior management and board of directors (Republic of Philippines, 2021[108]). A few countries, such as Morocco and Nepal, currently require banks to integrate environmental risk explicitly into credit risk ratings.

Available evidence on the effects of climate-related prudential policies

Based on existing analyses across conceptual, theoretical, and empirical research, climate-related prudential policies are found to have mixed effects on finance towards low-GHG activities, while bringing trade-offs with financial stability (Table 4.1). Conceptual, theoretical, and empirical analysis do not always come to the same conclusions in terms of direction and size of effects. Conceptual research currently expects potential positive effects across policy objectives for climate-related large exposure policies, as well as for some leverage and risk management and supervision policies, although effects may be small.

As adoption of these policies has been scarce, existing studies focus on conceptualisations, back-of-the-envelope calculations, theoretical and modelled effects. Furthermore, potential climate adjustments to existing policies have not all received the same attention in the literature. A substantial part of the literature on prudential policies concentrates on green supporting and brown penalising factors, but very few scientific and grey literature publications discuss the effects of climate-related liquidity or large exposure measures. Moreover, empirical research on the effects of individual policies can be difficult to discern as policies are often coupled. For example, guidelines and non-binding recommendations for climate risk integration into management are often coupled with disclosure measures.

Conceptual and theoretical research expects that a capital adequacy ratio with a green supporting factor would bring challenges to financial stability (Dankert et al., 2018[109]; Dafermos and Nikolaidi, 2021[110]; Dunz et al., 2021[101]; Oehmke and Opp, 2022[111]), while such research does not currently expect clear positive effects on limiting climate risks and increasing climate-related finance volumes.

- Some research points to a lack of evidence that low-carbon investments are substantially less risky, which would be needed to lower climate-related financial risk and enhance financial stability, justifying lower capital requirements (Dankert et al., 2018[109]; Coelho and Restoy, 2022[112]; Dafermos and Nikolaidi, 2022[113]). Other conceptual research suggests that climate-adjusted capital requirements, where carefully calibrated, could be effective in reducing climate-related financial risks and in supporting a smooth rather than abrupt climate transition (Oehmke, 2022[114]; Baranović et al., 2021[97]). Further theoretical research finds a decline in climate-related financial risks, albeit small (Dafermos and Nikolaidi, 2021[110]).
- At the same time, conceptual and theoretical research disagree on the effect of a green supporting factor towards increasing climate-related finance volumes. Some conceptual research questions the effectiveness of a green supporting factor, arguing that companies may finance emissions-intensive activities through sources other than loans (Oehmke, 2022[114]) and that the reduction in the cost of capital may be too small to influence investment decisions, similar to the empirically limited effect of the European Small and Medium Enterprise Supporting Factor (Dankert

et al., 2018[109]; EBA, n.d.[115]; 2DII, 2018[116]). Other theoretical research finds that lowering capital requirements for low-carbon investments through a green supporting factor may scale up green investments, but only in the short term (Dunz et al., 2021[101]) or if the green supporting factor remains small (Oehmke and Opp, 2022[111]). A large green supporting factor may crowd in investments, including GHG-intensive ones.

Table 4.1. Summary of literature on potential effects of climate-related prudential policies

Positive effect | No/minimal effect | Negative effect | Mixed evidence | No evidence

C = Conceptual analysis T = Theoretical analysis E = Empirical analysis

Dimension		Measure	Potential effect on the objective								
			Financial stability effects			Reduction of climate-related financial risks			Increases in climate-related finance volumes		
			C	T	E	C	T	E	C	T	E
Capital	Level and quality of capital	Capital adequacy ratio with a green supporting factor									
		Capital adequacy ratio with a brown penalising factor									
		Sectoral capital requirements									
		Counter-cyclical risk buffer									
		Systemic risk buffer									
	Leverage	Sectoral leverage ratios									
	Risk management & supervision	Climate-related stress tests									
		Internal capital adequacy assessment									
		Green asset ratio									
	Market discipline	Climate-related disclosure requirements									
Liquidity		Climate-related liquidity coverage ratio									
		Climate-related net stable funding ratio									
Large exposure		Climate-related lending limits/credit ceilings									
		Climate-related concentration charge									

Note: Colouring is based on the available literature, following the majority where dissenting; grey and academic literature was considered, literature had to provide structured argument and preferably some calculations to be included as conceptual, more literature was classified as theoretical evidence if it included models or simulations; literature relying on empirical data were classified as empirical.
Source: Authors, based on (D'Orazio, 2021[117]; Dafermos et al., 2022[118]; Dafermos and Nikolaidi, 2021[110]; Dunz et al., 2021[101]; Thomä and Gibhardt, 2019[119]; 2DII, 2018[116]; Benmir and Roman, 2020[120]; Oehmke and Opp, 2022[111]; Chamberlin and Evain, 2021[121]; Oehmke, 2022[114]) (Coelho and Restoy, 2023[122]; D'Orazio and Popoyan, 2019[50]; Grunewald, 2020[123]; Monnin, 2021[124]; Coelho and Restoy, 2022[112]; Battiston and Monasterolo, 2024[125]; Dikau and Volz, 2021[43]; Dikau and Volz, 2018[126]; Miguel, Pedraza and Ruiz-Ortega, 2024[127]; Lamperti et al., 2021[128]) (Baranović et al., 2021[97]; Miller and Dikau, 2022[98]; Schoenmaker and Van Tilburg, 2016[129]; Zhou et al., 2022[130]).

Conceptual and theoretical research on a capital adequacy ratio with a brown penalising factor also cautions about the financial stability effects of introducing this policy instrument. More studies expect positive effects on limiting climate risks. There are diverging expectations on the effect of this policy measure on increasing climate-related finance volumes.

- Theoretical research estimates lower economic output and higher loan defaults due to higher costs of capital for brown firms (Dafermos and Nikolaidi, 2021[110]; Oehmke and Opp, 2022[111]). Some theoretical work suggests the brown penalising factor should be targeted and limited in scope to avoid destabilising larger parts of the economy (Chamberlin and Evain, 2021[121]). For instance, the European Insurance and Occupational Pensions Authority is exploring the effects of a penalising factor applied to fossil fuel-related assets only (EIOPA, 2023[131]).
- Conceptual and theoretical research currently agree that the brown penalising factor would reduce climate-related financial risks. A brown penalising factor is expected to reduce climate-related financial risks by disincentivising exposure to potentially stranded GHG-intensive assets and increasing capital to better bear losses when climate-related risks do materialise (D'Orazio, 2021[117]; Berenguer, Cardona and Evain, 2020[132]; Oehmke and Opp, 2022[111]).
- Some conceptual and theoretical research expects that a brown penalising factor would increase finance volumes to low-carbon activities, as it limits banks' lending to brown assets and indirectly reorients lending to low-carbon activities (D'Orazio, 2021[117]; Dafermos and Nikolaidi, 2021[110]; Thomä and Gibhardt, 2019[119]). Other conceptual and theoretical research highlights the risk of limiting capital to GHG-intensive companies that are transitioning (Coelho and Restoy, 2022[112]) and loans being substituted for larger finance volumes of other types of financing (Thakor and Song, 2023[133]). Some research also highlights the importance of the specific design of this policy measure. A large brown penalising factor could crowd in low-carbon loans, while a brown penalising factor that is too small may even crowd out low-carbon loans (Oehmke and Opp, 2022[111]; Thakor and Song, 2023[133]). Additionally, the effectiveness of this policy measure in increasing climate-related finance volumes is expected to be dependent on fiscal climate policies, such as carbon taxes (Oehmke and Opp, 2022[111]; Dafermos and Nikolaidi, 2021[110]).

Based on limited research, other climate-related prudential instruments related to the level and quality of capital are also expected to have trade-offs between policy objectives.

- Conceptual research expects sectoral capital requirements to have negative effects on financial stability as the specification at the sector level may be too broad to effectively target only the most risk-exposed firms (D'Orazio, 2021[117]; Coelho and Restoy, 2022[112]). Theoretical research suggests that sectoral capital requirements enhance financial stability only when implemented alongside a carbon tax. In the absence of such a tax, higher sectoral capital requirements for high-emitting firms may simply drive these firms to raise capital outside the banking system rather than promoting a shift away from fossil-intensive practices (García-Villegas and Martorell, 2024[134]). Both conceptual and theoretical research expects a reduction of climate-related financial risks due to the reduced exposure to GHG-intensive activities (D'Orazio, 2021[117]; García-Villegas and Martorell, 2024[134]) and a possible increase in climate-related finance volumes (D'Orazio, 2021[117]).
- Other conceptual research points to mixed expectations on the effect of a climate-related countercyclical risk buffer. Similar to risk buffers varying with the business cycle, slowing credit expansion and reducing the risk of financial bubbles forming, climate-related countercyclical risk buffers may mitigate excessive credit growth towards GHG-intensive activities (D'Orazio and Popoyan, 2019[50]; Coelho and Restoy, 2022[112]). However, varying risk buffers are especially difficult to calibrate and may lead to more disruptions than other instruments when suddenly introduced (Coelho and Restoy, 2022[112]). There is no research on potential effects on climate-related capital flows of countercyclical risk buffers.
- Further conceptual research identifies the potential of systemic risk buffers to reduce climate-related financial risks, in particular, as it can be adjusted individually to reflect geographic and sectoral differences in exposure (Monnin, 2021[124]; Grunewald, 2023[135]; Busies et al., 2024[136]). There is no similar research on the effects on financial stability or increases in climate-related investment.

Within climate-related risk management and supervision policies, most existing research focuses on climate-related stress tests, finding mostly positive effects in terms of improved climate risk management, but little effect on climate-related finance volumes. Conceptual research expects such policy instruments to have a positive effect on financial stability by better informing policymakers on financial stability (D'Orazio, 2021[117]; DeMenno, 2022[137]; Schoenmaker and Van Tilburg, 2016[129]). Moreover, the supervisory process around climate-related stress tests is expected to offer more opportunities to improve banks' risk management and highlight priority areas to decrease climate risks (Coelho and Restoy, 2022[112]; Battiston and Monasterolo, 2024[125]). Empirical research suggests banks change their climate-related risk management practices after participating in a climate stress test. For example, the ECB's climate stress test required closer coordination between risk teams and management in participating banks, which may also facilitate incorporation of climate issues beyond the stress test (Calipel and Fidel, 2023[138]). Banks participating in the French supervisory agency's climate pilot stress test subsequently increased lending for green purposes (Fuchs et al., 2023[139]).

Some research on climate risk management policies more generally, in combination with disclosure policies, highlights the importance of capacity building. For example, Chinese regulation incentivising green lending, through integrating climate risks in risk management and related disclosure, found that larger, state-owned banks reduced their credit risk by incorporating environmental and social factors (Zhou et al., 2022[130]). However, smaller local banks experienced increased credit risk.

There is almost no research in relation to climate-related sectoral leverage ratios, internal capital adequacy ratios, green asset ratios, and liquidity-related instruments. Conceptually, a climate-related sectoral leverage ratio may be a transparent policy instrument to limit over-leveraging GHG-intensive sectors, potentially reducing climate-related financial risks (D'Orazio, 2021[117]). Little research has contributed to understanding the effects on financial stability or climate-related financial volumes. Further, the effects of internal capital adequacy assessment processes may be limited, but more research is needed. For example, the adoption of such a policy in Brazil required the explicit integration of climate (environmental) risks in banks' assessments of capital requirements. This led large banks to reallocate capital away from exposed sectors, but small banks expanded their lending activities to these sectors, with no substantial impact on climate-related finance volumes overall (Miguel, Pedraza and Ruiz-Ortega, 2024[127]). Literature on liquidity-related instruments, which remains scarce and only conceptual, expects positive to neutral effects on financial stability, mixed effects on the reduction of climate-related risks, and increases in climate-related financial flows (D'Orazio, 2021[117]; Baranović et al., 2021[97]).

A slightly larger number of conceptual research, and some initial theoretical research, on climate-related considerations for large exposure policies currently suggests positive effects across policy objectives. Both lending limits and concentration charges restrict financial institutions from holding large exposures to specifically defined sectors and thus limit their exposure to risks in those sectors (D'Orazio, 2021[117]; Baranović et al., 2021[97]; Miller and Dikau, 2022[98]). One expected advantage of lending restrictions is that it more directly limits identified climate risks and does not necessarily weigh on banks' capital requirements (Baranović et al., 2021[97]). However, it may be complex in operational terms, and sectors may need to be defined narrowly to strengthen resilience (Coelho and Restoy, 2023[122]). As activities exposed to climate-related risks differ within sectors, especially for GHG-intensive sectors with transitioning activities, climate performance needs to be defined at a granular level. This links back to the challenges discussed in Chapter 2 in relation to assessing progress towards climate alignment and applies to a range of policies discussed in this chapter.

4.2.3. Climate-related credit allocation policies

Credit allocation policies typically support certain economic development objectives by influencing the flow of credit to specific sectors that may otherwise not have sufficient access to credit (Dumlao, 2024[140]). These policies may overlap with climate-related prudential or monetary policies, depending on the stated purpose of the credit allocation policy. While this section covers their use for climate-related purposes, they have been and remain primarily driven by industrial policy goals.

Climate-related credit allocation policies directly promote climate-related credit measures and investments (D'Orazio, 2023[47]). Such policies are, for example, green lending quotas and concessional loans or direct credit guidance to priority sectors contributing to climate goals. Climate-related credit allocation quotas can, for instance, require bank lending to go to certain sectors or activities that contribute to climate change mitigation or resilience.

Climate-related credit allocation policies are more frequently adopted in Asia. As of 2023, over 30 such policies had been adopted in 16 countries (Figure 4.12, Panels A and C). This encompasses 6 AEs and 10 EMDEs, including 6 OECD member countries and 8 G20 jurisdictions. In a few countries, existing credit allocation policies with industrial policy goals were adjusted to integrate climate or sustainable development goals (e.g., in France and India). In other countries, climate-related credit allocation policies were established to focus on specific sectors, encourage lending or limiting credit towards specified sectors (e.g., in China and Fiji). Two-thirds of these policies are adopted by central banks (Figure 4.12, Panel B).

Experience with credit allocation policies for industrial policy goals suggests that the introduction of minimum quotas can lead to the accumulation of non-performing loans, negatively impacting financial stability (World Bank, 2024[71]; Dikau and Volz, 2021[43]). The analysis of the effects of credit allocation policies has mostly focused on their support for attaining (sustainable) development goals and is often combined with an analysis of other policies, such as refinancing (discussed in Subsection 4.2.4). There is limited theoretical or empirical evidence of the effect of specific climate-related credit allocation policies across policy objectives.

Figure 4.12. Adoption of climate-related credit allocation policies

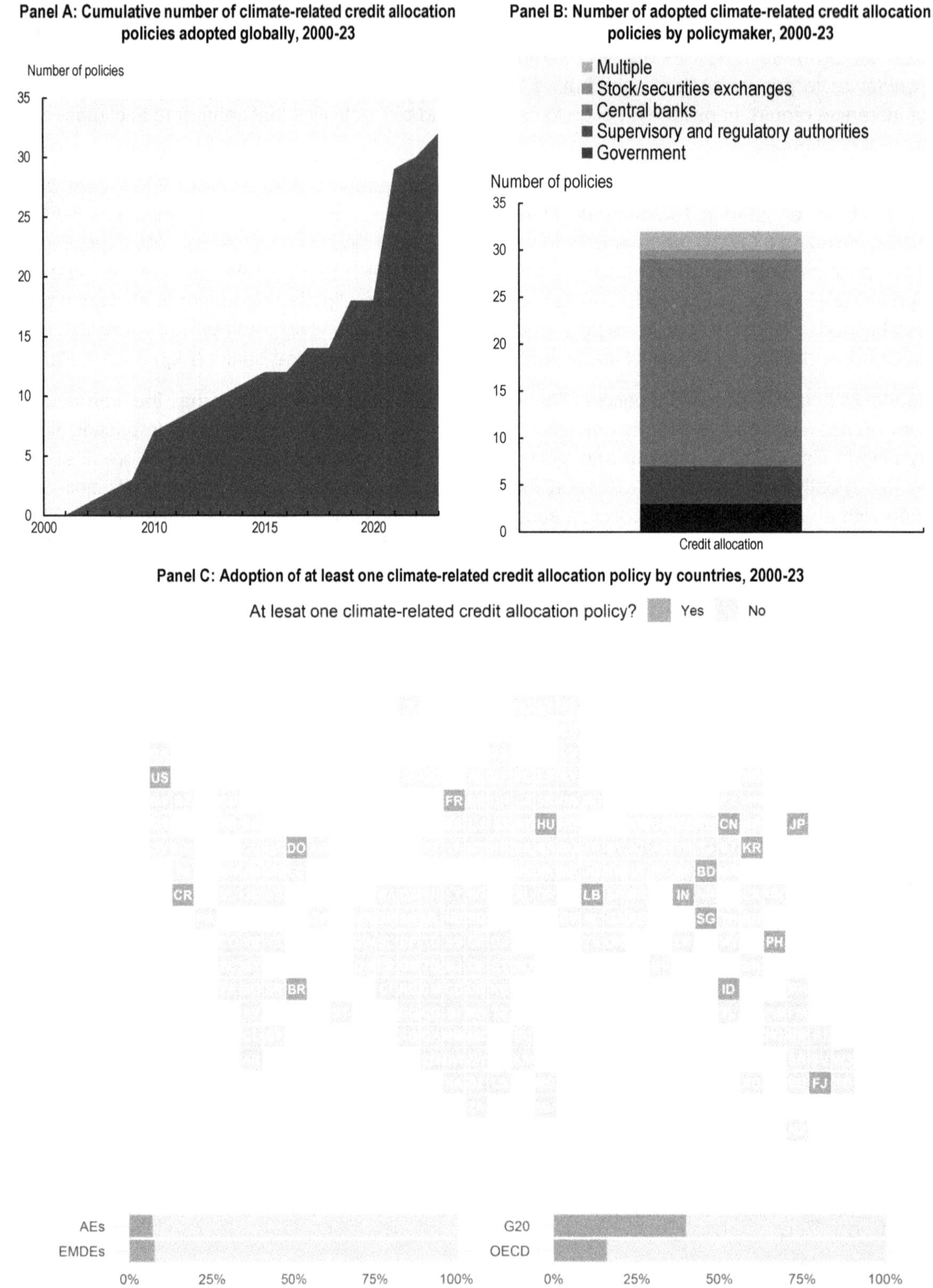

Note: AEs is advanced economies, based on the high-income country classification of the World Bank. EMDEs is emerging markets and developing economies, based on the World Bank classification for upper middle income, lower middle income, and low-income countries.
Source: Authors based on (D'Orazio, 2023[45]) and updated data.

4.2.4. Climate-related monetary policies

The most frequent aim of monetary policy is to maintain price stability. Price stability typically refers to an overall indicator of prices of produced goods and services, with monetary policy aiming to maintain low and steady inflation (Tamez, Weenink and Yoshinaga, 2024[77]). Monetary policy is usually the realm of central banks, sometimes of specific monetary authorities. It involves the use of tools such as interest rates and central bank asset holdings (Friedman, 2015[141]). The individual interpretations of stability differ, and several central banks also have additional aims in their policy objective (Dikau and Volz, 2021[43]). Other important macroeconomic objectives include exchange rate stability, economic growth, and job creation (Tamez, Weenink and Yoshinaga, 2024[77]).

In the context of pursuing price stability, monetary policy frameworks should, at a minimum account for the impact of climate change on price stability (Tamez, Weenink and Yoshinaga, 2024[77]). The integration of climate considerations into monetary policy formulation does not, however, automatically mandate central banks to utilise monetary policy instruments to contribute climate change adaptation or mitigation measures. As the use of monetary instruments reflects complex trade-offs and national contexts, the degree to which monetary policies can explicitly address climate considerations varies across jurisdictions and authorities (NGFS, 2021[52]).

Traditional monetary policies seem to benefit GHG emissions-intensive investments. Central banks' asset purchase programmes, for example, tend to be tilted towards emissions-intensive sectors, at least partially because asset purchase programmes focus on steadily performing, predictable incumbents while their novelty and unconventional funding structure put green investments at a disadvantage (Matikainen, Campiglio and Zenghelis, 2017[142]; Battiston and Monasterolo, 2019[143]; Papoutsi, Piazzesi and Schneider, 2022[144]). Within the scope of conventional financial stability mandates, such findings indicate a potential to adjust purchasing programmes and other monetary policies towards encouraging an orderly climate transition (Monnin, 2018[145]).

Degree of adoption of climate-related monetary policies

Monetary policies explicitly considering climate considerations are an emerging policy area, and such policies are currently limited (Figure 4.7, Panel A). There are three common monetary policy areas, through which central banks can integrate climate-related considerations into monetary policy, namely credit operations, collateral policies, and asset purchases (NGFS, 2021[52]).

- Credit operations refer to the central bank's lending activities to financial institutions, usually through short-term loans or liquidity provisions. They aim to ensure that banks have access to sufficient liquidity to meet their short-term obligations to help maintain stability in the financial system. To access these credit offers, banks must fulfil requirements, for example, in terms of the collateral they pledge. Climate-adjusted credit operations could steer central bank lending towards projects and actors that are less exposed to climate risks or aim to enhance climate change mitigation and resilience efforts. Climate-related considerations in this area can involve offering more favourable terms, such as lower interest rates or longer maturities, for loans that support environmentally sustainable projects or companies with strong environmental performance. Closely related are credit allocation policies (covered in Subsection 4.2.3), targeted refinancing operations and differentiated reserve requirements (explained below).
- Collateral policies, also referred to as collateral frameworks, define the range of assets that commercial banks can pledge to secure central bank credit operations, as well as the risk control measures that apply to them (NGFS, 2021[52]). Climate-related considerations can be integrated by adjusting the eligibility or valuation of collateral based on the climate-related characteristics of underlying assets. For instance, central banks might offer better collateral terms for green bonds associated with low GHG- assets or lower the value of assets tied to fossil fuel activities.

Asset purchases and holdings involve central banks buying and selling a variety of financial assets from both public and private sectors, typically to influence the amount of money circulating in the economy, exerting greater influence on longer-term interest rate levels and spreads while improving market liquidity (NGFS, 2021[52]). Climate-related considerations here may involve prioritising the purchase of green bonds or other securities that fund sustainable projects, while reducing exposure to or divesting from assets associated with high GHG emissions.

No consistent data collection is available for climate-related monetary policies, as these policies remain limited. Hence, the discussion here on the possible design of such policies builds on anecdotal evidence of a limited number of countries adopting such policies, as well as conceptual and theoretical analysis.

Climate-related credit operation policies can integrate climate considerations through (1) adjusting pricing of their credit offers to reflect counterparties' climate-related lending, (2) adjusting the pricing to reflect the composition of pledged collateral, or (3) adjusting counterparties' eligibility (NGFS, 2021[52]). This could take the form of lowering the interest rate of central bank lending facilities depending on the bank's portfolio decarbonisation (compared to a benchmark). It may entail making the interest rate depend on the climate characteristics of pledged collateral or only granting banks eligibility if they comply with thorough climate-related disclosure requirements. Closely related, targeted refinancing operations offer favourable conditions to access credit depending on green lending and thus can encourage financing green projects with longer time horizons. Reserve requirements can pursue monetary and prudential aims (IMF, 2022[146]). For climate purposes, they can be differentiated by the share of green lending and thus also potentially incentivise green financing.

Existing climate-related credit operations, although limited to date, tend to consist of additional lending facilities for banks financing transition-relevant projects. Often it is a form of conditioning low interest rates on lending to projects in specific areas, such as renewable energy or general mitigation and adaptation projects. For example, the Bank of Japan grants favourable conditions when banks commit to on-lend to projects such as renewable energy development and disclosure according to TCFD guidelines (BOJ, n.d.[147]). Some central banks have enhanced their climate-related credit facilities by coupling those with advantageous refinancing schemes. This enables banks to access favourable interest rates or maturities when their credit is due and they require refinancing. For instance, in the case of Bangladesh's Green Transformation Fund, the refinancing was linked to machinery imports aimed at improving water efficiency, waste management and increasing renewable energy use in exporting sectors (Green Finance Platform, n.d.[148]). A few countries introduced differentiated reserve requirements to encourage lending towards climate-critical activities. For example, Indonesia and the Philippines reduced reserve requirements to incentivise the provision of green lending for green projects, acknowledging no evidence yet on how to design such policies without interfering with traditional monetary policy objectives (World Bank, 2024[71]).

While not yet widely relied upon, another lever to integrate climate considerations into monetary policy can be the collateral framework. It can consider climate through four potential adjustments: (1) adjusting discount rates (haircuts), (2) adapting eligibility criteria with negative screening, (3) adopting eligibility criteria with positive screening, (4) aligning collateral pools of counterparties with sustainability objectives (NGFS, 2021[52]). So far, only a few central banks have adapted their collateral frameworks with climate-related considerations. For example, the European Central Bank included sustainability-linked bonds as an eligible asset for collateralisation, acknowledging that assets contributing to the transition of the economy often are more complex than previous eligibility requirements allowed (ECB, 2020[149]). Hungary's central bank, for example, applies preferential haircuts to green bonds (NGFS, 2024[150]).

Another type of climate-related monetary policy that has been adopted by some countries is the explicit integration of climate considerations into central bank portfolio asset purchases, for example by aligning bond purchase programmes (such as BoE, ECB). Such programmes typically cover the corporate sector but can be extended to sovereign bonds, including in the context of central banks' management of foreign exchange reserves (Fender et al., 2020[151]). Asset purchases on the open market are a normal tool of central banks to fulfil their price stability mandate. In times of very low interest rates, several central banks have also used outright purchases, also known as quantitative easing (QE) to pursue their mandate (ECB, 2022[152]). Climate-related adjustments to asset purchase programs could also be implemented for quantitative easing. Additionally, some authors have considered so-called "green QE", purchase programs of only green assets (Abiry et al., 2022[153]).

Generally, there are two approaches to considering the climate in asset purchases, namely introducing asset purchase tilting or negative screening (NGFS, 2021[52]). Both positive tilting and negative screening are based on available definitions and classifications of what the portfolio is tilted towards or what should be excluded from the eligible asset universe. Different approaches can be followed to define this, ranging from defining "green" or clean assets solely as certified green bonds (Schoenmaker, 2021[154]) to using the NACE sector code for differentiation, applying a carbon footprint metric, or coming up with a combination of all (Dafermos et al., 2022[118]; Battiston and Monasterolo, 2019[143]; Battiston et al., 2017[104]).

Available evidence on the effects of climate-related monetary policies

In terms of analysing effects of climate-related monetary policies, very limited theoretical analysis and no empirical analysis exists to date. Moreover, the different types of potential climate-related monetary policy instruments have been researched in varying depth, with currently more analysis on green tilting in asset purchases and haircut adjustments in the collateral framework.

Based on the best-available research, which is at this stage mostly conceptual, the effects of climate-related monetary policies are mostly expected to result in strong trade-offs between climate considerations and core pricing-related objectives (Table 4.2). Across monetary policy measures, existing research on the effects of climate-related monetary policies expects increases in climate-related finance volumes, a mix of positive and negative effects in terms of reducing climate-related financial risks, but no or negative effects on the effectiveness of monetary policy.

Only very limited conceptual research exists on climate-related credit operation policies, pointing to trade-offs between monetary and climate policy objectives (NGFS, 2021[52]). The adjustments of credit operations have not yet been researched through theoretical or empirical analyses. Some experiences with climate-related credit operation policies point to the importance of robust definitions and classifications of 'green activities' to make such policies effective (NGFS, 2024[150]).

With respect to climate-related collateral framework policies, most existing research has focussed on adjustments of discount rates, expecting no effect on monetary policy effectiveness, but positive effects on climate-related risk reductions and climate-related finance volumes. Both conceptual and theoretical research currently suggest minimal or no effects of adjusting haircuts or aligning collateral pools (NGFS, 2021[52]; Giovanardi et al., 2023[155]; Schoenmaker, 2021[154]). Increasing haircuts for GHG-intensive investments is expected to be more suitable than reducing haircuts for low-carbon investments, as the latter may be seen as more market-intrusive (McConnell, Yanovski and Lessmann, 2021[156]). Both conceptual and theoretical research expect positive effects on the reduction of climate-related financial risks, as the integration of climate risks into haircuts and eligibility may enhance protection from longer term risks that were not included so far (Dafermos et al., 2022[118]; Boneva, Ferrucci and Mongelli, 2021[157]; Schoenmaker, 2021[154]; McConnell, Yanovski and Lessmann, 2021[156]; Oustry et al., 2020[158]). Expanding eligibility for green investments, that may have unconventional financing structures, may increase climate-related finance volumes, and improve the financing landscape for low-carbon projects (Giovanardi et al., 2023[155]; Vestergaard, 2022[159]). Overall, adjusting collateral policies is expected to affect climate-related finance volumes positively (Schoenmaker, 2021[154]; McConnell, Yanovski and Lessmann, 2021[156]).

Table 4.2. Summary of literature on potential effect of climate-related monetary policies

Positive effect | No/minimal effect | Negative effect | Mixed evidence | No evidence

C = Conceptual analysis T = Theoretical analysis E = Empirical analysis

		Potential effect on the objective								
		Effect on monetary policy effectiveness			Reduction of climate-related financial risks			Increases in climate-related finance volumes		
Dimension	Measure	C	T	E	C	T	E	C	T	E
Credit operations	Adjusting pricing to lending benchmark									
	Adjusting pricing to collateral									
	Adjusting counterparties' eligibility									
Collateral	Haircut adjustment									
	Negative screening									
	Positive screening									
	Aligning collateral pools									
Asset purchases	Tilting									
	Negative screening									

Note: Colouring is based on the available literature, following the majority where dissenting; grey and academic literature was considered. Literature had to provide structured argument and preferably some calculations to be included as conceptual. Literature was classified as theoretical evidence if it included models or simulations. Literature relying on empirical data were classified as empirical.
Source: Authors, based on (NGFS, 2021[52]; Schoenmaker, 2021[154]; McConnell, Yanovski and Lessmann, 2021[156]; Dafermos et al., 2022[118]; Gros and Shamsfakhr, 2023[160]; Benmir and Roman, 2020[120]; Giovanardi et al., 2023[155]; Vestergaard, 2022[159]; Oustry et al., 2020[158]; Bressan, Monasterolo and Battiston, 2021[161]) (Abiry et al., 2022[153]).

Within climate-related adjustments of asset purchase program policies, existing research tends to point to limited effects on monetary policy effectiveness, while potentially reducing climate-related risks and increasing climate-related finance. Such research remains conceptual and theoretical.

- Existing research highlights that the expected effects of tilting or screening asset purchase programs depend on the exact definition of 'green' investments. Some research questions whether the green bond market is sufficiently deep for central banks to heavily invest in it, and whether monetary policy may be less effective if it has to rely on a very restricted subset of the market (Schoenmaker, 2021[154]). This could be especially constraining when tilting and screening methods are applied not only to corporate asset purchase programs but also to foreign reserve portfolios, which usually consist of short-term sovereign bonds and have to fulfil strict currency and liquidity requirements (see Chapter 3 Section 3.2 for evidence on current volumes of climate-related debt securities compared to the universe). To address the limited depth of the green bond market for corporate asset purchase programs, some researchers suggest buying bonds issued by national and regional development banks which then invest in green bonds and other climate solutions directly (Boneva, Ferrucci and Mongelli, 2021[157]). However, theoretical research has also shown that asset purchase tilting can be designed to not interfere with monetary policy effectiveness (Schoenmaker, 2021[154]). Furthermore, theoretical research suggests mixed interactions with fiscal policies such as carbon pricing, describing the potential of dedicated green asset purchase programs ('Green QE') to hedge the effects of a carbon tax or sharpen its effect (Papoutsi, Piazzesi and Schneider, 2022[144]; Benmir and Roman, 2020[120]).
- Conceptual evidence suggests that both tilting and screening approaches would support the reduction of climate-related financial risks (NGFS, 2021[52]). Conceptual and theoretical research on potential increases in climate-related finance volumes due to climate-related tilting or screening

of asset purchase programs emphasizes two effects. Financed emissions of central bank portfolios could be reduced dramatically (Schoenmaker, 2021[154]; Papoutsi, Piazzesi and Schneider, 2022[144]; Boneva, Ferrucci and Mongelli, 2021[157]). Additionally, research has addressed green quantitative easing as a mechanism to signal liquidity and lower the risk of green assets (Campiglio et al., 2018[162]; Ameli et al., 2019[87]). However, it is assumed that it may only marginally improve the financing situation for green projects or reduce emissions (Gros and Shamsfakhr, 2023[160]; Ferrari and Landi, 2023[163]; Abiry et al., 2022[153]).

- Furthermore, any effect of asset purchase programmes could not be a reliable continuous support for green investments as monetary policy considerations would take precedence over supporting a smoother transition. If core price stability objectives require selling assets, this would supersede climate-related allocations (ECB, 2021[164]).

On other monetary policies, theoretical analyses expect, for example, that a formal green interest rate allows the possibility of achieving both price stability and sustainability objectives (Roy, 2024[165]; Muller, 2021[166]). Further conceptual research argues that green-targeted long-term refinancing operations contribute more effectively to price stability objectives than asset purchase programs and would thus be well suited to counter the inflationary pressures expected from climate change disruptions (van 't Klooster and van Tilburg, 2020[167]).

Generally, as already pointed to in previous sections on climate-related transparency and information, and prudential policies, dissecting the effect of individual policies is challenging, as they are often part of policy packages. For example, stocks of climate-related financial policy in G20 countries are associated with lower emissions (D'Orazio and Dirks, 2021[72]). The adoption of climate-related financial policies in those countries went hand in hand with the development of the financial sector and economic development, which generally see emissions decrease.

4.3. Climate-related financial sector actions

Investors and financial institutions can take a variety of actions to influence the climate alignment of finance. Depending on their mandates, expectations, and perceived leverage in their relationships with investees and borrowers, financial sector actors can focus on different actions to reach their climate-related targets and implement climate transition plans. Such actions can notably relate to engagement, portfolio composition, strategy, and governance (as introduced in Chapter 2, Subsection 2.3.2). They can also take the form of voluntary disclosures (in the absence of or complementing disclosure policies discussed in Subsection 4.2.1, thereby providing data points to inform assessments and estimates as discussed in Chapters 2 and 3), as well as litigation, research including in cooperation with think tanks and NGOs among others (OECD, 2023[168]).

Private actions by financial sector actors can be direct responses to climate policy ambition and implementation or be established in the absence of policies based on voluntary frameworks and soft guidance. Such frameworks and guidance can come from coalitions, industry associations, and government-backed processes. For example, the OECD Guidelines for Multinational Enterprises provide government-backed recommendations to multinational enterprises (both non-financial and financial corporates) towards responsible business conduct, including in relation to risks and impacts of their activities on climate change (OECD, 2023[169]). Climate-related financial sector coalitions, such as the Institutional Investors Group on Climate Change (IIGCC), the Net Zero Asset Managers initiative (NZAM), and the Net-Zero Asset Owner Alliance (NZAOA), provide more specific guidance to asset owners and asset managers. Examples of coalitions for banks and insurers include Net-Zero Banking Alliance (NZBA) and Forum for Insurance Transition to NetZero. Members of these alliances combine significant shares of global assets, as shown in Chapter 3 (Figure 3.12).

The growing adoption of climate-related targets and plans, as part of broader strategies of financial institutions, is a key step towards aligning their portfolios with climate goals. Climate-related target setting and transition planning, based on climate-alignment assessments, set the strategic direction. Emissions reduction targets have received strong attention both among practitioners and researchers, resulting in wider adoption and methodological refinement of underlying measurements (CPI, 2024[170]; OECD, 2024[57]). Among 941 large global financial institutions (including 629 that are members of Net-Zero Alliances supported by the Glasgow Financial Alliance for Net Zero (GFANZ)), 42% had adopted a partial GHG emissions reduction target as of 2023, up from 4% in 2020 (

Figure 4.13). No financial institution in this sample had established a comprehensive emissions target, i.e., externally validated and climate-aligned targets, covering 90% or more of the relevant portfolio for both the near and long term. As targets set by financial institutions contribute to setting the foundation for actions to be directed towards net-zero transition and climate resilience plans, they are not sufficient in themselves to reduce GHG emissions and increase climate resilience, especially as they are not legally binding (McDonnell and Gupta, 2023[171]).

Figure 4.13. Disclosure of emissions reduction targets by large financial institutions

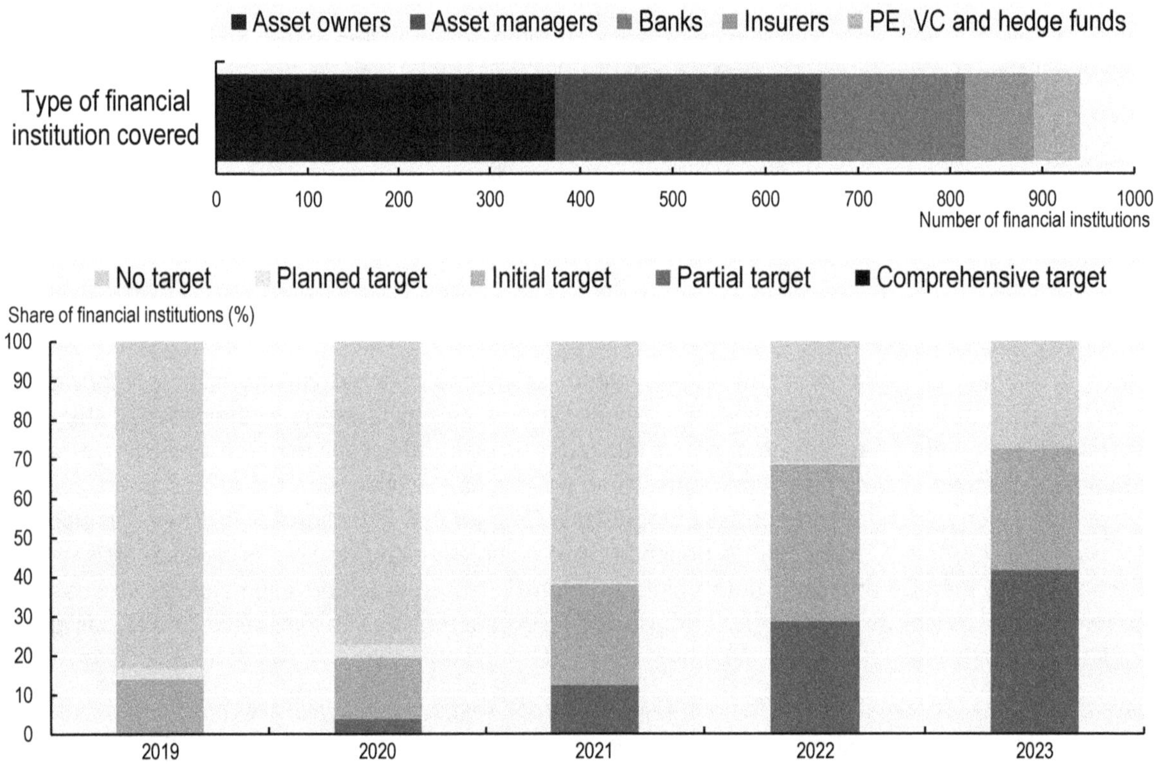

Note: This data covers 941 large financial institutions, including 629 members of Net-Zero Alliances supported by the Glasgow Financial Alliance for Net Zero (GFANZ). The indicator describes whether institutions have set clear and comprehensive targets for climate action (primarily reducing their emissions), whether those are quantitative targets or general, and whether they are disclosed transparently. No target is no evidence of a climate target. Planned target means a commitment to adopt a target. Initial target is a target has been adopted but it is partial, or information is incomplete. Partial target is transparently assessed aligned long-term and near-term targets, covering a portion of the relevant portfolio. Comprehensive target is an externally validated aligned long-term and near-term targets, covering 90% or more of the relevant portfolio.
Source: Authors, based on (CPI, 2024[170]).

Climate-related targets and commitments are typically actively pursued through a combination of engagement activities and portfolio construction practices, including divestment from carbon-intensive assets and scaled-up investments in climate solutions (NGFS, 2024[172]; OECD, 2023[54]; McDonnell and

Gupta, 2023[171]; NewClimate Institute, 2022[173]; PRI, 2021[174]), which are the focus of this section. Climate-oriented portfolio construction practices to increase climate-aligned activities and reduce exposure to misaligned activities relate to integrating climate alignment into existing and new investments such as (re)weighting, positive screening, and explicit funding of climate solutions. Divestment and exclusion from climate-misaligned activities represent the most drastic form of portfolio (re)construction and are thus discussed separately. For specific targets and asset classes other activities may be possible, such as direct management decisions for private equity holdings, e.g., in real estate and SMEs.

4.3.1. Climate-related engagement

Positive climate-related engagement by investors and financial institutions with clients and stakeholders aims to encourage climate alignment of the financial assets they hold. Investor stewardship, or active ownership, is "the use of investor rights and influence to protect and enhance overall long-term value for clients and beneficiaries, including the common economic, social, and environmental assets on which their interests depend" (PRI, 2023[175]). Generally, there are three types of possible engagements: engagement with investees in the real economy, market engagement with other financial market participants, and policy engagement with policymakers (NGFS, 2024[172]). For policy advocacy guiding documents in the investor community highlight the importance of aligning policy advocacy by underlying companies with climate goals advocated for by investors themselves (UNEP FI, 2023[176]).

Some financial sector actors rely on engagement with investees in the real economy to decarbonise their portfolios. Investors and financial institutions can in particular engage with companies to encourage or request them to consider climate change in their business decision-making processes, through direct dialogue with directors and key executives, shareholder meetings and courts (OECD, 2022[177]). In 2023, 12% of 941 large financial institutions disclosed on engagements with clients and investees positively influencing climate-related business practices and transparency (Figure 4.14). This share has remained stable over the past few years, although financial institutions planning to undertake climate-related engagements have doubled, representing about half of the institutions in the sample in 2023. Still, 32% disclosed no climate-related engagement activities in 2023.

Engagement can be done independently or as part of a group (such as through coalitions discussed above). Since requests are more likely to be accepted, the larger the holding of the requesting shareholders, alliances and coalitions are particularly attractive for actors focusing on stewardship. The significant increase in institutional investors' assets under management over the past fifteen years and the fact that a large portion of their assets tracks or replicates stock market indices have led to institutional ownership concentration, particularly for large firms (Medina, de la Cruz and Tang, 2022[178]). As most indices are weighted by market capitalisation, they tend to favour large companies over small ones. Therefore, the holdings of investors that follow these indices are concentrated in fewer and larger companies (Medina, de la Cruz and Tang, 2022[178]). Such increasing concentration of ownership and decision-making in capital markets may have important implications for stewardship actions by these largest institutional investors.

Climate-related engagement actions can follow available voluntary guidance, but policymakers could do more to guide good practices of market participants. Existing guidance by coalitions and industry associations for investors highlights the importance of communicating clear expectations and laying out an escalation path if expectations are not met (e.g., where implementation falls short of firms' transition plans and targets over time), including but not limited to divestments (IIGCC, 2024[179]). Where consistent with domestic mandates, policymakers can consider promoting guidance for investors and financial institutions who wish to engage in climate-aligned investing on the design and implementation of effective engagement strategies in relation to climate-related factors (OECD, 2022[180]).

Figure 4.14. Disclosure on engagement activities by large financial institutions with clients and investees

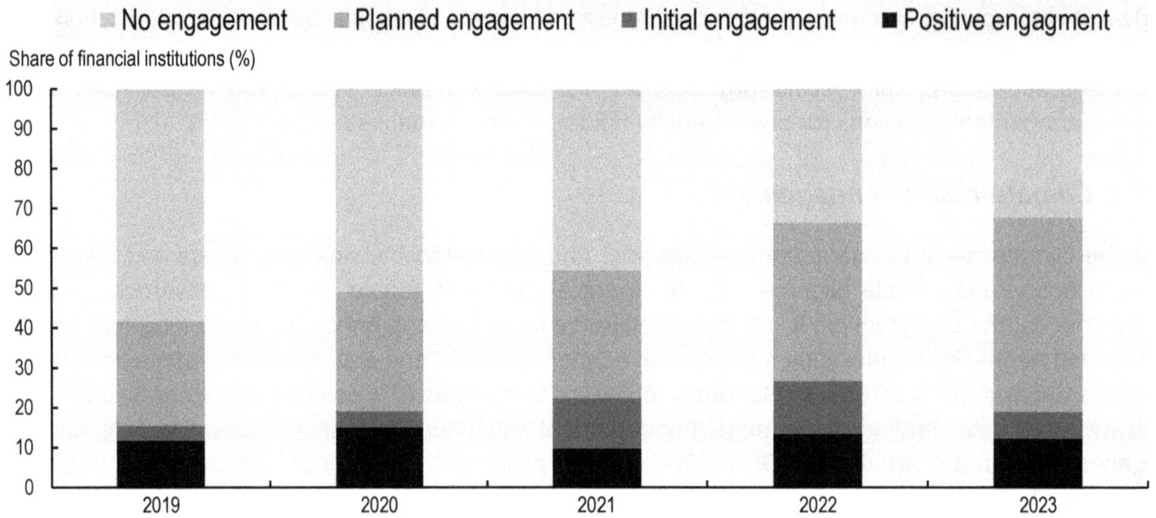

Note: This data covers 941 large financial institutions, including 629 members of Net-Zero Alliances supported by the Glasgow Financial Alliance for Net Zero (GFANZ). The indicator measures whether the organisation commits to engaging shareholders or clients on climate action and whether there is evidence of the organisation taking the necessary steps by mandating climate reporting requirements or through active ownership on portfolio companies. Positive engagement activities are measured by evidence of shareholder authority and voting rights, proven impact or engagement on business practices and models, with no evidence of negative actions that oppose the transition. No engagement is no evidence of climate-related engagement actions. Planned engagement is a commitment to engage on climate. Initial engagement is first steps at engaging on climate (including with suppliers), but possible presence of negative engagement, too. Positive engagement is indications of (general) positive engagement (including on business practices and transparency), and no negative action.
Source: Authors, based on (CPI, 2024[170]).

While climate-related engagement by financial institutions already seems to influence clients' climate transparency and target setting, their effectiveness in terms of reducing emissions is assessed as limited. Initial econometric evidence finds that investor demand for climate-related information results in greater corporate disclosure and contributes to firms' decisions to lower future carbon emissions (Kahn, Matsusaka and Shu, 2024[181]; Cohen, Kadach and Ormazabal, 2023[182]). Anecdotal evidence also indicates how investor engagement contributed to the uptake of climate targets among large listed companies (CA100+, 2024[183]). However, evidence of the effectiveness of engagement actions in reducing emissions is mixed. While individual cases suggest room for effective pressure and tangible effects (such as the decommissioning of coal plants), studies on a broader level find varying rates of success of shareholder climate-related demands being implemented (Kölbel et al., 2020[184]). One possible explanation relates to the cost of implementing the requested change, which is often higher for environmental requests than social or governance requests, with the latter having a higher observed success rate (Kölbel et al., 2020[184]). For costly environmental requests, the timing of shareholder resolutions may be particularly important (van der Kroft et al., 2024[185]). Moreover, the effectiveness of climate-related shareholder resolutions also varies across jurisdictions (2DII, 2024[186]).

4.3.2. Climate-oriented portfolio construction

Climate considerations can be embedded in all types of portfolio construction practices. Climate-oriented portfolio construction by investors and financial institutions changes the composition towards climate-aligned assets and away from climate-misaligned assets. Such practices can range from simple exclusion of companies that do not align with climate goals to full integration of climate-alignment considerations into the investment process, governance, and decision-making (OECD, 2020[187]).

Climate-oriented portfolio construction practices notably include:

- Divestment and exclusion, excluding assets that do not align with certain climate objectives.
- Norms-based/inclusive screening practices, which include assets that comply with climate policy goals, international climate standards or "best-in-class" firms based on climate performance scores.
- Climate-oriented rebalancing practices, which adjust portfolio exposure towards assets with higher climate performance scores, either through climate-tilted indices or active management.
- Thematic investing, which focuses on specific climate themes (e.g., mitigation, adaptation) which may prioritise specific climate objectives over maximising financial returns.
- Climate impact investing, which seeks financial returns by targeting non-financial climate outcomes through active engagement, shareholder activism, or divestment from climate-misaligned activities.
- Full climate-alignment integration, which systematically includes climate risks and opportunities across all aspects of investment processes, without relying solely on benchmarking or exclusions.

Generally, climate-related disclosure (Subsection 4.2.1) and climate-alignment assessments based on credible metrics and approaches (Chapter 2) are important information inputs for such practices (OECD, 2020[187]). These practices can be adopted to reduce exposure to risks from potential policy responses to climate change and/or contribute to the alignment of finance with climate goals. The remainder of this subsection focuses on divestment and exclusion practices, and climate-oriented tilting practices.

Divestment and exclusion practices

Climate-related divestment policies and exclusion policies are key actions for financial institutions to reduce exposure to climate-misaligned activities and influence market behaviour, typically following failed engagement efforts. Climate-related divestment policies are used by financial market participants to sell or exit from existing carbon-intensive holdings (PRI, 2022[188]). Divesting from assets within, but not across, a sector can send important market signals and enhance the competitive position of best-in-class actors in the sector. Exclusion policies are guidance and processes by financial institutions to avoid future capital allocation in emissions-intensive activities in their portfolios.

Divestment and exclusion actions can be motivated by the implementation of targets following failed attempts to engage and escalate stewardship. OECD principles and standards on responsible business conduct highlight that, where it is possible, continued relationship and engagement towards improvement over time is preferable. The need for disengagement should only take place after failed engagement attempts, where corrective actions or transitions are not feasible, or because of the severity of the adverse climate impact (OECD, 2023[169]). Both types of actions can be done for equity and fixed-income assets, but differences in asset characteristics can have important implications for the effectiveness of these actions (NewClimate Institute, 2022[173]).

In terms of implementation, climate-related divestment commitments relating to divestment from coal companies and assets doubled between 2020 and 2023 (IEEFA, 2023[189]; IEEFA, 2023[190]). Estimates of European pension funds divestment practices find that the majority is not divesting from fossil fuels. As of 2023, 60 (18%) out of 342 large European pension funds adopted fossil fuel-related targets (CPI, 2024[191]). An earlier estimate for 2019 finds that 129 (13%) of the 1 000 largest European pension funds had publicly committed to divest or already divested from fossil fuel holdings (Egli, Schärer and Steffen, 2022[192]). Looking at broader ESG practices, some evidence indicates that exclusion policies tend to be relatively more frequently adopted than divestment policies (NewClimate Institute, 2022[173]).

Despite an increase in the adoption of fossil fuel divestment and exclusion practices and actions, the global share of financial institutions with such policies remains limited. As of 2022, half of the largest 50 asset managers and less than a fifth of the largest 50 asset owners had exclusion policies targeted at emissions-intensive investee companies and clients (NewClimate Institute, 2022[173]). Only about a sixth of them had publicly committed to divest or already divested from fossil fuel holdings (NewClimate Institute, 2022[173]). An analysis in 2024 of 26 large banks found that none were committed to phasing out all financing for coal activities in line with 1.5°C warming, and only 2 were committed to ending project financing of new oil and gas fields (TPI, 2024[193]). Considering a larger pool of over 941 large financial institutions (including Alliance members), 46% of them had at least an initial divestment target in 2023, up from 15% in 2020 (Figure 4.15). Only 3% have a comprehensive fossil fuel divestment target, meaning financial institutions have comprehensive fossil fuel exclusion or phase-out policies or no remaining fossil fuel assets.

Figure 4.15. Adoption of fossil fuel phase out and exclusion goals by large financial institutions

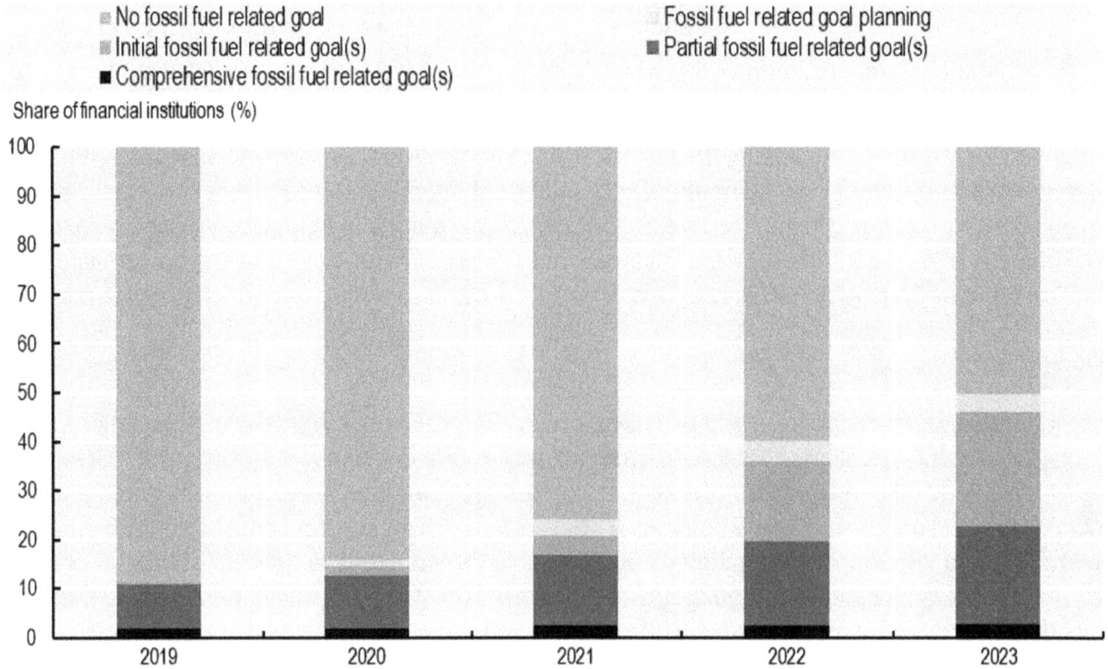

Note: This data covers 941 large financial institutions, including 629 members of Net-Zero Alliances supported by the Glasgow Financial Alliance for Net Zero (GFANZ). The indicator describes whether the institution has announced a clear target to divest from fossil fuels, with a clearly defined scope, and matched by fossil fuel exclusion policies. No phase out or exclusion goal(s) is no evidence of a fossil fuel related target. Phase out or exclusion target planning means there is a commitment to adopt fossil fuel related goals. Initial phase out or exclusion goals means the financial institution has a divestment goal, or other undefined fossil fuel policies. Partial phase out or exclusion goals means the financial institution has partial or undefined fossil fuel exclusion or phase-out policies. Comprehensive phase out or exclusion goals means the financial institution has comprehensive fossil fuel exclusion or phase-out policies or has no fossil fuel assets.
Source: Authors, based on (CPI, 2024[170]).

The effects of divestment and exclusion practices on reducing GHG emissions are uncertain. While some evidence finds that divestment policies by banks accelerated coal decommissioning (Green and Vallee, 2024[194]; Haushalter, Henry and Iliev, 2023[195]), several trade-offs and potential unintended consequences need to be considered, notably:

- Divestment and exclusion policies may increase the climate performance of financial institutions and investors adopting such policies, but they lose the ability to engage with and influence investees. Excluding investments from hard-to-abate firms removes the possibility to influence management decisions through engagement (NewClimate Institute, 2022[173]). Some research suggests that for any individual financial institution, engagement offers the highest potential to achieve real-economy impact (Caldecott et al., 2024[196]) or to generate socially desirable outcomes (Broccardo, Hart and Zingales, 2020[197]) compared with divestment strategies aiming at affecting cost of capital or liquidity.

- Divestment may also result in carbon leakage rather than actual GHG emission reductions in the real economy. There is an important difference between reducing emissions in an investment portfolio and reducing emissions in the real economy. Divesting from assets associated with adverse climate impacts removes the adverse climate impacts of investors' portfolios without necessarily reducing the overall impact on society and the environment, in case of purchase of the asset by another investor, or may in fact slow needed transition in high-emitting assets and sectors (OECD, 2023[169]). The credible threat of divestment, however, may incentivise more rapid actions on firm side to eventually transition to net-zero emissions.
- Divestment and exclusion policies can affect the cost of capital of financial assets being targeted, which in turn may reduce the capacity of underlying entities to transition. A wider literature assesses "sin stocks", finding that they tend to have a lower stock price and higher cost of capital (Hong and Kacperczyk, 2009[198]). Emerging evidence also shows that divestment pledges can affect the cost of capital in bond markets and liquidity, even slowing the expansion of certain sectors (Caldecott et al., 2024[196]; Cojoianu et al., 2020[199]). Such conceptual research hypothesised that in this context, divestment and exclusion policies may be most effective when capital for the affected firms is not easily substitutable. On the other hand, the lack of capital caused by divestment may prevent firms from investing in costly mitigation and adaptation projects and thus counteract the overarching alignment goal (Kacperczyk and Peydró, 2022[200]; Kahn, Matsusaka and Shu, 2024[181]).

Climate-oriented tilting practices

Investors following a positive portfolio tilt strategy on climate goals overweigh assets with a better climate performance in their equity portfolios, typically while maintaining sector weights compared to a target index or benchmark. They do so by reducing their ownership of climate-misaligned assets and substituting towards climate-aligned assets (Atta-Darkua et al., 2023[201]). Climate-oriented rebalancing practices remain a small but not insignificant share of financial market practices. In 2021, ESG-related tilts totalled 6% of the investment industry's assets (Pastor, Stambaugh and Taylor, 2023[202]).

Across financial sector actions and investment practices, it remains difficult to assess impacts on GHG emissions as available data generally does not allow to distinguish whether financed emissions decrease due to engagement with companies who in turn reduce emissions or due to reweighting towards already lower-emitting companies and away from emissions-intensive companies. Moreover, portfolio rebalancing practices are dependent on climate ratings, which are heterogenous across providers (as discussed in Chapter 2), meaning it is unclear whether such practices are currently contributing to real-economy decarbonisation (OECD, 2022[203]).

Another example of climate-oriented portfolio construction practices is the explicit increase in investments in "climate solutions" (IIGCC, 2024[179]). Impact investors have followed this approach, but studies find mixed results on their ability to push the capital and financing frontier faced by some green projects (Chen, 2022[204]; Cole et al., 2023[205]; Hartzmark and Shue, 2022[206]; Kölbel et al., 2020[184]). For conventional investors, banks, and asset managers, the mainstreaming of such climate-orientated portfolio construction remains, in most cases, limited to investment opportunities that fulfil their respective risk-return criteria. An estimate for large European pension funds finds that only 35 (10%) out of 342 funds adopted climate investment targets by 2023 (CPI, 2024[191]). An analysis in 2024 of 26 large banks showed that 15 had set specific quantitative targets to increase their total financing of climate solutions (TPI, 2024[193]).

Overall, the theoretical underpinning of portfolio construction practices (both negative/divestment and positive tilting) assumes that financing constraints will result in a higher cost of capital for emissions-intensive firms and thus, in combination with engagement strategies and escalation processes, increase pressure to lower emissions. It therefore relies heavily on the responsivity of firms to the cost of capital to induce climate action. Existing empirical evidence cannot consistently confirm such expectations.

References

2DII (2024), *A changing climate … for investor engagement on transition plans in France*, 2° Investing Initiative, https://2degrees-investing.org/resource/a-changing-climate-for-investor-engagement-on-transition-plans-in-france/. [186]

2DII (2018), *The Green Supporting Factor: Quantifying the impact on European bans and green finance*, https://2degrees-investing.org/wp-content/uploads/2018/04/2dii_The-Green-Supporting-Factor.pdf. [116]

Abiry, R. et al. (2022), *Climate change mitigation: how effective is green quantitative easing?*, European Central Bank, https://www.ecb.europa.eu/pub/pdf/scpwps/ecb.wp2701~72d8bfaa67.en.pdf. [153]

Allen, T. et al. (2020), *Climate-Related Scenarios for Financial Stability Assessment: An Application to France*, Banque de France Working Paper Series no. 774, https://publications.banque-france.fr/en/climate-related-scenarios-financial-stability-assessment-application-france. [103]

Ameli, N. et al. (2019), “Climate finance and disclosure for institutional investors: why transparency is not enough”, *Climatic Change*, Vol. 160/4, pp. 565-589, https://doi.org/10.1007/s10584-019-02542-2. [87]

Ang, G., D. Röttgers and P. Burli (2017), “The empirics of enabling investment and innovation in renewable energy”, *OECD Environment Working Papers*, No. 123, OECD Publishing, Paris, https://doi.org/10.1787/67d221b8-en. [23]

Atta-Darkua, V. et al. (2023), *Decarbonizing Institutional Investor Portfolios: Helping to Green the Planet or Just Greening Your Portfolio?*, https://doi.org/10.2139/ssrn.4212568. [201]

Attridge, S., B. Getzel and N. Gregory (2024), *Trillions or billions? Reassessing the potential for European institutional investment in emerging markets and developing economies*. [93]

Banco Central do Brasil (2011), *CIRCULAR 3,547 OF JULY 7, 2011*, https://www.bcb.gov.br/ingles/norms/brprudential/Circular3547.pdf. [105]

Bank of England (2022), *Results of the 2021 Climate Biennial Exploratory Scenario (CBES)*, https://www.bankofengland.co.uk/stress-testing/2022/results-of-the-2021-climate-biennial-exploratory-scenario. [42]

Bank of England (2019), *Enhancing banks’ and insurers’ approaches to managing the financial risks from climate change*, https://www.bankofengland.co.uk/-/media/boe/files/prudential-regulation/supervisory-statement/2019/ss319.pdf. [106]

Baranović, I. et al. (2021), *The challenge of capturing climate risks in the banking regulatory framework: is there a need for a macroprudential response?*, https://www.ecb.europa.eu/press/financial-stability-publications/macroprudential-bulletin/html/ecb.mpbu202110_1~5323a5baa8.en.html. [97]

Battiston, S. et al. (2017), “A climate stress-test of the financial system”, *Nature Climate Change*, Vol. 7/4, pp. 283-288, https://doi.org/10.1038/nclimate3255. [104]

Battiston, S. and I. Monasterolo (2024), *Enhanced scenarios for climate stress-tests*, https://www.lse.ac.uk/granthaminstitute/wp-content/uploads/2024/04/INSPIRE-Sustainable-Central-Banking-Toolbox-Paper-16.pdf. [125]

Battiston, S. and I. Monasterolo (2019), *How could the ECB's monetary policy support the sustainable finance transition?*, https://www.finexus.uzh.ch/en/news/cspp_sustainable_finance.html. [143]

Baudino, P. and J. Svoronos (2021), *Stress-testing banks for climate change – a comparison of practices*, BIS FSI Insights No 34, https://www.bis.org/fsi/publ/insights34.htm. [100]

Baylis, P. and J. Boomhower (2021), *Mandated vs. Voluntary Adaptation to Natural Disasters: The Case of U.S. Wildfires*, National Bureau of Economic Research, Cambridge, MA, https://doi.org/10.3386/w29621. [30]

Becker, M., F. Martin and A. Walter (2022), "The power of ESG transparency: The effect of the new SFDR sustainability labels on mutual funds and individual investors", *Finance Research Letters*, Vol. 47, p. 102708, https://doi.org/10.1016/j.frl.2022.102708. [75]

Beck, T. (2018), *Basel III & Unintended Consequences for Emerging Markets and Developing Economies - Part 4: Challenges on Infrastructure and SME Lending*, https://www.cgdev.org/blog/basel-iii-unintended-consequences-emerging-markets-developing-economies-part-iv-challenges. [94]

Benmir, G. and J. Roman (2020), *Policy interactions and the transition to clean technology*, https://www.lse.ac.uk/granthaminstitute/wp-content/uploads/2020/04/working-paper-337-Benmir-Roman-Jul21.pdf. [120]

Berenguer, M., M. Cardona and J. Evain (2020), *Integrating Climate-related Risks into Banks' Capital Requirements*, https://www.i4ce.org/wp-content/uploads/IntegratingClimate_EtudeVA.pdf. [132]

Bhandary, R., K. Gallagher and F. Zhang (2021), "Climate finance policy in practice: a review of the evidence", *Climate Policy*, Vol. 21/4, pp. 529-545, https://doi.org/10.1080/14693062.2020.1871313. [16]

BIS (2022), *Principles for the effective management and supervision of climate-related financial risks*, https://www.bis.org/bcbs/publ/d532.pdf. [81]

BIS (n.d.), *Basel Committee on Banking Supervision reforms – Basel III*, https://www.bis.org/bcbs/basel3/b3_bank_sup_reforms.pdf. [96]

BIS (n.d.), *Basel III: international regulatory framework for banks*, https://www.bis.org/bcbs/basel3.htm. [95]

Black, S. et al. (2023), *IMF Fossil Fuel Subsidies Data: 2023 Update. Working Paper No. 2023/169.*, International Monetary Fund, https://www.imf.org/en/Publications/WP/Issues/2023/08/22/IMF-Fossil-Fuel-Subsidies-Data-2023-Update-537281. [25]

BOJ (n.d.), *Funds-Supplying Operations to Support Financing for Climate Change Responses*, https://www.boj.or.jp/en/mopo/measures/mkt_ope/ope_x/index.htm (accessed on 10 October 2024). [147]

Boneva, L., G. Ferrucci and F. Mongelli (2021), *To Be or Not to Be "Green": How Can Monetary Policy React to Climate Change?*, ECB Occasional Paper No. 2021/285, https://www.ecb.europa.eu/pub/pdf/scpops/ecb.op285~be7d631055.en.pdf. [157]

Bressan, G., I. Monasterolo and S. Battiston (2021), "Reducing Climate Transition Risk in Central Banks' Asset Purchasing Programs", *SSRN Electronic Journal*, https://doi.org/10.2139/ssrn.3770192. [161]

Broccardo, E., O. Hart and L. Zingales (2020), *Exit vs. Voice*, National Bureau of Economic Research, Cambridge, MA, https://doi.org/10.3386/w27710. [197]

Busies, I. et al. (2024), "Designing a Macroprudential Capital Buffer for Climate-Related Risks", *SSRN Electronic Journal*, https://doi.org/10.2139/ssrn.4844507. [136]

CA100+ (2024), *Progress Update 2023*, https://www.climateaction100.org/wp-content/uploads/2024/01/Climate-Action-100-Progress-Update-2023.pdf. [183]

Caldecott, B. et al. (2024), "How sustainable finance creates impact: transmission mechanisms to the real economy", *Review of World Economics*, https://doi.org/10.1007/s10290-024-00541-9. [196]

Calipel, C. and L. Fidel (2023), *Climate stress tests: what co-benefits can we expect for transition financing?*, https://www.i4ce.org/wp-content/uploads/2023/03/Climate-stress-tests-what-cobenefits-can-we-expect-for-transition-financing_au3003323.pdf. [138]

Camilleri, A. et al. (2018), "Consumers underestimate the emissions associated with food but are aided by labels", *Nature Climate Change*, Vol. 9/1, pp. 53-58, https://doi.org/10.1038/s41558-018-0354-z. [74]

Campiglio, E. (2016), "Beyond carbon pricing: The role of banking and monetary policy in financing the transition to a low-carbon economy", *Ecological Economics*, Vol. 121, pp. 220-230, https://doi.org/10.1016/j.ecolecon.2015.03.020. [85]

Campiglio, E. et al. (2018), "Climate change challenges for central banks and financial regulators", *Nature Climate Change*, Vol. 8/6, pp. 462-468, https://doi.org/10.1038/s41558-018-0175-0. [162]

Chamberlin, B. and J. Evain (2021), *Indexing capital requirements on climate : What impacts can be expected?*, https://www.i4ce.org/en/publication/indexing-capital-requirements-on-climate-what-impacts-can-be-expected/. [121]

Chen, S. (2022), *Green Investors and Green Transition Efforts: Talk the Talk or Walk the Walk?*, https://doi.org/10.2139/ssrn.4254894. [204]

Chhun, B. et al. (2024), "Environmental domain tagging in the OECD PINE database", *OECD Environment Working Papers*, No. 232, OECD Publishing, Paris, https://doi.org/10.1787/be984b0a-en. [15]

Coelho, R. and F. Restoy (2023), *Macroprudential policies for addressing climate-related financial risks: challenges and trade-offs*, Bank for International Settlements, https://www.bis.org/fsi/fsibriefs18.pdf. [122]

Coelho, R. and F. Restoy (2022), *The regulatory response to climate risks: some challenges*, Bank for International Settlements, https://www.bis.org/fsi/fsibriefs16.pdf. [112]

Cohen, S., I. Kadach and G. Ormazabal (2023), “Institutional investors, climate disclosure, and carbon emissions”, *Journal of Accounting and Economics*, Vol. 76/2-3, p. 101640, https://doi.org/10.1016/j.jacceco.2023.101640. [182]

Cojoianu, T. et al. (2020), “Does the fossil fuel divestment movement impact new oil and gas fundraising?”, *Journal of Economic Geography*, Vol. 21/1, pp. 141-164, https://doi.org/10.1093/jeg/lbaa027. [199]

Cole, S. et al. (2023), *What Do Impact Investors Do Differently?*, National Bureau of Economic Research, Cambridge, MA, https://doi.org/10.3386/w31898. [205]

Cong, Y., M. Freedman and J. Park (2020), “Mandated greenhouse gas emissions and required SEC climate change disclosures”, *Journal of Cleaner Production*, Vol. 247, p. 119111, https://doi.org/10.1016/j.jclepro.2019.119111. [66]

Costa, H. et al. (2024), “The role of financing constraints and environmental policy on green investment”, *Economics Letters*, Vol. 239, p. 111741, https://doi.org/10.1016/j.econlet.2024.111741. [13]

Council of the European Union (2021), *Proposal for a Directive of the European Parliament and of the Council*, https://data.consilium.europa.eu/doc/document/ST-15882-2023-INIT/en/pdf. [107]

CPI (2024), *Net Zero Finance Tracker*, https://netzerofinancetracker.climatepolicyinitiative.org/. [170]

CPI (2024), *State of European Pension Funds’ Net-Zero Transition*, https://bit.ly/3ZTBGWj. [191]

D’Orazio, P. (2023), “A global database for climate-related financial policies”, *BMC Research Notes*, Vol. 16/1, https://doi.org/10.1186/s13104-023-06418-8. [47]

D’Orazio, P. (2023), “Climate change and macro-financial risks: financial policy responses for an orderly low-carbon transition”, *Environmental Research: Climate*, Vol. 2/1, p. 013002, https://doi.org/10.1088/2752-5295/acb790. [69]

D’Orazio, P. (2021), “Towards a post-pandemic policy framework to manage climate-related financial risks and resilience”, *Climate Policy*, Vol. 21/10, pp. 1368-1382, https://doi.org/10.1080/14693062.2021.1975623. [117]

D’Orazio, P. and M. Dirks (2021), “Exploring the effects of climate-related financial policies on carbon emissions in G20 countries: a panel quantile regression approach”, *Environmental Science and Pollution Research*, Vol. 29/5, pp. 7678-7702, https://doi.org/10.1007/s11356-021-15655-y. [72]

D’Orazio, P. and L. Popoyan (2019), “Fostering green investments and tackling climate-related financial risks: Which role for macroprudential policies?”, *Ecological Economics*, Vol. 160, pp. 25-37, https://doi.org/10.1016/j.ecolecon.2019.01.029. [50]

D’Orazio, P. and S. Thole (2022), “Climate-related financial policy index: A composite index to compare the engagement in green financial policymaking at the global level”, *Ecological Indicators*, Vol. 141, p. 109065, https://doi.org/10.1016/j.ecolind.2022.109065. [46]

Dafermos, Y. et al. (2022), *Greening collateral frameworks*, https://www.lse.ac.uk/granthaminstitute/publication/greening-collateral-frameworks/. [118]

Dafermos, Y. and M. Nikolaidi (2022), *Greening capital requirements*, https://www.lse.ac.uk/granthaminstitute/wp-content/uploads/2022/10/INSPIRE-Sustainable-Central-Banking-Toolbox-Policy-Briefing-Paper-8.pdf. [113]

Dafermos, Y. and M. Nikolaidi (2021), "How can green differentiated capital requirements affect climate risks? A dynamic macrofinancial analysis", *Journal of Financial Stability*, Vol. 54, p. 100871, https://doi.org/10.1016/j.jfs.2021.100871. [110]

Dankert, J. et al. (2018), *A Green Supporting Factor — The Right Policy?*, https://www.suerf.org/wp-content/uploads/2023/12/f_99be9f83741d1275639df2c1e4d0072f_3473_suerf.pdf. [109]

DEFRA (2010), *The contribution that reporting of greenhouse gas emissions makes to the UK meeting its climate change objectives*, https://www.gov.uk/government/publications/the-contribution-that-reporting-of-greenhouse-gas-emissions-makes-to-the-uk-meeting-its-climate-change-objectives. [64]

DeMenno, M. (2022), "Environmental sustainability and financial stability: can macroprudential stress testing measure and mitigate climate-related systemic financial risk?", *Journal of Banking Regulation*, Vol. 24/4, pp. 445-473, https://doi.org/10.1057/s41261-022-00207-2. [137]

Dikau, S. et al. (2024), "Prudential net zero transition plans: the potential of a new regulatory instrument", *Journal of Banking Regulation*, https://doi.org/10.1057/s41261-024-00247-w. [44]

Dikau, S. and U. Volz (2021), "Central bank mandates, sustainability objectives and the promotion of green finance", *Ecological Economics*, Vol. 184, p. 107022, https://doi.org/10.1016/j.ecolecon.2021.107022. [43]

Dikau, S. and U. Volz (2018), *Central Banking, Climate Change, and Green Finance. ADBI Working Paper Series No. 867*, Asian Development Bank, https://www.adb.org/publications/central-banking-climate-change-and-green-finance. [126]

D'Orazio, P. (2023), "Dataset for the climate-related financial policy index (CRFPI)", *Data in Brief*, Vol. 48, p. 109044, https://doi.org/10.1016/j.dib.2023.109044. [45]

Downar, B. et al. (2021), "The impact of carbon disclosure mandates on emissions and financial operating performance", *Review of Accounting Studies*, Vol. 26/3, pp. 1137-1175, https://doi.org/10.1007/s11142-021-09611-x. [61]

Dubash, N. et al. (2022), "National and Sub-national Policies and Institutions", in *Climate Change 2022: Mitigation of Climate Change*, Cambridge University Press, https://doi.org/10.1017/9781009157926.015. [6]

Dumlao, L. (2024), "MANDATORY CREDIT ALLOCATION AND GOVERNMENT GUARANTEE IN THE PHILIPPINES", *Financial and credit activity problems of theory and practice*, Vol. 2/55, pp. 48-63, https://doi.org/10.55643/fcaptp.2.55.2024.4322. [140]

Dunz, N. et al. (2021), "ECB's Economy-Wide Climate Stress Test", *SSRN Electronic Journal*, https://doi.org/10.2139/ssrn.3929178. [101]

EBA (n.d.), *Capital Requirements Regulation (CRR) Article 4*, https://www.eba.europa.eu/regulation-and-policy/single-rulebook/interactive-single-rulebook/14406. [115]

ECB (2024), *Climate and nature plan 2024-2025*, https://www.ecb.europa.eu/ecb/climate/our-climate-and-nature-plan/shared/pdf/ecb.climate_nature_plan_2024-2025.en.pdf. [38]

ECB (2022), *What is the ECB's asset purchase programme?*, https://www.ecb.europa.eu/ecb-and-you/explainers/tell-me-more/html/asset-purchase.en.html. [152]

ECB (2021), *From green neglect to green dominance?*, https://www.ecb.europa.eu/press/key/date/2021/html/ecb.sp210303_1~f3df48854e.en.html. [164]

ECB (2020), *ECB to accept sustainability-linked bonds as collateral*, https://www.ecb.europa.eu/press/pr/date/2020/html/ecb.pr200922~482e4a5a90.en.html. [149]

Egli, F., D. Schärer and B. Steffen (2022), "Determinants of fossil fuel divestment in European pension funds", *Ecological Economics*, Vol. 191, p. 107237, https://doi.org/10.1016/j.ecolecon.2021.107237. [192]

EIOPA (2023), *Prudential treatment of sustainability risks, consultation paper*, https://www.eiopa.europa.eu/system/files/2023-12/Consultation%20Paper%20on%20the%20Prudential%20Treatment%20of%20Sustainability%20Risks.pdf. [131]

Emambakhsh, T. et al. (2022), *Climate-related risks to financial stability*, https://www.ecb.europa.eu/press/financial-stability-publications/fsr/special/html/ecb.fsrart202205_01~9d4ae00a92.en.html#toc3. [59]

Erel, I. (ed.) (2023), "Can Banks Save Mountains?", *The Review of Corporate Finance Studies*, Vol. 12/4, pp. 761-791, https://doi.org/10.1093/rcfs/cfad013. [195]

European Parliament (2024), *Transparency and integrity of Environmental, Social and Governance (ESG) rating activities*, https://www.skadden.com/-/media/files/publications/2024/07/eu-adopts-legislation/regulation-on-the-transparency-and-integrity-of-environmental-social-and-governance-rating-activitie.pdf?rev=7fbda3bab974456bbfd078f080a48a4d&hash=CB500ED0B2FCDDCB0FBE63174DE. [51]

Fender, I. et al. (2020), *Reserve management and sustainability: the case for green bonds?*, https://www.bis.org/publ/work849.htm (accessed on 2 October 2024). [151]

Ferrari, A. and V. Landi (2023), *Toward a Green Economy: The Role of Central Bank's Asset Purchases, Working Paper Series No 2779*, European Central Bank, https://www.ecb.europa.eu/pub/pdf/scpwps/ecb.wp2779~a4eca2101a.en.pdf. [163]

Friedman, B. (2015), "Monetary Policy since the 2007–2009 Financial Crisis", in *International Encyclopedia of the Social & Behavioral Sciences*, Elsevier, https://doi.org/10.1016/b978-0-08-097086-8.71037-3. [141]

FSB (2023), *FSB Roadmap for Addressing Financial Risks from Climate Change Progress report*, https://www.fsb.org/wp-content/uploads/P130723.pdf. [39]

FSB (2022), *Supervisory and Regulatory Approaches to Climate-related Risks*, https://www.fsb.org/uploads/P131022-1.pdf. [41]

FSB (2022), *Supervisory and Regulatory Approaches to Climate-related Risks: Final report*, https://www.fsb.org/2022/10/supervisory-and-regulatory-approaches-to-climate-related-risks-final-report/. [82]

Fuchs, L. et al. (2023), *Climate stress tests, bank lending, and the transition to the carbon-neutral economy*, https://www.bankingsupervision.europa.eu/press/conferences/shared/pdf/20230502_research_conference/Nguyen_paper.pdf. [139]

García-Villegas, S. and E. Martorell (2024), *Climate transition risk and the role of bank capital requirements*, Banco de España, Madrid, https://doi.org/10.53479/36292. [134]

Gasparini, M. et al. (2024), "Model-based financial regulations impair the transition to net-zero carbon emissions", *Nature Climate Change*, Vol. 14/5, pp. 476-481, https://doi.org/10.1038/s41558-024-01972-w. [84]

Gaukrodger, D. (2022), *Investment treaties and climate change: The Alignment of finance flows under the Paris Agreement*, https://www.oecd.org/investment/investment-policy/oecd-background-investment-treaties-finance-flow-alignment.pdf. [36]

Gersbach, H. and J. Rochet (2012), "Aggregate Investment Externalities and Macroprudential Regulation", *Journal of Money, Credit and Banking*, Vol. 44, pp. 73–109, http://www.jstor.org/stable/23321957. [90]

Giovanardi, F. et al. (2023), *The effectiveness of green collateral policy as an instrument of climate policy*, Deutsche Bundesbank, https://www.bundesbank.de/en/publications/research/research-brief/2023-57-green-collateral-policy-805516. [155]

Green Finance Platform (n.d.), *Bangladesh's Green Transformation Fund (GTF)*, https://www.greenfinanceplatform.org/policies-and-regulations/bangladeshs-green-transformation-fund-gtf (accessed on 10 October 2024). [148]

Green, D. and B. Vallee (2024), *Measurement and Effects of Bank Exit Policies*, https://doi.org/10.2139/ssrn.4090974. [194]

Grill, M., A. Popescu and E. Rancoita (2024), *Climate Transition Risk in the Banking Sector: What Can Prudential Regulation Do?*, ECB Working Paper Series No 2910, https://www.ecb.europa.eu/pub/pdf/scpwps/ecb.wp2910~c4d2c82f8c.en.pdf. [83]

Gros, D. and F. Shamsfakhr (2023), *Shades of Green Monetary Policy: Would a green tilt help?*, https://www.europarl.europa.eu/RegData/etudes/IDAN/2023/755709/IPOL_IDA(2023)755709_EN.pdf. [160]

Grunewald, S. (2023), "Macroprudential policies and climate risks", *SSRN Electronic Journal*, https://doi.org/10.2139/ssrn.4327142. [135]

Grunewald, S. (2020), *Climate Change as a Systemic Risk – Are Macroprudential Authorities up to the Task?*, European Banking Institute Working Paper Series – no. 62, https://doi.org/10.2139/ssrn.3580222. [123]

Hartzmark, S. and K. Shue (2022), *Counterproductive Sustainable Investing: The Impact Elasticity of Brown and Green Firms*, https://doi.org/10.2139/ssrn.4359282. [206]

Haščič, I. et al. (2015), "Public Interventions and Private Climate Finance Flows: Empirical Evidence from Renewable Energy Financing", *OECD Environment Working Papers*, No. 80, OECD Publishing, Paris, https://doi.org/10.1787/5js6b1r9lfd4-en. [35]

He, S., L. Xu and D. Shi (2023), "How does environmental information disclosure affect carbon emissions? Evidence from China", *Environmental Science and Pollution Research*, Vol. 30/41, pp. 93998-94014, https://doi.org/10.1007/s11356-023-28883-1. [60]

Hong, H. and M. Kacperczyk (2009), "The price of sin: The effects of social norms on markets", *Journal of Financial Economics*, Vol. 93/1, pp. 15-36, https://doi.org/10.1016/j.jfineco.2008.09.001. [198]

IEA (2023), *Fossil Fuel Subsidies Database*, https://www.iea.org/data-and-statistics/data-product/fossil-fuel-subsidies-database. [27]

IEA (2023), *Fossil Fuels Consumption Subsidies 2022*, IEA, https://www.iea.org/reports/fossil-fuels-consumption-subsidies-2022. [22]

IEEFA (2023), *200 and counting – Global financial institutions committed to coal divestment has doubled in three years*, https://ieefa.org/articles/200-and-counting-global-financial-institutions-committed-coal-divestment-has-doubled-three (accessed on 12 August 2024). [190]

IEEFA (2023), *200 and counting: Global financial institutions are exiting coal*, https://ieefa.org/resources/200-and-counting-global-financial-institutions-are-exiting-coal (accessed on 12 August 2024). [189]

IIGCC (2024), *Net Zero Investment Framework*, https://www.iigcc.org/net-zero-investment-framework. [179]

IMF (2023), *Fossil Fuel Subsidies*, https://www.imf.org/en/Topics/climate-change/energy-subsidies. [26]

IMF (2022), *Monetary and Capital Markets Department: Technical Assistance Handbook: Reserve Requirements*, https://www.imf.org/en/Publications/miscellaneous-publications/Issues/2022/01/18/monetary-and-capital-markets-department-technical-assistance-handbook. [146]

Jung, H., R. Engle and R. Berner (2023), *CRISK: Measuring the Climate Risk Exposure of the Financial System*, Federal Reserve Bank of New York Staff Reports, no. 977, https://www.newyorkfed.org/medialibrary/media/research/staff_reports/sr977.pdf. [102]

Kacperczyk, M. and J. Peydró (2022), *Carbon Emissions and the Bank-Lending Channel*, https://doi.org/10.2139/ssrn.3915486. [200]

Kahn, M., J. Matsusaka and C. Shu (2024), *Divestment and Engagement: The Effect of Green Investors on Corporate Carbon Emissions*, https://doi.org/10.3386/w31791. [181]

Kölbel, J. et al. (2020), "Can Sustainable Investing Save the World? Reviewing the Mechanisms of Investor Impact", *Organization & Environment*, Vol. 33/4, pp. 554-574, https://doi.org/10.1177/1086026620919202. [184]

Kraft, A., R. Vashishtha and M. Venkatachalam (2017), "Frequent Financial Reporting and Managerial Myopia", *The Accounting Review*, Vol. 93/2, pp. 249-275, https://doi.org/10.2308/accr-51838. [86]

Krogstrup, S. and W. Oman (2019), *Macroeconomic and Financial Policies for Climate Change Mitigation: A Review of the Literature*, International Monetary Fund, https://www.imf.org/en/Publications/WP/Issues/2019/09/04/Macroeconomic-and-Financial-Policies-for-Climate-Change-Mitigation-A-Review-of-the-Literature-48612. [49]

Lamperti, F. et al. (2021), "Three green financial policies to address climate risks", *Journal of Financial Stability*, Vol. 54, p. 100875, https://doi.org/10.1016/j.jfs.2021.100875. [128]

Linehan, R. (2024), *US Must Correct Unintended Consequences of Basel III That Suppress Infrastructure Financing*, https://www.wilsoncenter.org/article/us-must-correct-unintended-consequences-basel-iii-suppress-infrastructure-financing. [92]

LSEG (2024), *Scope for improvement: Solving the Scope 3 conundrum*, https://www.lseg.com/content/dam/ftse-russell/en_us/documents/research/solving-scope-3-conundrum.pdf. [56]

Magyar Nemzeti Bank (2022), *Monetary policy for sustainability*, https://www.mnb.hu/letoltes/zold-jegybanki-eszkoztar-strategia-tanulmanykotet-eng-0209.pdf. [99]

Matikainen, S., E. Campiglio and D. Zenghelis (2017), *The climate impact of quantitative easing*, The Grantham Research Institute on Climate Change and the Environment, https://www.lse.ac.uk/granthaminstitute/wp-content/uploads/2017/05/ClimateImpactQuantEasing_Matikainen-et-al-1.pdf. [142]

McConnell, A., B. Yanovski and K. Lessmann (2021), "Central bank collateral as a green monetary policy instrument", *Climate Policy*, Vol. 22/3, pp. 339-355, https://doi.org/10.1080/14693062.2021.2012112. [156]

McDonnell, C. and J. Gupta (2023), "Beyond divest vs. engage: a review of the role of institutional investors in an inclusive fossil fuel phase-out", *Climate Policy*, Vol. 24/3, pp. 314-331, https://doi.org/10.1080/14693062.2023.2261900. [171]

Medina, A., A. de la Cruz and Y. Tang (2022), "Corporate ownership and concentration", *OECD Corporate Governance Working Papers*, No. 27, OECD Publishing, Paris, https://doi.org/10.1787/bc3adca3-en. [178]

Mésonnier, J. and B. Nguyen (2021), *Showing off cleaner hands: mandatory climate-related disclosure by financial institutions and the financing of fossil energy*, Banque de France, https://www.banque-france.fr/sites/default/files/medias/documents/wp800.pdf. [67]

Miguel, F., A. Pedraza and C. Ruiz-Ortega (2024), "Climate-change regulations: Bank lending and real effects", *Journal of Financial Stability*, Vol. 70, p. 101212, https://doi.org/10.1016/j.jfs.2023.101212. [127]

Miller, H. and S. Dikau (2022), *Preventing a 'climate Minsky moment': environmental financial risks and prudential exposure limits*, https://www.lse.ac.uk/granthaminstitute/publication/preventing-a-climate-minsky-moment/. [98]

Monasterolo, I. et al. (2017), "Vulnerable yet relevant: the two dimensions of climate-related financial disclosure", *Climatic Change*, Vol. 145/3-4, pp. 495-507, https://doi.org/10.1007/s10584-017-2095-9. [53]

Monnin, P. (2021), *Systemic Risk Buffers – The Missing Piece in the Prudential Response to Climate Risks*, https://www.cepweb.org/systemic-risk-buffers-the-missing-piece-in-the-prudential-response-to-climate-risks/. [124]

Monnin, P. (2018), *Central banks should reflect climate risks in monetary policy operations*, SUERF Policy Note No. 41, https://www.suerf.org/publications/suerf-policy-notes-and-briefs/central-banks-should-reflect-climate-risks-in-monetary-policy-operations/. [145]

Muller, L., A. Lacroix and B. Ruffieux (2019), "Environmental Labelling and Consumption Changes: A Food Choice Experiment", *Environmental and Resource Economics*, Vol. 73/3, pp. 871-897, https://doi.org/10.1007/s10640-019-00328-9. [73]

Muller, N. (2021), *On the Green Interest Rate.*, National Bureau of Economic Research, Cambridge, MA, https://doi.org/10.3386/w28891. [166]

Nachtigall, D. et al. (2022), "The climate actions and policies measurement framework: A structured and harmonised climate policy database to monitor countries' mitigation action", *OECD Environment Working Papers*, No. 203, OECD Publishing, Paris, https://doi.org/10.1787/2caa60ce-en. [5]

Narbel, P. (2013), *The Likely Impact of Basel III on a Bank's Appetite for Renewable Energy Financing*, NHH Dept. of Business and Management Science Discussion Paper No. 2013/10, https://doi.org/10.2139/ssrn.2341519. [89]

NewClimate Institute (2022), *Making finance consistent with climate goals?*, https://newclimate.org/resources/publications/making-finance-consistent-with-climate-goals. [173]

NGFS (2024), *Adapting central bank operations to a hotter world: current progress and insights from practical examples*, https://www.ngfs.net/sites/default/files/medias/documents/ngfs_adapting_central_bank_operations_to_a_hotter_world_final.pdf. [150]

NGFS (2024), *Technical Document – Decarbonisation strategies for corporate portfolios of central banks*, https://www.ngfs.net/sites/default/files/media/2024/05/16/ngfs_technical_document_on_decarbonisation_strategies_for_corporate_portfolios_of_central_banks_0.pdf. [172]

NGFS (2021), *Adapting central bank operations to a hotter world: Reviewing some options*, https://www.ngfs.net/en/adapting-central-bank-operations-hotter-world-reviewing-some-options. [52]

NGFS (2020), *Guide for Supervisors: integrating climate-related and environmental risks into prudential supervision*, https://www.ngfs.net/en/guide-supervisors-integrating-climate-related-and-environmental-risks-prudential-supervision. [78]

OECD (2024), *Global Corporate Sustainability Report 2024*, OECD Publishing, Paris, https://doi.org/10.1787/8416b635-en. [57]

OECD (2024), *Green Budgeting in OECD Countries 2024*, OECD Publishing, Paris, https://doi.org/10.1787/9aea61f0-en. [20]

OECD (2024), *Policy Instruments for the Environment (PINE) Database*, July 2024 version, http://oe.cd/pinedatabase. [9]

OECD (2023), "Aligning finance flows and private sector action with a resilient net-zero transition", in *Net Zero+: Climate and Economic Resilience in a Changing World*, OECD Publishing, Paris, https://doi.org/10.1787/9f689459-en. [31]

OECD (2023), "Assessing net-zero metrics for financial institutions: Supporting the monitoring of financial institutions' commitments", *OECD Business and Finance Policy Papers*, No. 37, OECD Publishing, Paris, https://doi.org/10.1787/dedcfe56-en. [54]

OECD (2023), "Financing adaptation amid increasing climate risks", in *Net Zero+: Climate and Economic Resilience in a Changing World*, OECD Publishing, Paris, https://doi.org/10.1787/09e304e3-en. [28]

OECD (2023), *Managing Climate Risks and Impacts Through Due Diligence for Responsible Business Conduct: A Tool for Institutional Investors*, OECD Publishing, Paris, https://doi.org/10.1787/8aee4fce-en. [168]

OECD (2023), *Net Zero+: Climate and Economic Resilience in a Changing World*, OECD Publishing, Paris, https://doi.org/10.1787/da477dda-en. [3]

OECD (2023), *OECD Guidelines for Multinational Enterprises on Responsible Business Conduct*, OECD Publishing, Paris, https://doi.org/10.1787/81f92357-en. [169]

OECD (2023), *OECD Guidelines for Multinational Enterprises on Responsible Business Conduct*, OECD Publishing, Paris. [19]

OECD (2023), *OECD Inventory of Support Measures for Fossil Fuels 2023*, OECD Publishing, Paris, https://doi.org/10.1787/87dc4a55-en. [24]

OECD (2023), *Scaling Up the Mobilisation of Private Finance for Climate Action in Developing Countries: Challenges and Opportunities for International Providers*, Green Finance and Investment, OECD Publishing, Paris, https://doi.org/10.1787/17a88681-en. [34]

OECD (2023), *The Climate Action Monitor 2023: Providing Information to Monitor Progress Towards Net-Zero*, OECD Publishing, Paris, https://doi.org/10.1787/60e338a2-en. [10]

OECD (2022), *Climate Change and Corporate Governance*, Corporate Governance, OECD Publishing, Paris, https://doi.org/10.1787/272d85c3-en. [177]

OECD (2022), "ESG ratings and climate transition: An assessment of the alignment of E pillar scores and metrics", *OECD Business and Finance Policy Papers*, No. 06, OECD Publishing, Paris, https://doi.org/10.1787/2fa21143-en. [203]

OECD (2022), *FDI Qualities Policy Toolkit*, OECD Publishing, Paris, https://doi.org/10.1787/7ba74100-en. [33]

OECD (2022), "Policy guidance on market practices to strengthen ESG investing and finance a climate transition", *OECD Business and Finance Policy Papers*, No. 13, OECD Publishing, Paris, https://doi.org/10.1787/2c5b535c-en. [180]

OECD (2020), *ESG Investing: Practices, Progress and Challenges*, OECD Publishing, Paris, https://doi.org/10.1787/b4f71091-en. [187]

OECD (2019), *Aligning Development Co-operation and Climate Action: The Only Way Forward*, The Development Dimension, OECD Publishing, Paris, https://doi.org/10.1787/5099ad91-en. [21]

OECD (2015), *Aligning Policies for a Low-carbon Economy*, OECD Publishing, Paris, https://doi.org/10.1787/9789264233294-en. [4]

OECD (2008), *OECD Environmental Outlook to 2030*, OECD Publishing, Paris, https://doi.org/10.1787/9789264040519-en. [7]

OECD (Forthcoming), *The IFCMA's climate policy database: A proposal for a policy instruments typology and data structure*. [2]

Oehmke, M. (2022), *Bank capital regulation and climate change*, European Systemic Risk Board, https://www.esrb.europa.eu/pub/asc/insights/shared/pdf/esrb.asc.insight_03_11_22~c72a4ae30d.en.pdf. [114]

Oehmke, M. and M. Opp (2022), *Green Capital Requirements*, https://doi.org/10.2139/ssrn.4040098. [111]

Oustry, A. et al. (2020), *Climate-related Risks and Central Banks' Collateral Policy: a Methodological Experiment*, Banque de France, https://publications.banque-france.fr/en/climate-related-risks-and-central-banks-collateral-policy-methodological-experiment. [158]

Papoutsi, M., M. Piazzesi and M. Schneider (2022), *How unconventional is green monetary policy?*, https://web.stanford.edu/~piazzesi/How_unconventional_is_green_monetary_policy.pdf. [144]

Pastor, L., R. Stambaugh and L. Taylor (2023), *Green Tilts*, National Bureau of Economic Research, Cambridge, MA, https://doi.org/10.3386/w31320. [202]

PRI (2023), *Definitions for responsible investment approaches*, https://www.unpri.org/investment-tools/definitions-for-responsible-investment-approaches/11874.article#Stewardship. [175]

PRI (2022), *Discussing divestment: Developing an approach when persuiing sustainability outcomes in listed equities*, https://www.unpri.org/download?ac=16109. [188]

PRI (2021), *Stewardship*, https://www.unpri.org/introductory-guides-to-responsible-investment/an-introduction-to-responsible-investment-stewardship/7228.article. [174]

Republic of Philippines (2021), *Sustainable Finance Framework*, https://www.treasury.gov.ph/wp-content/uploads/2022/01/Republic-of-Philippines-Sustainable-Finance-Framework-vF-with-disclaimer.pdf. [108]

Roy, A. (2024), "Green monetary policy to combat climate change: Theory and evidence of selective credit control", *Journal of Climate Finance*, Vol. 6, p. 100035, https://doi.org/10.1016/j.jclimf.2024.100035. [165]

Scherer, B. and M. Hasaj (2023), "Greenlabelling: How valuable is the SFDR Art 9 label?", *Journal of Asset Management*, Vol. 24/7, pp. 541-546, https://doi.org/10.1057/s41260-023-00319-y. [76]

Schoenmaker, D. (2021), "Greening monetary policy", *Climate Policy*, Vol. 21/4, pp. 581-592, https://doi.org/10.1080/14693062.2020.1868392. [154]

Schoenmaker, D. and R. Van Tilburg (2016), "What Role for Financial Supervisors in Addressing Environmental Risks?", *Comparative Economic Studies*, Vol. 58/3, pp. 317-334, https://doi.org/10.1057/ces.2016.11. [129]

Shi, D., C. Bu and H. Xue (2021), "Deterrence effects of disclosure: The impact of environmental information disclosure on emission reduction of firms", *Energy Economics*, Vol. 104, p. 105680, https://doi.org/10.1016/j.eneco.2021.105680. [58]

Smoleńska, A. and J. van 't Klooster (2022), "A Risky Bet: Climate Change and the EU's Microprudential Framework for Banks", *Journal of Financial Regulation*, Vol. 8/1, pp. 51-74, https://doi.org/10.1093/jfr/fjac002. [80]

Stechemesser, A. et al. (2024), "Climate policies that achieved major emission reductions: Global evidence from two decades", *Science*, Vol. 385/6711, pp. 884-892, https://doi.org/10.1126/science.adl6547. [8]

Steffen, B. (2021), "A comparative analysis of green financial policy output in OECD countries", *Environmental Research Letters*, Vol. 16/7, p. 074031, https://doi.org/10.1088/1748-9326/ac0c43. [17]

Stiroh, K. (2022), *Climate Change and Double Materiality in a Micro- and Macroprudential Context*. [40]

Sullivan, R. and A. Gouldson (2012), "Does voluntary carbon reporting meet investors' needs?", *Journal of Cleaner Production*, Vol. 36, pp. 60-67, https://doi.org/10.1016/j.jclepro.2012.02.020. [65]

Tamez, M., E. Emre and A. Gullo (2024), "Banking Law and Climate Change: Key Legal Issues", *IMF Working Papers*, Vol. 2024/193, p. 1, https://doi.org/10.5089/9798400288388.001. [79]

Tamez, M., H. Weenink and A. Yoshinaga (2024), *Central Banks and Climate Change: Key Legal Issues, IMF Working Paper No. 24/192*, International Monetary Fund, https://doi.org/10.5089/9798400288395.001. [77]

Tandon, A. (2021), "Transition finance: Investigating the state of play: A stocktake of emerging approaches and financial instruments", *OECD Environment Working Papers*, No. 179, OECD Publishing, Paris, https://doi.org/10.1787/68becf35-en. [70]

Thakor, A. and F. Song (2023), "Banks, Markets, and the Color of Finance", *SSRN Electronic Journal*, https://doi.org/10.2139/ssrn.4581551. [133]

Thanassoulis, J. (2014), "Bank pay caps, bank risk, and macroprudential regulation", *Journal of Banking & Finance*, Vol. 48, pp. 139-151, https://doi.org/10.1016/j.jbankfin.2014.04.004. [91]

The Global Adaptation Mapping Initiative Team (2021), "A global assessment of policy tools to support climate adaptation", *Climate Policy*, Vol. 22/1, pp. 77-96, https://doi.org/10.1080/14693062.2021.2002251. [29]

Thomä, J. and K. Gibhardt (2019), "Quantifying the potential impact of a green supporting factor or brown penalty on European banks and lending", *Journal of Financial Regulation and Compliance*, Vol. 27/3, pp. 380-394, https://doi.org/10.1108/jfrc-03-2018-0038. [119]

Tienhaara, K. et al. (2022), "Investor-state disputes threaten the global green energy transition", *Science*, Vol. 376/6594, pp. 701-703, https://doi.org/10.1126/science.abo4637. [37]

Tomar, S. (2024), *Greenhouse Gas Disclosure and Emissions Benchmarking*, SMU Cox School of Business Research Paper No. 19-17, European Corporate Governance Institute – Finance Working Paper No. 818/2022, https://doi.org/10.2139/ssrn.3448904. [62]

TPI (2024), *State of transition in the banking sector*, Transition Pathway Initiative Centre, London School of Economics and Political Science, https://www.transitionpathwayinitiative.org/publications/2024-state-of-transition-in-the-banking-sector-report-2024. [193]

Trencher, G. et al. (2022), "The rise of phase-out as a critical decarbonisation approach: a systematic review", *Environmental Research Letters*, Vol. 17/12, p. 123002, https://doi.org/10.1088/1748-9326/ac9fe3. [14]

UK Department for Environment, Food & Rural Affairs (2021), *Climate change adaptation reporting: third round*, https://www.gov.uk/government/publications/climate-change-adaptation-reporting-third-round#full-publication-update-history. [55]

UNEP FI (2023), *Aligning Climate Policy Engagement with Net-Zero Commitments: A foundation for asset owner engagement of asset managers*, https://www.unepfi.org/industries/aligning-climate-policy-engagement-with-net-zero-commitments/. [176]

UNFCCC SCF (2023), *Report of the Standing Committee on Finance. Addendum. Synthesis of views regarding ways to achieve Article 2, paragraph 1(c), of the Paris Agreement*, https://unfccc.int/documents/632307. [1]

van 't Klooster, J. and R. van Tilburg (2020), *Targeting a sustainable recovery with Green TLTROs*, https://www.positivemoney.eu/wp-content/uploads/2020/09/Green-TLTROs.pdf. [167]

van der Kroft, B. et al. (2024), *Timing Sustainable Engagement in Real Asset Investments*, National Bureau of Economic Research, Cambridge, MA, https://doi.org/10.3386/w32646. [185]

Venmans, F., J. Ellis and D. Nachtigall (2020), "Carbon pricing and competitiveness: are they at odds?", *Climate Policy*, Vol. 20/9, pp. 1070-1091, https://doi.org/10.1080/14693062.2020.1805291. [12]

Vestergaard, J. (2022), *How can central banks help mitigate climate change? A money view perspective on green central banking, SECO Working Paper, No. 2022*, Roskilde University, Department of Social Sciences and Business, Socio-Economic Research Centre (SECO). [159]

Wang, Q. et al. (2023), "Reexamining the impact of foreign direct investment on carbon emissions: does per capita GDP matter?", *Humanities and Social Sciences Communications*, Vol. 10/1, https://doi.org/10.1057/s41599-023-01895-5. [32]

WEF (2022), *3 actions to accelerate emerging market climate transition*, https://www.weforum.org/agenda/2022/06/3-actions-to-accelerate-emerging-market-climate-transition/. [68]

WEF (2013), *Financial Regulation – Biased against Clean Energy and Green Infrastructure?*, https://www.weforum.org/publications/financial-regulation-biased-against-clean-energy-and-green-infrastructure/. [88]

World Bank (2024), *Finance and Prosperity 2024*, https://www.worldbank.org/en/publication/finance-and-prosperity-2024. [71]

World Bank (2024), *State and Trends of Carbon Pricing 2024*, World Bank, http://hdl.handle.net/10986/41544. [11]

World Bank (2021), *Toolkits for Policymakers to Green the Financial System*, World Bank Group, http://documents.worldbank.org/curated/en/374051622653965991/Toolkits-for-Policymakers-to-Green-the-Financial-System. [48]

WWF & Frankfurt School of Finance & Management (2019), *Finance fit for Paris (3fP)-Tracker Handbook*, https://www.fs-unep-centre.org/project/3fp-tracker/. [18]

Zhang, Y. and J. Liu (2020), "Overview of research on carbon information disclosure", *Frontiers of Engineering Management*, Vol. 7/1, pp. 47-62, https://doi.org/10.1007/s42524-019-0089-1. [63]

Zhou, X. et al. (2022), "Bank green lending and credit risk: an empirical analysis of China's Green Credit Policy", *Business Strategy and the Environment*, Vol. 31/4, pp. 1623-1640, https://doi.org/10.1002/bse.2973. [130]

Note

[1] Credit institutions mainly refer to banks and certain other instutitions fulfilling banking services (e.g., (EBA, n.d.[115])).

5 Conclusion: lessons learnt for the way forward

Achieving net-zero emissions and building resilience to climate change requires aligning finance with such goals, as emphasised by Article 2.1c of the Paris Agreement. This inaugural edition of the OECD Review on aligning finance with climate goals brought together best-available information, data and research to support building the evidence base to design an effective policy landscape that incentivises and enables reaching this goal. It did so by reviewing approaches to assess the climate alignment of finance, the current degree of climate alignment of finance, as well as financial public policies and financial sector actions adopted that may influence the climate alignment of finance.

5.1. Good practices in ensuring the environmental integrity and policy relevance of climate-alignment assessments

Public policy and private actions to contribute to aligning finance with climate policy goals and avoid misaligned new investments must be informed by robust assessments of progress towards such alignment. However, efforts to increase the climate alignment of finance are currently fragmented, in part due to the absence of a common framework to credibly assess progress. Such assessments need to rely on credible methodologies and best-available evidence. Against this backdrop, the present review highlighted significant progress that has been made in assessing the climate alignment of finance, but also several gaps and greenwashing risks that may undermine climate-alignment assessments.

The review points to five key good practices to ensure the environmental integrity and policy relevance of climate-alignment assessments:

- **Place best-available estimates of finance to activities contributing to or undermining climate goals in the context of total financial flows and stocks.** This needs to be done across all layers of finance, from real-economy investments to financial assets across asset classes, financial institutions, and financial jurisdictions.
- **Rely on a pertinent set of core yet complementary metrics.** Across layers of finance, different metrics highlight different aspects of climate performance. Due to the complexity of climate-alignment assessments, no silver-bullet metric can credibly and transparently capture all dimensions. Combining a set of key complementary metrics provides a more holistic and nuanced assessment of the degree of progress and actions towards climate alignment.
- **Transparently disclose underlying methodological assumptions and choices.** A range of complex methodological choices and assumptions influence the results of climate-alignment assessments of finance. Key climate performance metrics can follow different calculation approaches. Transparency on these approaches and assumptions facilitates the comparability of different assessments and analyses of their environmental integrity.

- **Assess the reliability and comparability of input data.** The credibility of climate-alignment assessments is highly depended on the accuracy, granularity, and coverage of underlying input data, all of which differ depending on the source. Such data can be reported, based on mandatory or voluntary disclosure practices, or estimated. Moreover, different disclosure policies can propose different reporting approaches and scope. Increased transparency on data gaps and estimation methods in disclosures is needed.
- **Rely on best-available reference points against which to assess climate alignment, that reflect the characteristics of assets and the ambition needed to reach climate policy goals.** Climate-alignment assessments require matching granular data on investment and financing with climate-related characteristics of underlying assets or actors and analysing the consistency of such characteristics with existing climate policy goals as reference points. Notably, climate change mitigation scenarios can provide a credible reference point for target setting and alignment assessments when the selected scenario can be considered as consistent with the Paris Agreement, matches the granularity of the financial asset or entity under consideration, and provides transparency on climate outcomes and underlying assumptions.

Assessing progress towards achieving Article 2.1c of the Paris Agreement also requires assessing the climate alignment of drivers influencing the climate alignment of finance. Such assessments depend on the credibility of climate-alignment assessments of financial flows and stocks.

5.2. Actions to better assess and drive climate alignment in finance

Different communities play different roles in informing and influencing assessments of and developments in the climate alignment of finance, including public policymakers and financial sector participants. Each community can take a range of actions to enhance alignment assessments, improve the availability and credibility of data, and more generally support efforts to redirect finance towards aligned activities that result in progress towards net zero GHG emissions and climate resilience in the real economy. This section highlights sets of three key actions based on the evidence compiled in this review.

Government ministries, notably economic, environmental, and financial ministries, can influence assessments and drivers of the climate alignment of finance through a wide set of policy tools. Based on this review, governments, ideally in coordination across ministries, could:

- **Promote disclosure of key complementary metrics that is interoperable across jurisdictions and considers not only climate-related risks but also the alignment perspective.** In doing so, policymakers need to reflect best-available climate science as well as disclosure and reporting capacities. Aside from real-economy policies such as economic or regulatory policies, disclosure policies are one of the main financial policy tools available to governments. Across jurisdictions, a range of voluntary and mandatory disclosure policies are in place. Their interoperability should be improved, while maintaining sufficient specificity to avoid greenwashing. Moreover, disclosure policies need to address financial institutions explicitly, as well as place more efforts on climate resilience-related disclosure to help build the evidence base for resilience alignment of finance.
- **Support climate-alignment efforts through improved availability of granular input data and reference points that are both tangible and ambitious.** Access to granular and accurate data is essential for scenario development and analysis in the financial sector. Policymakers can provide mechanisms to support the availability of geography and sector specific data, which is critical to inform the design of scenarios. For example, they can support improved data in national energy accounts, as well as, for providers of international development finance, help increase the capacities of developing countries in this area.
- **Identify and revise policies incentivising and enabling domestic and international financial flows going to climate-misaligned activities.** A range of real-economy policies remain in place

that continue to support finance going to activities that are misaligned with climate goals. As the financial system and real economy are inherently linked, respective policy ecosystems affect each other. The effectiveness of climate-related financial system policies depends on the effectiveness of climate-related real-economy policies.

Financial system policymakers, such as central banks, and regulatory and supervisory authorities, focus on ensuring the stability, efficiency, integrity, and functioning of the financial system. Financial system policymakers may, depending on their mandates, develop tailored financial sector policies to address climate risks and, in some cases, address climate alignment of finance explicitly. Considering these varying mandates, central banks and regulatory and supervisory authorities could:

- **Collect and, to the extent possible, make publicly available detailed data on finance exposed to activities misaligned with and contributing to climate goals.** For this, financial policymakers could work together with national statistical offices to develop green finance statistics for jurisdictions, as per ongoing efforts under the System of National Accounts. Moreover, data collected for financial stress tests or other risk assessments can be highly relevant to climate policymakers in the context of alignment assessments and to inform their policymaking.
- **Develop disclosure requirements of key complementary metrics for financial institutions.** Climate-related disclosure by financial institutions is currently scarce, likely due to the relatively limited climate-related disclosure requirements for these institutions across jurisdictions globally. A key set of complementary metrics could provide insights into the climate risks and performance of financial institutions.
- **Assess the effects of existing policies.** Central banks and regulatory and supervisory authorities can further assess the effects on core financial and price stability objectives of integrating climate-related considerations. Additionally, they could, to the extent consistent with their mandates, consider the impacts of their policies on climate goals.

Investors and financial institutions, including commercial banks, asset owners, and asset managers, **can** play a key role in shifting finance towards activities aligned with climate goals. While certain actions may be mandated or incentivised through policies, investors and financial institutions also have taken actions voluntarily. Building on this, they can take further actions to support assessments of climate-alignment in finance, and help drive the transition to net-zero emissions and climate resilience:

- **Disclose on a broader set of metrics and asset classes in a comparable and transparent manner.** Climate-alignment assessments of investors and financial institutions remain limited. These actors could voluntarily disclose aggregate volumes of financial flows or stocks in activities contributing to or undermining climate goals, as well as take part in climate-alignment assessments organised by government authorities in their jurisdiction(s).
- **Assess impacts of climate-related actions and unintended consequences of existing practices.** The evidence base on best practices in financial sector actions is still developing. Financial institutions could consider sharing information on their ex-post assessments of actions intended in influencing the climate alignment of their portfolios. Such assessments should prioritise assessing impacts in terms of GHG reductions and improved climate resilience in the real economy.
- **Explore new ways to increase financial flows to activities contributing to climate goals by systematically embedding climate considerations in financial decision-making.** Beyond targets, financial institutions need to scale up efforts to shift finance towards climate-aligned activities, by integrating climate considerations in their investment decision-making and actions more broadly, rather than only for specific "green" assets. They can also further share experiences with policymakers on existing and perceived barriers to scaling up climate-aligned finance and to financing the transition of misaligned activities.

Data, assessment, and rating providers provide information on which many actions and decisions are based, including for climate-alignment assessments of finance. They could further:

- **Develop assessments across all asset classes and layers of finance to address blind spots**. The development of new metrics and methodologies to assess both finance to activities contributing to or undermining climate goals can prioritise private equity, corporate loans, as well as assessments of financial flows and stocks at the level of financial institutions.
- **Disclose methodological assumptions and calculation approaches behind available climate performance metrics and data.** Metrics that inform climate-alignment assessments can be complex. Data and rating providers can rely on a range of methodological assumptions and approaches. While choices based on different perspectives can be valid, transparency on those choices is important to enable users to understand advantages and limitations of the data on which they rely, as well as their applicability for their use case.
- **Include information on the scope and comparability of available climate-related metrics and data.** Climate performance data used for climate-alignment assessments may be based on different scopes or disclosed through different reporting regimes. Data and rating providers could provide further metadata to provide clarity on these elements to users. This should for instance include information on the type of asset classes and share of total activities within a portfolio that are covered by the climate metric and assessment being put forward. Such information is critical to qualify results and avoid their misuse, as well as to reduce risks of greenwashing.

Climate science and policy researchers can play a crucial role in supporting environmental integrity in climate-alignment assessments of finance. This community encompasses climate scientists, climate scenario providers, climate policy academics, environmental economists, or sustainable finance researchers, as well as NGOs, which can contribute in different ways. Three key actions are to:

- **Increase the transparency and comprehensiveness of disclosure of climate change scenario data.** Scenarios are key inputs into climate-alignment assessments of finance. To ensure scenarios used in the financial sector are fit for purpose, further information could be shared by scenario providers. They could disclose more complete temperature outcome data, with peak and end-of-the-century temperatures associated with several likelihoods. Increased transparency of country-level and sectoral-level specificity in their models would also be helpful for uses in finance.
- **Develop new approaches to credibly assess the climate alignment for financial asset classes and layers of finance that are insufficiently covered, including in relation to climate change resilience.** Climate policy researchers can contribute to methodological developments where approaches are still maturing such as for corporate loans or private equity. They can also provide crucial independent and third part evaluation of the extent to which existing financial sector assessments and practices result in real economy impacts. This could include developing evidence to prioritise metrics and comparing methodological approaches and assumptions.
- **Develop theoretical and empirical analysis on the impacts of climate-related policies and actions.** While investors and financial institutions can proactively invest in climate solutions and the climate transition, their decisions ultimately depend on the credibility and effective implementation of ambitious climate policies. Such policies, in turn, need to be informed by improved evidence base, which researchers can contribute to developing such evidence, notably by using emerging best-available data on the evolution of financial flows and stocks aligned or misaligned with climate mitigation policy goals, and by conducting trial and pilot studies for climate resilience. Both empirical analysis where policies have been adopted and theoretical analysis on policies that could be adopted can help support building an effective policy landscape.

www.ingramcontent.com/pod-product-compliance
Lightning Source LLC
Chambersburg PA
CBHW061220240926
51846CB00006B/1293
* 9 7 8 9 2 6 4 7 5 6 7 2 4 *